PREFACE

This book is an introduction to computer programming, using the C programming language. It presupposes no previous programming experience. However, readers familiar with other programming languages will find many explanations herein that have proven useful to other experienced programmers in C language training sessions.

The book treats the C language as a general purpose computer language for programmers concerned with portability and efficiency. No special application area is favored; examples are chosen primarily to illustrate the specific features of C. The focus is tutorial rather than reference; no attempt is made to supercede the compiler manuals for syntactic details. The topic sequence has evolved over five years of teaching C language. I have tried to strike a balance between imparting the fundamentals of programming (which are independent of language and environment) and passing on useful details of the library, compilation procedures, and software maintenance. The goal is to give you the information you need to be a competent programmer in a real software engineering environment.

I hope the book will communicate, beyond the technical details, the delights of working in C language. C is a wonderfully designed tool for programming a variety of modern computers, elegant in its simplicity and yet powerful for many uses. Using it, you can create small, efficient applications that will not be limited to a single computer hardware. As you use it in your computing projects, you may come to appreciate the enthusiastic reception that it has found among professional programmers.

Appendix A presents a concise guide to the C language and the library commonly provided by UNIX (and many other) systems. This guide is not meant to replace the detailed syntactic reference provided by your compiler vendor. It is rather a summarization of the rules for writing *readable* C programs.

Appendix B discusses environmental questions in detail, such as how to compile a program, sizes of bytes and words, and compiler-dependent features. This appendix also contains full listings of all programs shown in the text. Frequent checkpoint questions, prefaced by **Question**, are answered in Appendix B of the book.

Programming exercises, marked as **Exercise**, are left to the reader's ingenuity.

It is a pleasure to acknowledge the encouragement and assistance of many people who have helped in this project. First of all, to P. J. Plauger go my special thanks, both for his role in producing the book and in bringing C language to many diverse environments. He would, in fact, have been a co-author of the book except for unforeseen demands upon his time. All the occurrences of "we" and "our" in the book are not meant as a "royal we" — I have kept them in hopes of our collaborating on future versions.

As it stands, the "we" herein often refers to the other seminar instructors of Plum Hall Inc, notably Steve Schustack and David Graham, whose concern for the clear presentation of the language has sharpened many of the examples. Others who commented on various drafts of the material include C. Gelber, John Justice, Brian Kernighan, Ian MacLeod, Ed Rathje, Greg Rose, Teri Whynman, and my mother, Ruby Schunior. My thanks to them do not, of course, mean that they necessarily agree with all points in the presentation — the author who writes, programs, tests, and sets type himself has no one to blame for mistakes that remain.

For steadfast support and encouragement, my heartfelt thanks go to my family — Halls, Pritchetts, Richters, Schuniors, Schanzes, and Whynmans.

A special thanks also goes to Dave Plauger, Tana Plauger, and the rest of the Whitesmiths, Ltd., staff. Don Bolinger wrote the text formatter `ctext` and made a pre-release version available for the typesetting. And Whitesmiths provided the solid compilers used to test the programs, which were run without changes on three different machine architectures. Their Idris operating system provided reliable support for all the operational aspects of preparing the book. A similar thanks goes to VenturCom, Inc., for the Venix version of UNIX which was used at many times in the project.

The original author of C language, Dennis Ritchie of Bell Laboratories, deserves the appreciation of all of us in the C language community. It is for many of us a strong recommendation of C that it was *not* designed by a committee.

I am delighted to acknowledge Plum Hall's magnificent staff, Sonya Whynman and Linda Deutsch, for everything they did in bringing this book into being.

And most of all, thanks to Joan Hall, my wife and Plum Hall's president, who made a good instructor out of the assistant professor I once was.

Thomas Plum

LEARNING TO PROGRAM IN C

£12·95

Thomas Plum

Prentice-Hall, Inc.

Englewood Cliffs, New Jersey 07632

Library of Congress Cataloging in Publication Data

PLUM, THOMAS (date)
    Learning to program in C.

    Bibliography: p.
    Includes index.
    1. C (Computer program language).   I. Title.
QA76.73.C15P58 1983   001.64'24   83-2144
    ISBN 0-13-527854-6
    ISBN 0-13-527847-3 (pbk.)
    ISBN (Plum Hall edition): 0-911537-00-7

For Joan

© 1983 by Plum Hall Inc., Cardiff, New Jersey 08232

This Prentice-Hall, Inc., edition published 1983.

All rights reserved. No part of this book may be
reproduced, in any form or by any means,
without permission in writing from the publisher.

We wish to thank the following for their kind permission to reproduce excerpts from copyrighted material:

Rules of Blackjack, from *Gaming Guide*. Copyright © 1980 by Bally Park Place Hotel and Casino. Reprinted by
permission.

Acknowledgement of trademarks: UNIX is a trademark of Bell Laboratories; PDP-11 and VAX are trademarks of
Digital Equipment Corporation; CP/M is a trademark of Digital Research Corporation; Venix is a trademark of
VenturCom, Inc.; Idris is a trademark of Whitesmiths, Ltd.; MC68000 is a trademark of Motorola Inc. C is not a
trademark, nor are the names of the software development commands such as cc.

This book was set in Times Roman, Megaron, and Standard Typewriter by the author, using a Varityper 5410 driven
by PDP 11/23 and MC68000 computers with ctext under the Idris operating system, assisted by tbl and spell
under the Venix version of the UNIX operating system.

Printed in the United States of America

10 9 8 7 6 5 4 3 2 1

ISBN 0-13-527854-6

ISBN 0-13-527847-3 {PBK}

Prentice-Hall International, Inc., *London*
Prentice-Hall of Australia Pty. Limited, *Sydney*
Editora Prentice-Hall do Brasil, Ltda., *Rio de Janeiro*
Prentice-Hall Canada Inc., *Toronto*
Prentice-Hall of India Private Limited, *New Delhi*
Prentice-Hall of Japan, Inc., *Tokyo*
Prentice-Hall of Southeast Asia Pte. Ltd., *Singapore*
Whitehall Books Limited, *Wellington, New Zealand*

CONTENTS

iii

CHAPTER 0:   INTRODUCTION

The Computer: TIME Magazine's "Man of the Year" for 1982.
("Machine of the Year," actually)

0.1   Introduction

Of special significance for C language fans is that "the computer" is a tangible piece of hardware for many people. Quite recently, as late as 1976, one might have predicted that computing would become increasingly centralized, with widespread terminal access to giant computing centers. The decreasing costs of microcomputers and minicomputers have caused a quite different result. Computer users are commonly aware of the memory size and processor speed of the machines that they use, and the computer as *machine* (as opposed to a *remote abstraction*) is a fact of life in most offices, and in many homes too. The situation is favorable for a language such as C, which embodies in an elegant way many of the common features of modern computing machines.

Indeed, many of the people that we have trained in C language are by occupation not programmers, but rather engineers, who come to the study of C with considerable knowledge of circuitry and processors. For them, C programming becomes another important tool in their engineering toolkit.

Another group interested in C are the systems programmers, who write the programs that other programmers use — notably compilers and operating systems, which we will examine in the next section. In such work, efficiency — making programs fast and small — is a major consideration. Often, there is also a payoff for portable programs that can run on a variety of different machines.

Also, there are the programmers who write applications packages which adapt the computer to the specialized needs of its users. Here again, the combination of efficiency and portability provided by C makes it ideal for the serious software producer.

All these users of C reap the benefits of its role as a small language close to the features of computing machines. C has had these benefits from the start. It evolved from the language B, an adaptation in 1970 by Ken Thompson of Martin Richards' BCPL. The UNIX operating system, originally written in PDP-11 assembler, was rewritten in C shortly after C was created in 1972. The results of the rewrite were overwhelmingly positive, and very shortly C displaced assembler programming in the UNIX environment. (For a fuller account of the history of C, see Ritchie *et. al.* [1978].)

During most of its history, C has been closely associated with the UNIX operating system, its original home and first major application. Much of the current interest in C is fed by the independent popularity of UNIX. However, the association is largely historical rather than intrinsic, and certain recent trends have promoted the independent status of C language. A series of C compilers for non-UNIX environments have been produced by several independent vendors, notably Whitesmiths, Ltd., as well as by Bell Laboratories. Indeed, the early years of the 80's have seen a proliferation of microprocessor versions of C, with an accompanying interest in the language from serious hobbyists.

To suggest a deliberate oxymoron, we could call C a "portable assembler" for modern computers. "Portable," in the sense that the same program can be run on a variety of different computers; "assembler," in the sense that these programs are small and fast, with complete control over the data in the machine. Thus, one simple criterion for the suitability for C to a given application is a positive answer to these two questions: "Is assembler language being considered?" And "Might it be useful for the program to run on different hardware?"

Given the variety of uses for C, we will not attempt to give a "cookbook" approach to programming. Our major goal is to give you a clear understanding of the language and its underlying behavior in the computer. The program examples and exercises are chosen not primarily as useful software — although some of them will be useful — but rather as illustrations of the features of C language. Our sequence of topics and explanations have evolved over several years of teaching C language to working professionals. For many of our trainees, their first serious programming project was to be done in C language, so our book covers programming fundamentals as well as the details of C language. Knowing that any sentence in the book may later be quoted in isolation, we will avoid simplifying things with "half-truths" to be undone later in the presentation, but certain topics (such as separate compilation of functions) will be postponed entirely until all the pieces can be put into place.

Thus, the organization of the book is as follows. Chapter 1 ("Computers and C") describes the characteristics of modern computers. Using a deliberately introductory approach, we presuppose only that you have some acquaintance with a computer. The experienced computer user can safely skim this chapter.

Chapter 2 ("Data") provides an introduction (or refresher) on bits, binary, octal, hexadecimal, and character codes. Declaration of scalar variables is covered in detail. (The enum type, from some recent compilers, is not covered in this book.) The "atoms" of a program are defined. Then, a presentation of assignment, flow of control, output, program size, #define and #include provide a foundation for real program examples.

Chapter 3 ("Operators"), the longest chapter, covers most of the operators of C language. Character input/output is explained early, to permit interactive programs. Precedence and associativity are described throughout the chapter, and summarized at the end. The address-of operator, in its uses for the scanf function, lays groundwork for later discussions of arrays and pointers. A scheme for portable defined types is presented. The chapter concludes with environmental information about input and output. (Opening and closing named files, and the numerous library functions that process them, are not included in this book.)

Chapter 4 ("Statements and Control Flow") covers all C control structures in full detail. Both syntax and readability are described for each topic. The chapter introduces the *design* of control structures, to facilitate the careful planning required for reliable programs.

Chapter 5 ("Functions") covers all syntactic aspects of C functions. Separate compilation and linkage are described, as well as the extended syntax checker, lint. Two-dimensional arrays are postponed to this chapter so that their initialization can be described.

Chapter 6 ("Software Development") discusses analysis, design, implementation, and maintenance. A real case study problem ("Blackjack") is covered in full detail.

Chapter 7 ("Pointers") covers the basics of pointers in C. The advanced applications — dynamic storage allocation, linked lists, and pointers to functions — are not covered in this introductory book.

Chapter 8 ("Structures") covers the C language struct. Not included are union, self-referencing structures, and bit fields.

Appendix A constitutes a "pocket guide" to C, summarizing readable syntax rules and the most common C library. Also included are formats for printf and scanf, common C bugs, C "idioms," and ASCII codes.

Appendix B contains answers to all checkpoint questions in the text, as well as listings of the programs and notes about environmental dependencies. Its structure was deliberately chosen to allow compiler vendors an easy framework for describing differences and special features of their compilers.

First, the basics.

CHAPTER 1: COMPUTERS AND C

Before we begin the study of programming, we will describe the general characteristics of the computers that we will be using. The machines that are programmed in C have many features in common. To avoid slanting the presentation to a particular machine, we start with a story about a computer-like hotel clerk named Igor who works at the Transylvanian Hilton.

1.1   Igor and the Numbers Game

Igor and his storage mechanism constitute our *computing system.*

1.   The system has a *main memory* (or *storage*) consisting of equal-sized, numbered receptacles.

At the Transylvanian Hilton, the storage is embodied in a wall of pigeonholes, each of which can contain one slip of paper. Each pigeonhole is labeled with a number. The hotel happens to have 1024 slots, or *1K* in computer lingo; the slot numbers run from 0 to 1023. The slots look like this:

```
|___0|___1|___2|___3|___4|___5|___6|___7|
|    |    |    |    |    |    |    |    |
|____|____|____|____|____|____|____|____|
|___8|___9|__10|__11|__12|__13|__14|__15|
|    |    |    |    |    |    |    |    |
|____|____|____|____|____|____|____|____|
|__16|__17|__20|__21|__22|__23|__24|__25|
|    |    |    |    |    |    |    |    |
|____|____|____|____|____|____|____|____|

                 . . .

|1016|1017|1018|1019|1020|1021|1022|1023|
|    |    |    |    |    |    |    |    |
|____|____|____|____|____|____|____|____|
```

2.   *Input:* Information from the outside world can be entered into the slots, either by giving it to Igor, or by someone else directly placing it into a slot. *Output:* Information can be passed to the outside world by copying the information from a slip and giving it to someone. Again, Igor can do this, or someone else can do it directly.

It makes for a simpler system if Igor does all the input and output himself, but if he is very busy, he may have an assistant to do the copying.

3.   Igor has a repertory of *wired-in (i.e., built-in) capabilities.*

We have already mentioned that he can put information into a slot and copy out what is in a slot. He can copy information from one slot to another, and perform simple calculations like addition, subtraction, multiplication, and division. He can, for example, copy down a number from each of two slots, add them together, and store the result in a slot. The wired-in capabilities are referred to as Igor's *hardware* — "hard," because it cannot be changed.

4.   Igor can only do these few simple operations, but he is *fast and reliable.*

It is essential that Igor work flawlessly for days or even months. This reliability is essential for the proper functioning of the system.

5.   Some of the storage is devoted to *instructions for the processor.*

The manager has discovered that it is useful to store Igor's instructions in a section of slots otherwise unused for information storage. After carrying out the instruction contained in one slot, Igor then proceeds to the *next sequential slot* for further instructions. Also, one slot may contain an instruction directing him to some other slot. Upon arriving for work in the morning, Igor looks in a designated slot for instructions, and starts to work. A complete set of instructions constitutes a *program.* A collection of programs for Igor constitutes his *software* — "soft," because it can be changed relatively easily.

Given this set of capabilities, we can describe a simple program for Igor: totaling a customer's bill.

Slot	Contents
0	Copy slot 9 into slot 13
1	Copy slot 10 to Accounting Department
2	Copy slot 11 to Accounting Department
3	Copy an input from Accounting Department to slot 12
4	If no more inputs, go to slot 7 for further instructions
5	Add slot 12 to slot 13
6	Go to slot 3 for further instructions
7	Copy slot 13 to customer
8	Go to slot 14 for further instructions
9	"0.00"
10	"Please send the charges for room number: "
11	"123"
12	
13	
14	

Now we begin the "numbers game." Written out as above, the instructions are long-winded and cumbersome. But it is possible to streamline matters by assigning a number code to each of Igor's instructions and write them in this more compact form.

6. The processor's wired-in capabilities are identified by numeric *instruction codes*.

Here are some instruction codes for Igor:

Code   Meaning

1   Go to slot __ for further instructions.
2   If no more inputs, go to slot __ for further instructions.
3   Add slot __ to slot __.
4   Copy slot __ to Accounting Department.
5   Copy an input from Accounting Department to slot __.
6   Copy slot __ into slot __.
7   Copy slot __ to customer.

Using these codes, Igor's program looks like this:

Slot	Contents
0	6, 9, 13
1	4, 10
2	4, 11
3	5, 12
4	2, 7
5	3, 12, 13
6	1, 3
7	7, 13
8	1, 14
9	"0.00"
10	"Please send the charges for room number: "
11	"123"
12	
13	
14	

To summarize: our system (Igor plus slots) has these properties:

1.   The storage consists of equal-sized, numbered slots.

2.   Data is moved from the outside world to slots (input), and from slots to the outside world (output).

3.   The clerk has a fixed set of wired-in capabilities.

4.   The clerk is fast and reliable.

5.   Instructions to the clerk are placed in the storage.

6.   The wired-in capabilities are identified by numeric instruction codes.

1.2   Basics of a Real Computer

Now we will convert our story about Igor and the slots into a description of a real computer. The role played by Igor is assigned to a piece of hardware known as the *central processing unit (CPU)*. The role of the slots is played by another piece of hardware, the *main memory*. The transmission of information to and from the system will be done by a *terminal*. These units have all six of the characteristics described above, plus some new ones.

7.   Each character is entered in the storage as a *character code* number.

When a key is pressed at a terminal, it sends the numeric code for that character to the system. Similarly, when a code is sent to a terminal, the corresponding character appears on the screen or printout.

There are two common schemes of character codes: the ASCII code (American Standard Code for Information Interchange) and the EBCDIC code (Extended Binary Coded Decimal Information Code). The EBCDIC ("EBB-see-dick") code is used almost exclusively by IBM equipment; non-IBM processors usually use ASCII ("ASK-ee"). However, even IBM machines will provide a better environment for C if ASCII is used internally. Here and throughout the book, we will assume that our processor uses the ASCII code.

In each scheme, the code for the digit 1 is one greater than the code for 0, the code for 2 is one greater than the code for 1, etc. through the digit 9. In other words, the digits occupy ten adjacent position in the code table, one above the next, in the same sequence as the digits themselves — their natural "collating sequence," to use the technical term. In both schemes, the collating sequence places A below B, B below C, etc., but the letter codes are not all adjacent in the EBCDIC scheme.

Here is a partial table for ASCII:

```
|space 32 | @    64 |  `    96 |
|  !    33 | A    65 | a     97 |
|  "    34 | B    66 | b     98 |
|  #    35 | C    67 | c     99 |
|  $    36 | D    68 | d    100 |
|  %    37 | E    69 | e    101 |
|  &    38 | F    70 | f    102 |
|  '    39 | G    71 | g    103 |
|  (    40 | H    72 | h    104 |
|  )    41 | I    73 | i    105 |
|  *    42 | J    74 | j    106 |
|  +    43 | K    75 | k    107 |
|  ,    44 | L    76 | l    108 |
|  -    45 | M    77 | m    109 |
|  .    46 | N    78 | n    110 |
|  /    47 | O    79 | o    111 |
|  0    48 | P    80 | p    112 |
|  1    49 | Q    81 | q    113 |
|  2    50 | R    82 | r    114 |
|  3    51 | S    83 | s    115 |
|  4    52 | T    84 | t    116 |
|  5    53 | U    85 | u    117 |
|  6    54 | V    86 | v    118 |
|  7    55 | W    87 | w    119 |
|  8    56 | X    88 | x    120 |
|  9    57 | Y    89 | y    121 |
|  :    58 | Z    90 | z    122 |
|  ;    59 | [    91 | {    123 |
|  <    60 | \    92 | |    124 |
|  =    61 | ]    93 | }    125 |
|  >    62 | ^    94 | ~    126 |
|  ?    63 | _    95 |
```

(The codes below 32 and those above 126 are special control characters, and not shown here; see Appendix A for a full table.) Using these codes, each of the messages can be entered into the storage as a number. A common convention is to terminate each message with a zero. Thus, "Please" becomes 80, 108, 101, 97, 115, 101, 0.

If ever you should need to know the ASCII codes for a character, you can find it here or in Appendix A. However, memorizing any of this information is a waste of brainpower. Once you know that these numeric codes are used in the storage and that they produce readable characters when printed, you have learned all that is needed.

So far, all that has changed from Igor's program is the numerical storage of the characters. The program has now been encoded entirely into numbers: numbers for the slots, numbers for the instruction codes, and numbers for the characters. The next step, however, alters the way that these numbers are arranged in the storage.

8.   Each slot in the storage can hold only one small number, and is called a *byte*. Each byte has an *address*, a number which identifies its location in the memory.

Each character code is held in a separate byte, and each of the instructions will probably take several bytes for its storage. The CPU must be capable of determining how many bytes each instruction occupies.

With the introduction of this eighth property, we say good-bye to Igor; converting his program into one-byte numbers would be unrewarding. We are now strictly into the world of real computers.

1.3   Basic Architecture

Each of the slots in the memory is known technically as a *byte*, and as we have seen, is capable of holding one small number. The byte may be (1) an actual number, or (2) part of a machine instruction, or (3) the code for a printing character.

Let us look for a moment at a specific byte whose address is, say, 1660. (Our real machines will usually have many K bytes of memory, in contrast to Igor's more limited slot storage.) Assume that the code for a printing character is stored there, say the character A whose code is 65 in the ASCII code. Somewhere else in the memory are machine instructions that will send that character to a terminal. When those instructions are executed, the number 65 is sent to a terminal. The end result is that an A appears on the terminal screen.

To understand the machinery that makes this possible, we will draw a "block diagram" picture of a typical C machine. In the figure below we see four "blocks" (i.e., functional pieces) of hardware that are interconnected by an "omnibus connection" (omnibus: "for everything"), or *bus*. The four blocks are

CPU: the Central Processing Unit;

Memory: all the bytes of machine storage;

Disk Controller: which sends data to and from a disk drive;

Terminal Controller: similar connection to a terminal.

In our short scenario above, the CPU reads an instruction from the memory and does what that instruction directs it to do. In this case, the instruction tells the CPU to fetch the byte from location 1660 and to send that byte to the terminal controller. The terminal controller then accepts that byte (value 65), and sends it to the terminal.

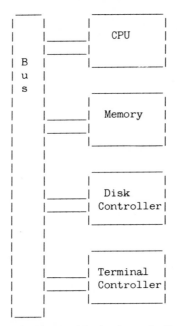

Each of these hardware blocks is typically a *printed circuit board,* and the bus is typically a piece of hardware that the boards plug into, with typically 50 to 100 separate connections between the boards. The time required for the byte-copying is limited mainly by the speed of execution of the boards and the time required for signals to move between them over the bus. The ultimate limit on the speed is the speed of light — the electrical signals travel about 1 billion feet per second, or one foot in one billionth of a second (one nanosecond). (Note: the American "billion" equals the British "thousand million" — but the American and British "nano" are equal.) On a typical C machine, this scenario takes a few millionths of a second. The terminal at the end of the process is usually the limiting bottleneck; terminals range in speed from 10 characters per second to several thousand per second.

The disk typically transfers data much faster than the terminal. Let us modify the scenario above to include the disk. Suppose the user has some data on the disk which is to be printed on the terminal. To be very concrete about it, the user has the disk (or diskette) in hand, inserts it into the disk drive, and executes a program to print some information. After a lot of instructions have been executed that find the appropriate information on the disk, an instruction will be executed that transfers some characters from the disk to the memory. Once the information is in the memory, instructions like our scenario above can transfer it one character at a time to the terminal.

This account will generally be true of any machine that you can use to *execute* your C programs. If you also use your machine to *prepare* C programs, it will also have a collection of software known as an *operating system.* In the operating system are various instructions which make the hardware easier for the programmer to use to produce useful programs.

To summarize: both data and instructions reside in the memory. Certain machine instructions cause the transfer of data to or from the disk or the terminal, producing a result that the user can see. The basic hardware is usually augmented with an operating system to make the hardware easier to use.

1.4   A Common Environment

One of the great advantages of a language such as C is that it makes it possible to develop software for a great variety of machines and operating systems. The word *environment* is often used to denote the combination of a machine with an operating system; in this sense, C works in a variety of environments. Once you have mastered C in your environment, it is a relatively easy step to write for other environments.

However, this variety poses problems for us in writing a book that attempts to tell you how to do things step-by-step. One solution often taken is to describe the use of the language at a level sufficiently vague to apply to all environments. We prefer to take a more concrete approach: we will give specific pictures and recipes for a specific environment and also tell you what needs to be changed in other environments.

Thus, throughout this book there will be a *Common Environment:* a PDP-11 computer using the UNIX (Version 7) operating system. One of the characteristics of the PDP-11 is that machine addresses are *2-byte* numbers, ranging from 0 to 64K. Whenever addresses are shown in our diagrams, they will be shown as 2-byte numbers. Throughout the book, whenever a figure or example contains a value that depends upon your machine, we will provide a space nearby with a notation like **[1-1 mach]** where you can jot your machine's corresponding value. Similarly, instances depending on operating system will be marked by **[1-2 os]**, and those depending on the C compiler will be marked **[1-3 cc]**. In Appendix B you will find environment-dependent values wherever these notations are shown.

We strongly recommend that your study of C should make use of a real computer on which you can do the exercises. We have sent advance copies of this book to all the compiler vendors known to us, and some have prepared an information sheet with specific details keyed to the topic sequence in Appendix B. If your environment is different from our Common Environment, please write to your vendor for this information.

This is the information that you need at this point (ask a knowledgeable local person if you do not have the information yourself):

What machine are you working on?   **[1-1 mach]** _____
(Our Common Environment: PDP-11)

What is its address size?   **[1-1 mach]**   _____
(Our Common Environment: 2 bytes, ranging from 0 to 64K-1)

Which operating system are you using?   **[1-2 os]** _____
(Our Common Environment: UNIX Version 7)

Which compiler are you using?   **[1-3 cc]**   _____
(Our Common Environment: UNIX cc)

1.5   A Sample Program

The first program to run in any environment is one which simply announces that it is working. In the C language community, the standard first program says

```
hello, world
```

and then quits. The following C program does nothing but print this message. (For any program in this book which you could enter and run on your computer, a duplicate listing will be found in Appendix B.)

```
hello.c [1-4]:
    main()
       {
       write(1, "hello, world\n", 13);
       }
```

The program is found in a file named `hello.c` and contains four lines. A file like this, which contains a C program that you can print and read, is known as a *source file* **[1-5 os]** and its readable contents are known as *source code*, or, colloquially, just *code*. The word main says that this is a *main program*, one that can be executed by itself. The *opening brace* ({) marks the beginning of the program, and the *closing brace* (}) marks its end. The line

```
    write(1, "hello, world\n", 13);
```

writes the 13 characters between the quotes to your terminal (specified by the 1). The code \n stands for *newline*, which causes the display to end the current line and start a new one, much like the RETURN key on a typewriter. It consists of two characters in the source file, but in the eventual program it counts as one character.

If you have access now to a computer, we suggest that you try out each of the steps in the following recipe. Since all the steps of this recipe involve environment-dependent details, refer to Appendix B if your environment is different. **[1-6 os] [1-7 mach] [1-8 cc]**

(1) To get our C program into the computer, we need to use a *text editor*, a program that creates or modifies files of text such as programs. The result of editing is a source file named `hello.c`.

(2) If we have made any mistakes in entering the program, or wish to make changes to an existing program, we again use the text editor to make the changes.

(3) We use the *compiler* to produce an executable program. In our Common Environment, the compiler is invoked with the command

```
cc hello.c
```

The compiler then goes to work. During its work, it produces a file of *assembler code*, a human-readable version of the machine instructions needed for the program. If you do not tell the compiler to stop with the assembler code, it goes on to produce a file known as an *object-code file*, or *object file*. The object file is simply a series of numbers, the actual hardware instructions to execute your program. The compiler then turns the job over to the *linker*, which combines the instructions for the `hello.c` program with instructions from a *link library*. The instructions for `write`, for example, are found in this library. The end result is an executable program, named `a.out` in our Common Environment.

(4) We execute or "run" the executable program, and should obtain the printout

```
hello, world
```

The whole sequence is summarized in the figure below. This type of diagram is known as a *data flow diagram;* each box represents a program receiving input from the arrows flowing into it and producing output on the arrows flowing out of it.

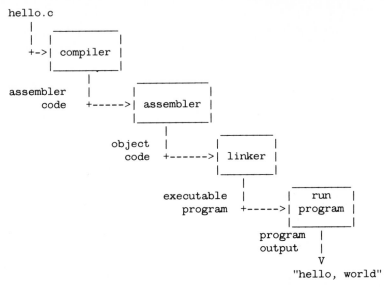

The last step in the process — running the executable program — deserves further explanation. After the compilation process, the program (known as a.out in the UNIX environment) exists as a *file* on a disk, containing machine instructions. When the user asks to *run*, or execute, the program, the process of "asking" is mediated by the *operating system*, which reads the user's commands from a terminal and then executes them. The operating system is itself a program which occupies space in the memory; that part of the operating system which continually "resides" in the memory is known as the *resident*. After the operating system locates the a.out file on the disk and reads it into the memory, the memory then looks something like this:

```
 _____
|                 |
| Operating       |
| System          |
| Resident        |
|                 |
|_____|
|                 |
| Instructions    |
| and Data        |
| for             |
| a.out           |
|_____|
```

Thus, the loading process has read the instructions and data for a.out into the machine memory. In the diagram, the memory also contains an operating system. Between the two of them, they contain all that is necessary for a.out to do its work.

Such is the picture when the program compiles successfully. Quite often, while learning the language you will have errors in your program which the compiler will complain about. We would like to prepare you now for handling the situation intelligently.

One common type of error is a *syntax error* — the format of your program is not what the compiler expects. Unfortunately for the learner, many C compilers are not great at telling you a human-oriented description of the underlying problem. For example, edit your `hello.c` file and remove the semicolon, to produce

```
helbad.c:
    main()
        {
        write(1, "hello, world\n", 13)
        }
```

On compiling the result, you may encounter messages such as this:

```
helbad.c:4: Statement syntax
```

Each such message tells you what file was being compiled, what line number the compiler was reading, and a description of the problem. In this case, the compiler complains about the syntax of line 4, but line 4 actually is all right — the problem is that the program is missing the semicolon on line 3. Often, the real problem will be *one line sooner* or *one line later* than the compiler tells you.

Continue this exercise by removing other components of the program and observe the results. If you are lucky, you can get the compiler to give you quite a long list of error messages. In this case, *fix the first error* and see how many messages go away as a result.

A *linkage error* is a different type of error. If, for example, we misspell the name **write** as **qrite**, we will receive a message like this:

```
undefined: _qrite
```

which means, simply, that the name **qrite** cannot be found in our link library. The correction is usually obvious, as it is in this case.

CHAPTER 2: DATA

C language machines store data in the binary number system, so we first present a introduction to the binary system. Then we show how data is stored in variables and constants. And after some discussion of the octal and hexadecimal number systems, we are ready to show programs that print results.

2.1 Bits and Numbers

In this section, we will look at some interesting things that can be done in a world with only two numbers, zero (0) and one (1). The operations on these numbers were invented by George Boole in the 1840's; hence, the system is known as Boolean algebra.

The three basic operations of Boolean algebra are AND (&), OR (|), and NOT (~). Their rules — "0 & 0 is 0", "0 & 1 is 1", etc. — can be written in tables:

```
    AND                 OR                  NOT
     &   0   1           |   0   1           ~
       --------            --------            ----
   0 |  0   0         0 |  0   1         0 |  1
     |                  |                  |
   1 |  0   1         1 |  1   1         1 |  0
```

Or to put the rules into words, one number AND another number produces 1 only if both numbers are 1; one number OR another number produces 0 only if both numbers are 0; and the negation (NOT) of a number changes 0 into 1 and 1 into 0.

This is certainly a tiny system of arithmetic, with only two numbers. It is interesting because it models some facts of *logic*, when we interpret zero (0) as *false* and one (1) as *true*. "Sentences that can be *true* or *false*" are sometimes known as *assertions*, or to give more credit to Professor Boole, as *Boolean expressions*. Here is an example of a Boolean expression, in words:

"1 is less than n AND n is less than 100".

If n is 50, this expression is *true*. Why? First of all, because it is "obvious", but also, "1 is less than n" is *true*, "n is less than 100" is *true*, and therefore, since "*true* AND *true*" is *true*, the result is *true*. (Or expressed in Boolean numbers, 1 & 1 is 1.)

As we will see in Section 3.5, these operations (& | ~) appear in C language, where we will give them the names *bit-and*, *bit-or*, and *bit-not*. For the moment, we turn instead to *arithmetic*, with the operations *plus*, *minus*, *multiply*, and *divide*. In order to get more interesting arithmetic using *bits* (the digits 0 and 1), we need to use more of them together. The simplest combination we can make is to put two bits together into one number, which would give us these four numbers: 00, 01, 10, 11. Give the leftmost bit the value 2, and the rightmost bit the value 1, and we have an "unsigned two-bit" *binary* arithmetic:

```
0    00
1    01
2    10
3    11
```

Familiar facts of arithmetic have new faces:

```
   0    00        0    00        1    01        1    01
 + 0    00      + 1    01      + 2    10      + 1    01
 ---- ----      ---- ----      ---- ----      ---- ----
   0    00        1    01        3    11        2    10
```

But how about 2 + 2? The usual arithmetic result would not fit into two bits; but if we allow our numbers to go to three bits, we can express the result.

```
   2    010
 + 2    010
 ---- -----
   4    100
```

But how about 4 + 4? Hmmm. We could keep expanding the size of our numbers to hold bigger and bigger values, but this is not how real computers work. The C machine has data types that are big enough for a fixed number of bits, and no more. Many C compilers provide variables that can hold eight bits for numbers from 0 to 255:

```
   0    00000000
   1    00000001
   2    00000010
   3    00000011
   4    00000100
 . . .      . . .
 253    11111101
 254    11111110
 255    11111111
```

How to convert from binary to decimal? Here is one method that will be of some use later. We are working here with 8-bit numbers, but the same method will work for any size binary number.

Write down the binary number, and next to it label two columns for "ones" and "zeros." For example,

```
01110101    ones | zeros
                 |
                 |
                 |
```

Starting at the rightmost digit, write a 1 below "ones" if that digit is a 1, or below "zeros" if that digit is a 0. In this case:

```
01110101    ones | zeros
                 |
              1  |
                 |
```

As we work from right to left, each digit is worth 2 times the value of the one to its right. So the next digit, the second one from the right, has value 2. In this case, the digit is a zero, so put a 2 under the zeros column.

```
01110101    ones | zeros
                 |
              1  |
                 |   2
                 |
```

Continue the process from right to left until all digits have been recorded either under ones or zeros. The numeric value of the binary number is the sum of the entries in the "ones" column. We can double-check by summing both columns and adding them together; they should total 255, because

$$255 = 1 + 2 + 4 + 8 + 16 + 32 + 64 + 128.$$

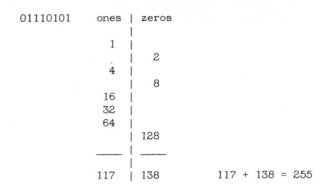

```
01110101      ones | zeros
                   |
              1    |
                   |   2
              4    |
                   |   8
             16    |
             32    |
             64    |
                   | 128
             ____  | ____
                   |
            117    | 138        117 + 138 = 255
```

Question [2-1] What is the decimal value of the following binary numbers?

    00001111   01010101   10000001

  _____   _____   _____

How do we add two binary numbers? The process works just like the usual process of decimal addition, except that the sum of 1 and 1 is not 2, but "0 with carry 1." For example, adding the numbers 7 and 2:

```
  00000111    Starting from the right, 1 + 0 is 1.
+ 00000010    Going leftwards, 1 + 1 is 0 carry 1.
----------    Third digit, carry 1 + 1 + 0 is 0 carry 1.
  00001001    Fourth digit, carry 1 + 0 + 0 is 1.
              The other four digits are all 0.
```

Just for practice, convert the result into decimal by the two-column procedure given above. Your result should look like this:

```
00001001      ones | zeros
                   |
              1    |
                   |   2
                   |   4
              8    |
                   |  16
                   |  32
                   |  64
                   | 128
             ____  | ____
                   |
              9    | 246        9 + 246 = 255
```

Noticing how much easier it was here to just add the "ones" column, we suggest leaving off the "zeros" column, since it served mainly for cross-checking.

All these rules can be reduced to the more mathematical interpretation of a *"base two"* (or *base-2*) number system. Recalling that "two to the power N" (or 2^N) means "two times two times two..." repeated N times, and that 2^0

equals 1, then the binary number 10110001 equals

$$1\times2^7 + 0\times2^6 + 1\times2^5 + 1\times2^4 + 0\times2^3 + 0\times2^2 + 0\times2^1 + 1\times2^0$$

or 177 decimal.

So far we have dealt only with non-negative numbers in our binary system (and nothing bigger than 8 bits, at that). Let us look at some different interpretations of the bits that will allow both positive and negative numbers. The leftmost (or *high-order*) bit will be known as the *sign bit*. If it is a zero, the signed number will have the same value as before; but if the sign bit is a 1, the number value is taken as negative.

The first scheme for signed numbers is known as the *twos complement system*. In this system, when we add two numbers we get the same binary result whether either of the numbers was interpreted as signed or unsigned. In other words, if we add 11111111 and 00000001, we get 00000000, when the result is truncated to eight bits:

```
    11111111
+   00000001
    ---------
    00000000
```

As an unsigned 8-bit number, the bits 11111111 equal 255, and if we add them to 1, we get zero, with a "carry" from the leftmost bit. But in our new signed interpretation, 11111111 equals -1 (negative one), 11111110 equals -2, etc:

Binary value	Unsigned 8-bit value	Signed 8-bit value (twos complement)
00000000	0	0
00000001	1	1
00000010	2	2
00000011	3	3
. . .	. . .	. . .
11111101	253	-3
11111110	254	-2
11111111	255	-1

The rightmost column shows the *twos complement* interpretation of the number.

We arranged the numbers in the table running from 00000000 to 11111111, to show that the set of numbers which we originally interpreted as 0 to 255 can also be interpreted as positive and negative numbers. Arranging the table according to the (twos complement) signed value would look like this:

Binary value	Unsigned 8-bit value	Signed 8-bit value (twos complement)
10000000	128	-128
10000001	129	-127
10000010	130	-126
10000011	131	-125
. . .	. . .	. . .
11111100	252	-4
11111101	253	-3
11111110	254	-2
11111111	255	-1
00000000	0	0
00000001	1	1
00000010	2	2
. . .	. . .	. . .
01111111	127	127

How, then, to convert an 8-bit binary number to its signed (twos complement) decimal representation? For now, the simplest rule is to first convert to unsigned decimal, which we covered earlier. Then if the sign bit of the binary number was a 1 bit, subtract 256 from the unsigned value. A more general rule will be presented in Section 3.6.

The name "twos complement" comes from the fact that when we add a number with its twos complement value, the sum at each position is two — zero with "carry," in binary. There is an alternative scheme called "ones complement" where the sum at each position is a one. In other words, to find the ones complement of a binary number, change each 0 bit to a 1, and each 1 bit to a 0. The previous table looks like this in ones complement:

Binary value	Unsigned 8-bit value	Signed 8-bit value (ones complement)
10000000	128	-127
10000001	129	-126
10000010	130	-125
10000011	131	-124
. . .	. . .	. . .
11111100	252	-3
11111101	253	-2
11111110	254	-1
11111111	255	-0
00000000	0	0
00000001	1	1
00000010	2	2
. . .	. . .	. . .
01111111	127	127

Notice that in ones complement arithmetic there are two binary values for zero: 00000000 and 11111111. Another peculiarity of the ones complement system is the "end-around carry" — if the binary sum produces a high-order carry, a 1-

bit is added to the low-order end. For example, when adding "negative zero" (11111111) to itself, ordinary binary addition would give the 8-bit sum 11111110, with a high-order carry. After end-around carry, the result becomes "negative zero" itself, 11111111.

Most C machines work with twos complement arithmetic, and we will show twos complement values whenever they occur in diagrams [2-2 mach]. The existence of C compilers on ones complement machines does raise some portability questions that will be addressed in Section 3.21.

Question [2-3] What is the 8-bit sum? What does each number equal in decimal? Do each problem both in unsigned and twos complement signed interpretation.

```
        binary        unsigned      signed
                      decimal       decimal (twos complement)


       00101011 =    _____       _____
     + 10000011 =    _____       _____
     -----------

       _____        _____       _____



       11110000 =    _____       _____
     + 00001111 =    _____       _____
     -----------

       _____        _____       _____



       10000000 =    _____       _____
     + 00001010 =    _____       _____
     -----------

       _____        _____       _____
```

Now compute these 8-bit sums, using ones complement interpretation:

```
binary              signed
                    decimal (ones complement)

  00101011 =        _____
+ 10000011 =        _____
-----------

  _____           _____


  11110000 =        _____
+ 00001111 =        _____
-----------

  _____           _____


  11111101 =        _____
+ 11111110 =        _____
-----------

  _____           _____
```

2.2 Integer Variables

Recall from Section 1.2 that the memory of a computer is subdivided into bytes, each of which holds one small number. One of the important things that a C compiler does is to associate a *name*, chosen by the programmer, with one or more of the machine memory locations. In a program, each such name is known as a *variable* — so named because its *value* (or "contents") can vary as the program is run. Each C variable has a *type*, which specifies its *representation* and its *size*.

The two basic representations for data are

integers (whole numbers with no fractional part) — the *signed* integers and the *unsigned* integers; and

floating-point numbers (numbers with a "floating" decimal point).

We will describe floating-point variables in the next section. Here let's look at the three basic sizes of integer variables found in C: 1-byte variables (known as char in C), 2-byte variables (known as short), and 4-byte variables (known as long). **[2-4 mach]**

A programmer-chosen name is *declared* to be a certain type of variable by a C statement called a *declaration* statement. Here are some declarations:

```
char c;
short i;
long lnum;
```

In the machine memory, the storage for these variables would look like this (where each box represents one byte of the memory):

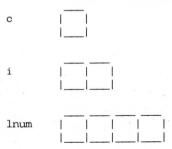

The numeric values of these variables are stored using the binary number representation. On most C machines each byte contains 8 bits, so a char can hold a number from -128 to 127, a short can hold from -32768 to 32767, and a long can hold from -2147483648 to 2147483647 **[2-5 mach] [2-6 cc]**.

There is also an integer type known simply as int. The size of an int depends upon the machine hardware. On some machines, such as our standard PDP-11 environment, an int is a 2-byte variable, the same as a short. On other machines, an int is a 4-byte variable, the same as a long **[2-7 mach]**. Because of this variability in the size of an int, we prefer to use either short or long variables.

C provides both signed and unsigned integer variables. Variables of the type unsigned int are the same size as an int, but are interpreted according to the unsigned arithmetic that we showed earlier. (The type unsigned int can be abbreviated to unsigned.) Some compilers provide other unsigned types: if the word unsigned is prefixed to an integer type, the contents of the variable are interpreted as always being zero or greater. Thus an unsigned char can hold numbers from 0 to 255; an unsigned short can hold from 0 to 65535; and an unsigned long can hold from 0 to 4294967295 **[2-8 cc]**.

As we saw above, each variable is given a *type* by means of a declaration statement. When the program is run, each variable will have an address in the machine memory. The hardware eventually uses this address as its means of locating the variable when the program runs. For example, if the program contains these declarations

```
        short i;
            ...
        short j;
```

the variables might look like this in the memory (where each oblong box represents the 2-byte storage for one short):

```
NAME      ADDRESS     STORAGE


 i         2000      |  _____  |
                     | |_____| |


 j         3000      |  _____  |
                     | |_____| |
```

For purposes of illustration we have shown the variables at particular locations. The actual locations they occupy are up to the compiler, and of no concern to the programmer. All that matters is that each one has an address in the memory.

As a notational convenience, variables with the same type can be declared in the same declaration statement, by listing them with commas between them:

```
short i, j;
```

When a value is *assigned* to a variable, its storage holds that value until another value is assigned. Thus when the C *assignment statement*

```
i = 7;
```

is executed, the value 7 is put into the storage of i; in this example, the two bytes at machine address 2000 are set to the value 0000000000000111, i.e., 7. When the assignment statement

```
j = i;
```

is executed, the 2-byte value at location 2000 is copied into the 2-byte storage at location 3000. The resulting memory locations look like this:

```
NAME      ADDRESS     STORAGE


 i         2000      |  _____  |
                     | |   7   | |


 j         3000      |  _____  |
                     | |   7   | |
```

To summarize, a *variable* has a *name* and a *type,* which are specified in a declaration statement. When the program is run, the variable has a *value,* and *location (address).* The *type* of the variable determines the *size* (number of bytes) and *representation* (integer or floating-point) of the variable.

2.3   Floating-point Variables

So far, all numbers we have seen are whole-number integers, with no fractional part. *Floating-point* variables are the C mechanism for handling fractional numbers. The fundamental concept is that of *scientific notation:* any number can be expressed as a decimal fraction multiplied by a power of ten. The value 3.14159, for example, can be written

$$.314159 \times 10^1$$

Similarly, -10000 can be written as

$$-.1 \times 10^5$$

The machine storage for a floating-point number has three parts:

sign (either positive or negative);

fraction (a number somewhat less than 1); and

exponent.

The fraction and exponent are generally binary rather than decimal in C machine storage, but the distinction is important only at a more advanced level of programming. The exact form of the storage of floating-point numbers varies with the machine, but all standard C compilers offer two flavors of floating-point numbers:

float which holds at least 6 decimal digits; and

double which holds at least 15 decimal digits.

The exponent in the floating-point storage allows for numbers to be as small as 10^{-38} or as large as 10^{38}.

Floating-point numbers are thus accurate only to the number of digits in their storage; they can never *exactly* represent fractions such as one-third. However, accuracy to 15 places (or even 6) is often quite sufficient.

2.4   Constants

We have seen that *variables* have a *name, type,* and (when the program is run) a *location* and *value.* C programs also contain *constants*, which specify an unchanging value. Each constant has a *type*, but does not have a *location*, except for the "string constants" which we will see soon.

Integer constants consist of one or more numeric digits (possibly prefaced with a sign), such as 0, or 1, or -12345. The *type* of integer constants is int; however, on a machine where int is smaller than long, an integer constant too big to fit an int will have the type long. Also, a constant can be forced to have type `long` by appending the letter L to the number.

A *numeric constant* containing a decimal point is a floating-point constant, such as 3.14159 or -9.99. A floating-point constant can also be written in E-format, such as 1E-37 (which means 1×10^{-37}) or -1E5 (which means -1×10^5). The *type* of floating-point constants is `double`.

Character constants are a means of specifying the numeric value of a particular character. For example, the character constant 'a' is the value which, when sent to a terminal, will print an a. Similarly, the character constant '0' is the value which, when sent to a terminal, will print a 0. In the ASCII character set, the code for '0' is 48. Note that there is a character constant for an actual zero numeric value; it is written '\0'. This *null character* is very different from the character constant '0'; when the null character is sent to a terminal, the terminal does absolutely nothing in response. (Its uses in C language will be described momentarily.) There are some other special character constants:

```
'\n'    newline
'\t'    tab
'\b'    backspace
'\r'    carriage return
'\f'    form feed
'\\'    backslash
'\''    single-quote (apostrophe)
'\ddd'  arbitrary bit pattern
```

The *type* of character constants is `char`. (The number *ddd* contains one, two, or three digits and is written in the *octal* system; see Section 2.5.)

A *string constant* consists of characters surrounded by double-quotes, such as the famous

```
"hello, world\n"
```

String constants, unlike the others, actually have a *location* in the machine memory. The characters in the string are stored in memory, and the numeric value of the constant is the *address* of this memory. In addition, the compiler stores the *null character* '\0' at the end of the string to mark the end of it. Assuming the ASCII character set, the string constant "0" looks something like this in the memory:

```
         _____
3000    | 48 |  0 |
        | '0'|'\0'|
         -----------
```

and the value of the constant is its address (in this hypothetical case, 3000) -- whereas the value of '0' is simply the number 48 (the ASCII code for '0'). Our representation of the string storage shows both the numeric ASCII code for each byte and the corresponding character constant.

The shortest string constant is the *null string,* which is written "" and is stored in memory as a single null character, `'\0'`.

Question [2-9] What is the *type* of each constant:

What does this string constant look like in memory:

"000"

2.5   Octal and Hexadecimal Numbers

So far, we have written binary numbers using only the bits 0 and 1. You can easily see a couple of problems with this system. It tends to get verbose even for the small 8-bit numbers we have used so far. Also, it compounds the odds of making mistakes with the larger numbers. For a more compact notation of binary numbers, we can use *octal* and *hexadecimal* numbers.

To convert a number from binary to octal, group the bits into groups of three, starting at the right. Next, write down one digit for the binary value of each group of three (or fewer) bits. Here is an example:

```
11001010  -->  11 001 010  -->  3 1 2
```

The translation between octal and binary can be given by a table:

binary	octal
000	0
001	1
010	2
011	3
100	4
101	5
110	6
111	7

In C programs, any numeric constant that starts with a leading zero is interpreted as an octal number. Therefore, if we wanted to write the binary number 11001010 in a C program, we could write it as 0312. C also employs octal numbers (without the leading zero) in the *arbitrary bit pattern* style of

character constants.   The character constant '\23' has the decimal value of
19, for example.

Converting from octal to binary is very easy: translate each octal digit
into the corresponding group of three bits.

Question [2-10] Write down the octal equivalent for each binary number:

10110010   11111111

0__ __ __   0__ __ __

1101100100110110   1111111111111111

0__ __ __ __ __ __   0__ __ __ __ __ __

Question [2-11] Write down the binary equivalent (8 or 16 bits) for each octal
number:

014   0177

_____   _____

0200   014662   052525

_____   _____   _____

Octal numbers constitute a *"base-8"* arithmetic system: the octal number
0123 corresponds to

$1 \times 8^2 + 2 \times 8^1 + 3 \times 8^0$

or 83, in decimal.

As you see, the octal number system serves as a shorthand for writing
binary numbers, using groups of three bits each.   An alternative system, which
uses groups of four bits each, is the *hexadecimal* number system.   (The roots
of the name "hexadecimal" are "hexa" for "six" and "deci" for "ten," hence
"based on sixteen.")

To convert a number from binary to hexadecimal, start with the rightmost four bits and convert them to a hexadecimal digit.   Then working
leftwards, keep grouping into four-bit digits. The table for hexadecimal digits
includes the usual 10 decimal digits and the letters "A" through "F" to stand
for digits with values 10 through 15:

binary	hexadecimal	binary	hexadecimal
0000	0	1000	8
0001	1	1001	9
0010	2	1010	A
0011	3	1011	B
0100	4	1100	C
0101	5	1101	D
0110	6	1110	E
0111	7	1111	F

In C programs, hexadecimal constants appear with 0x prefixed to them; e.g., 0x1F is the number 31. For various historical reasons, most of the early work in C language favored the octal number system — witness its favored role in constants such as '\23'. However, most modern C machines have data sizes of 8, 16, and 32 bits, which divide more conveniently into 4-bit digits. In our book, we will show both octal and hexadecimal where appropriate, but generally favor decimal numbers in our programs and diagrams.

To convert from hexadecimal to binary, just convert each digit to its corresponding binary value.

Question [2-12] Write down the hexadecimal equivalent for each binary number:

10110010   11111111

0x__ __   0x__ __

1101100100110110   1111111111111111

0x__ __ __ __   0x__ __ __ __

Question [2-13] Convert from the hexadecimal to the corresponding binary:

0xFE   0x40

_____   _____

0x7FFF   0x9A6E

_____   _____

2.6   Atoms of a C Program

One of the first things that the compiler does when reading a program is to split it into "words and punctuation." These basic pieces of a program are known as its *atoms*. Each variable name constitutes one atom; so does each constant. Here is a complete list of the categories of atoms:

1. *Names* or *identifiers*, chosen by the programmer. Identifiers may be as long as you like, but the compiler will only look at the first eight characters of the name. Characters beyond eight are ignored. Identifiers are composed of letters and numbers, and must start with a letter. The underscore character _ counts as a letter, but names that *start* with an underscore are usually reserved for the system software. The compiler sees the difference between lower-case characters and upper-case characters; the names MAIN, Main, and main are three different names in C. The most common C style is to use only lower-case characters for your identifiers. Examples that illustrate these rules:

    Legal identifiers: i   j   x1   total   user_id

    Illegal identifiers: %_of_change   57flavors

    Bad style, but legal: TOTAL   _x

    There are some "conventional" meanings for simple names: c is a character; i, j, and n are integers; x, y, and z are floating-point. Over 90% of the hundreds of C programmers we surveyed share these conventions.

2. *Constants:* As we saw in the previous section, C has the following types of constants:

    Decimal integer constants (both int and long): 63   9999   -40   -40L

    Octal integer constants: 077   040   0   0L

    Hexadecimal integer constants: 0x37   0xFFFF   0x9000   0x9000L

    Character constants: 'a'   '0'   '\0'   '\n'

    String constants: "help"   "hello, world\n"   ""

    Floating-point constants: 1.5   .001   1E-5   -1000.

3. *Whitespace:* any number of blanks, tabs, and newlines may be used to separate the atoms in a program. Good style dictates that you use tabs and spaces to arrange your program in a readable layout, but to the compiler, all whitespace is the same.

4. *Comments* may be used anywhere whitespace is allowed. A comment starts with the two characters /* and continues (possibly over several lines) to the two characters */.

5.   *Separators* are the punctuation of C:

    ,   ;   {   }   =   (   )   :

6.   *Operators* (such as "plus", "minus", "times", or "divided-by") are described in Chapter 3. Examples:

    +   -   *   /

7.   *Keywords* are "built-in" names of the language. These are *reserved* names, meaning that you are not allowed to use them as identifiers. A complete list of C keywords **[2-14 cc]**:

auto	double	if	static
break	else	int	struct
case	entry	long	switch
char	extern	register	typedef
continue	float	return	union
default	for	short	unsigned
do	goto	sizeof	while

Notice that the comment format in C allows multi-line comments; all comments extend until the closing */. It is always good style to place a comment before each program to describe what is done in that program. A useful style for such *prolog comments* is to align the asterisks in the second position of each line, as in the programs that follow.

Since all whitespace is treated the same by the compiler, these two programs would compile the same:

hello2.c **[2-15]**:
```
/* hello2 - print greeting
 */
main()
    {
    write(1, "hello, world\n", 13);
    }
```

hello3.c **[2-16]**:
```
/* hello3 - print greeting */
main
(
)
{
write
(
1
,
"hello, world\n"
,
13
)
;
}
```

The second program, hello3.c, has been written with one atom per line, just to show what the atoms are.

Question [2-17] Write the category of atom next to each line of hello3.c.

2.7   Flow of Control

An *assignment statement* such as

```
c = 'A';
```

assigns the value to the right of the equal-sign to the variable on the left of the equal-sign. After the assignment, the new value is remembered in the storage of the variable until yet another new value replaces it. The best verbalization of the assignment operator is "gets," as in "c *gets* 'A'." It should definitely *not* be read as "equals."

We now combine some declarations, constants, and assignment statements to make a simple C program. Each line of the program is identified by a *line number* at the left-hand margin. (The line numbers are added for illustration only and are not part of the source file.)

```
asst.c:
   1  /* asst - examples of assignment
   2   * (No output is produced)
   3   */
   4  main()
   5      {
   6      char c;
   7      short i;
   8
   9      c = 'A';
  10      i = 65;
  11      c = 'X';
  12      i = -4;
  13      }
```

For this program, or any other one, its life history can be divided into four stages or "times":

Edit-time: The source file is created using a text editor.

Compile-time: The compiler reads the source file and creates an executable program.

Load-time: The executable program is loaded into the memory of the computer.

Run-time: Control of the computer is given to the executable program that is loaded in memory.

Thus, "run-time" is the time when the program actually performs what it was programmed to do. In order to understand what happens at run-time, you need to know that the computer has a mechanism for keeping track of where it is in the execution of a program. On most C machines, this mechanism is known as the *program counter (PC)*. At each instant of time as the machine is running, the PC contains the location of the next instruction that it is about to execute.

After the executable program is loaded into the memory by the operating system, the operating system turns control of the machine over to the executable program by loading the PC with the address of the first instruction of the program. After that, the PC keeps track of where it is in the program, until the program is finished. Then the PC reverts to an address in the operating system again.

Each C statement may create more than one machine instruction in the executable program, and each machine instruction may consist of several bytes. However, for the time being, we will treat the PC as though it kept track of the execution by the *line number* of the program, rather than by actual machine addresses. Thus, when our program is started, the PC starts at line 9, the first executable statement of the program. (The declaration statements on lines 6 and 7 do not generate any executable code; they just give information to the compiler.) After the code for line 9 is executed, the PC points to line 10. This statement is then executed by the machine, and the PC points to line 11, and so forth. The time that these events take is measured in *microseconds* (millionths of a second), but they still follow each other in strict sequence. This strict sequence is known as the *flow of control*. If you are looking at a printed program in front of you, you can simulate the flow of control by moving your finger from top to bottom of the program listing. The PC is the machine's equivalent of your pointing finger.

The run-time flow of control looks like this:

PC=9   The storage of the variable c receives the value 65 (the ASCII code for 'A'). Its eight bits in memory now look like this: 01000001. (Before this statement is executed, the variable has what is known as a "garbage" value — whatever bits happened to be lying in the memory.)

PC=10   The storage of the variable i receives the value 65; its 16 bits in memory look like this: 0000000001000001. The variable c continues to hold the value it received before.

PC=11   The storage of the variable c is changed to 98 (the ASCII code for 'X'); i is still 65.

PC=12   The storage of the variable i is changed to -4; its bits now look like this: 1111111111111100. c is still 98.

PC=13   The end of the program is reached, and control returns to the operating system.

This program has not produced any observable result; all it has done is to store some values into certain locations inside the machine, then abandon them.

In order to see what is going on during the execution of the program, we must perform some *output*, the subject of our next section. Our sample program has simply illustrated the sequential flow of control through an executable program: execution starts with the first executable statement and proceeds statement-by-statement until the end of the program. Each assignment statement stores a certain value into the storage of some variable, and that value abides in that location until something else is stored in that variable.

2.8   Output and Printf

To see what our program is doing, we need to add *output* to our
program. The most common way of producing output is the function `printf`.
Its simplest use is to print messages — the string constants that we saw in
section 2.4:

```
printf("hello, world\n");
```

A more significant use of `printf` is to print variables using an output format:

```
printf("%d\n", c);
```

Here we are printing the char variable c, using the *format* "%d\n". The format says to print as a decimal number and then to return the cursor or carriage to start a new line. Other output conversions are available: %o specifies
octal format, %x specifies hexadecimal format, %u specifies unsigned decimal
format, and %c prints as an ASCII character. More than one format is allowed by a single call to `printf`, and ordinary printing text may be interspersed with the formats, as in

```
printf("c: dec=%d oct=%o hex=%x ASCII=%c\n",
    c, c, c, c);
printf("i: dec=%d oct=%o hex=%x unsigned=%u\n",
    i, i, i, i);
```

Naturally, the ASCII format should not be used if the variable being printed
does not contain a legal ASCII character. Adding the calls to `printf` gives

```
asst2.c [2-18]:
    /* asst2 - print assigned values
     */
    main()
        {
        char c;
        short i;

        c = 'A';
        i = 65;
        printf("c: dec=%d oct=%o hex=%x ASCII=%c\n",
            c, c, c, c);
        printf("i: dec=%d oct=%o hex=%x unsigned=%u\n",
            i, i, i, i);
        c = 'X';
        i = -4;
        printf("c: dec=%d oct=%o hex=%x ASCII=%c\n",
            c, c, c, c);
        printf("i: dec=%d oct=%o hex=%x unsigned=%u\n",
            i, i, i, i);
        }
```

Note that the same variable can be printed using several different formats; the choice of output format is given entirely by the format string, not by the type of the variable being printed.

Some practical suggestions on entering and compiling this program: The procedure of editing the source file is just as we saw in Section 1.5. But if you use the simple recipe for compilation

```
cc asst2.c
```

you will create a file named a.out **[2-19 cc]**, which will effectively destroy the executable version of your hello.c program. For simple learning examples such as these, it matters little — less space on your disk or diskette will be taken up by seldom-used executable programs. But as you advance, you will obviously not want to re-compile a program every time you want to use it. The more sophisticated formula for compilation is **[2-20 cc]**

```
cc -o asst2 asst2.c
```

The option -o asst2 says to place the executable program in a file named asst2. Then to execute it, you run asst2 instead of a.out. Try this option on the compilation of asst2.c.

Question [2-21] What does the output of asst2 look like?

There are also floating-point formats available from printf. Suppose the variable **x** is either float or double, and contains the value 123.5. We could print it in *fixed-point* format with one decimal place using the format "%.1f" (which would print 123.5), or in E-notation using the format "%.4e" (which would print 0.1235e3). In either case, after the % in the format, we find a *precision* specifier, which tells how many decimal fraction places to print.

All these formats shown so far will accept an additional specification of *printing width*, by giving the desired width immediately after the percent-sign of the format. For example, the statement

```
printf("%6c %6d %6o %6x\n", c, c, c, c);
```

will allow six print positions for each output. (This allows printouts with lined-up columns of numbers.) Without the width specification, C takes only as many positions as are needed to print the data.

We can obtain leading zeroes on the output by placing a zero before the output field width. Thus,

```
printf("%3d 0x%02x 0%03o\n", 10, 10, 10);
```

will produce

```
10 0x0A 0012
```

Question [2-22] If each format in `asst2.c` is changed to a 6-position width (without leading zeroes), what does its output look like?

In the floating-point formats, the width and precision may be combined. If `dollars` is a `float` or `double` variable, we could print numbers up to 999,999.99 with the format `"%10.2f"`, as in

```
printf("%10.2f\n", dollars);
```

The comma after the thousands place cannot be specified, but we have left one space for a possible leading minus-sign.

To summarize the formats with a few examples:

ASCII character:	%c	%6c	
decimal integer:	%d	%6d	%03d
unsigned integer:	%u	%6u	%03u
octal integer:	%o	%6o	%03o
hexadecimal integer:	%x	%6x	%02x
fixed-point:	%.1f	%10.2f	
E-notation:	%.3e	%10.6e	

Note that the number of formats must match the number of items separated by commas appearing after the formats. If there are too many items, some data will be left unprinted. If there are too few items, extra garbage will be printed.

Exercise 2-1. Write and test a program which will print (decimal, octal, hex) the value of the special character constants:

```
'\n'     newline
'\t'     tab
'\b'     backspace
'\r'     carriage return
'\f'     form feed
'\\'     backslash
'\''     single-quote (apostrophe)
'\123'   arbitrary bit pattern  (e.g., 0123)
```

2.9   Program Size

Now you know that you can get output either with the `write` function (seen in `hello.c`) or the `printf` function (seen in `asst2.c`). Which to choose? As often happens, there are tradeoffs: The `printf` function is powerful, but large; the `write` function is very bare-bones, but takes little space in the computer memory. Indeed, about all you can do with `write`, given the C language we have covered so far, is to write messages such as `hello, world`.

Your operating system most likely has a command to tell you how much memory your program will require when run. In our Standard Environment (UNIX), the `size` command will give the answer **[2-23 os]**. The execution looks something like this:

```
cc -o hello hello.c
size hello
180+22+4 = 206b = 0316b

cc -o asst2 asst2.c
size asst2
2326+402+1040 = 3768b = 07270b
```

Forget for the moment about the first numbers with plus-marks between them; they concern "text" and "data" segments of the program, which we will cover in Section 5.8. Notice the difference in the total program size: 206 bytes (0316 octal) versus 3768 bytes (07270 octal). Those of you who work on large, time-shared computers will not care much, but if you are programming for a small, dedicated engineering application, the size of the resulting program is important.

Exercise 2-2. Determine the size required by `hello` on your system. Then modify `hello.c` to use the `printf` function, and determine the size of the resulting program.

2.10   Define and Include

C language has a mechanism called `#define`, which can make program constants easier to read. Consider the following revision of `hello2.c`:

```
hello4.c [2-24]:
    /* hello4 - print greeting
     */
    #define STDOUT   1
    #define MESSAGE "hello, world\n"
    #define LENGTH   13
    main()
        {
        write(STDOUT, MESSAGE, LENGTH);
        }
```

The very first step in compilation is the *preprocessor* which processes lines starting with a # such as

```
    #define STDOUT    1
```

The result of the preprocessing is to replace any occurrence of STDOUT with 1, any occurrence of MESSAGE with "hello, world\n", and any occurrence of LENGTH with 13. After all this replacing, our program looks *exactly* like hello2.c did to the compiler. We have simply specified the constants in a way that will be easier for someone to change later. As a general rule, any constant that could conceivably be modified later should be given a readable upper-case name via #define.

Of course, the name STDOUT is something of a mystery here. The mystery will be cleared up in Section 3.22.

A collection of commonly-used #define constants can be entered once into a file, and can be brought into a C source program using #include. Such a file is known as an *include-file* or *header file*. At this point, you should refer to Appendix B.2.10, and create the file local.h that you will find listed there. Be sure to type the upper and lower case characters just as you see them there. We will explain the items from that file as we come to them. For now, just notice that it defines the name STDOUT so that you could successfully compile the following hello5.c program.

```
hello5.c [2-25]:
    /* hello5 - print greeting
     */
    #include "local.h"
    #define MESSAGE "hello, world\n"
    #define LENGTH   13
    main()
        {
        write(STDOUT, MESSAGE, LENGTH);
        }
```

We are introducing include-files quite early, because they are commonly used on large projects to collect conventional values used throughout the project. The name local.h is chosen merely to suggest the "local" name that your organization may adopt for its standard include-file.

CHAPTER 3: OPERATORS

The operators of C are a faithful reflection of the built-in machine operations of modern computers. They provide the programmer with nearly all the capabilities that are available in assembler languages, without limiting the program to one specific computer hardware.

3.1 Arithmetic Operators

Arithmetic is the school subject dealing with addition, subtraction, multiplication, and division, and is pronounced "a-RITH-me-tick." In C, we have the *arithmetic operators,* in which the adjective "arithmetic" is pronounced "a-rith-MET-ick." There are five arithmetic operators:

+   plus (addition)

–   minus (subtraction)

*   times (multiplication)

/   divided by (division)

%   modulo (remainder)

All these operators are *dyadic* ("dye-ADD-ick") operators, meaning that they will accept two *operands* (the things being operated upon). (Another term for "dyadic operator" is *"binary operator,"* but we are avoiding this term to avoid confusion with "binary numbers.") Examples are a + b ("a plus b") and c / d ("c divided by d"). Furthermore, the "minus" operator can be used as a *monadic* ("moan-ADD-ick"), or *unary* ("you-NARY"), operator, meaning that it is applied to only one operand. "Unary minus" is the operation that takes the negative value of a number, as in –x ("negative x").

In programming languages, an *expression* is the name for the construction formed by an operator and its operands. (An operand by itself also constitutes an expression.) Examples of expressions are

```
a + b        c / d        -x      x
```

When this statement is executed

```
x = y + z;
```

the (run-time) value of **y** and the value of **z** are added together, and the result is assigned to **x**. More interestingly, when

```
x = y + z * w;
```

is executed, a *temporary result* is created for the product of **z** and **w**. The value of this temporary and the value of **y** are added together, and the result is assigned to **x**. This last statement illustrates a *precedence rule* of C; multiplication has *higher precedence* than addition, and hence it *binds tighter* to its operands. If we wanted to add **y** and **z** before the multiplication, we would need to use *parentheses* like this:

```
x = (y + z) * w;
```

Note that one expression may form a part of a bigger expression. Thus in the above statement there are eight expressions:

```
x
y
z
w
y + z
(y + z)
(y + z) * w
x = (y + z) * w
```

When one expression forms a part of a bigger expression, it is known as a *subexpression*. Of the eight expressions above, seven are subexpressions; the largest one is not a subexpression — it is the *full expression*. (The concept of the full expression will be important when we discuss "side-effects" later.)

These examples illustrate a portion of the *precedence hierarchy* of C. Using only the operators shown so far, the hierarchy would look like this:

( )	parentheses	TIGHTEST
-	unary minus	
* / %	multiplicative	
+ -	additive	
=	assignment	LOOSEST

Unary minus groups the tightest of the arithmetic operators:

```
x = y * -z;
```

multiplies **y** by negative **z**.

There is a conventional method of depicting the grouping of expressions in programming languages: the *expression tree.* Such a tree is formed by placing the operands of each operator slightly below the operator, joined by a connecting line. Thus, each subexpression forms a tree, and the whole expression forms a tree. These trees grow downward, in contrast to biological trees, which grow upward. The reason for this convention probably comes from "organization charts" in which the president or "big cheese" is usually at the top. In C, the "big cheese" operator at the top of the tree is the one which is not part of any subexpression. The expression tree for

        i = (j + k) * -m

looks like this:

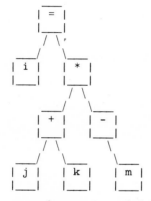

Notice that no parentheses are needed in the tree, because the information that they convey in the expression is conveyed by the tree notation. Another way to fully depict the grouping of an expression is the *fully parenthesized form,* in which every subexpression (except a simple variable or constant) has parentheses around it. For the expression

        i = (j + k) * -m

the fully parenthesized form looks like

        i = ((j + k) * (-m))

which, if used in an actual program, would be considered verbose, unreadable C. This tree (like the expression that generates it) does not specify the *order of evaluation* of its subexpressions. The only rule for arithmetic operators is that before an operator can be evaluated, its operands must first be evaluated. Thus the compiler is free to evaluate (j + k) first and then evaluate -m, or it could do them in the other order.

Question [3-1] Draw expression trees for the following expressions:

```
a + b % c            -a / b            a * -b
```

Question [3-2] How many subexpressions are there in this expression? _____
List them.

```
(a + b) * (c + d) + e
```

Let us look at the *semantics* (i.e. "meaning") of these operators in more detail. All of them can be applied to all the variable types that we have seen so far — both integers and floating-point. Addition and subtraction accomplish their usual result. Division, when applied to integers, produces a whole-number result with no fraction; thus, 6 / 4 is equal to 1, with no fraction or remainder. If it is the remainder that we are interested in, the % operator will tell it; 6 % 4 yields 2, an integer result. When applied to floating-point numbers, division yields a fractional answer (to as much precision as can be held in a float or double). Thus, 6. / 4. will yield 1.5 exactly. The remainder operator (%) is therefore not defined for floating-point data.

Of course, with either integer or floating-point data, division by zero is not a good idea, and the results are unpredictable.

Question [3-3] What does this program print?

```
arith.c [3-4]:
    /* arith - arithmetic practice
     */
    main()
        {
        printf("%d %d %d %d\n",
            1 + 2, 5 / 2, -2 * 4, 11 % 3);
        printf("%.5f %.5f %.5f\n",
            1. + 2., 5. / 2., -2. * 4.);
        }
```

Notice that we are able to put these arithmetic expressions right into the output list of the `printf` statements. This is one of the excellent features of C: an expression may be used anywhere a value is allowed.

Question [3-5] If a equals 8, b equals 2, and c equals 4, what is the resulting value of each expression:

```
a + b % c              -a / b              a * -b
```

_____   _____   _____

3.2   Relational Operators

So far, the program examples we have shown are all "straight-through" programs: the machine executes the first instruction, then goes on to the next, then the next, and so forth until the program is finished. Now we will introduce *loops* and *conditionals*, both of which alter the straight-through flow of control through the program. The following program, `blast.c`, illustrates a *loop*, known in C as the `for` statement:

```
blast.c [3-6]:
    /* blast - print countdown
     */
    main()
        {
        short n;

        for (n = 10; n >= 0; n = n - 1)
            printf("%d\n", n);
        printf("Blast off!\n");
        }
```

English translation of program:

> Start the variable n at 10.
> Count it down to zero, printing each value.
> Print "Blast off!" when done.

A flow chart for this program looks like this:

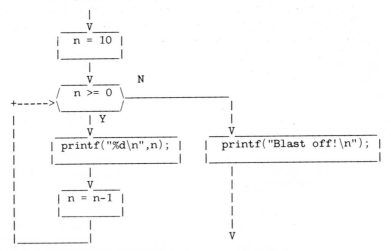

We will generally prefer to show program logic with a *program outline* (or *pseudo-code*), which is formatted like a program but contains a readable mixture of English and programming abbreviations:

> *for n = 10 down to 0*
>   *print n*
> *print "Blast off!"*

The loop can also be written with the **while** statement:

```
n = 10;
while (n >= 0)
    {
    printf("%d\n", n);
    n = n - 1;
    }
```

The flow-chart is the same as above. The expressions to initialize and to
step the variable n must be written in separate statements, because the while
statement contains only a single test within the parentheses. The *body* of the
loop (the statements that are controlled by it) becomes two statements, and
braces are required around the body any time it contains more than one statement.

The simplest form of *conditional* statement in C is the if statement,
such as this example:

```
if (n == 3)
    printf("We have ignition!\n");
```

The statement under the if is executed only if the condition in the parentheses
is *true*. If we add this if statement to blast.c, we obtain

blast2.c [3-7]:
```
/* blast2 - print countdown
 */
main()
    {
    short n;

    for (n = 10; n >= 0; n = n - 1)
        {
        printf("%d\n", n);
        if (n == 3)
            printf("We have ignition!\n");
        }
    printf("Blast off!\n");
    }
```

Notice the braces around the body of the for statement; they became necessary when the body grew to more than one line.

C has a full set of *relational operators*, such as the == ("is equal to")
that we just used. Here is the full set of relational operators:

```
<=      less than or equal to

<       less than

>=      greater than or equal to

>       greater than

==      equal to

!=      not equal to
```

Each of these operators takes two operands and produces a numerical result which is either 1 or 0 according to whether the relation is *true* or *false*. The while statement tests the *result* of the comparison: a *zero* stands for *false*, and any *non-zero* value stands for *true*. We will call this behavior of the while statement a *semi-Boolean* logic, because "zero equals *false*" is the proper Boolean interpretation, but "non-zero equals *true*" is the semi-Boolean interpretation.

The precedence of the relational operators is just below that of the arithmetic operators. This allows us to write expressions such as

```
a + b < c + d
```

with the meaning "a plus b is less than c plus d". Incidentally, when code makes sense in English when read aloud, we say that it "passes the telephone test" — i.e., would make sense when read aloud over the telephone. This is a rough test for program readability; when code fails the telephone test, try rewriting it. (For this and other useful style rules, see Kernighan and Plauger [1978].)

3.3   Logical Operators

The results of relational operators can be combined using the *logical operators:*

```
&&      and

||      or

!       not
```

For example,

```
a < b && b < c
```

is *true* (equals 1) if a is less than b *and* b is less than c; otherwise it is *false* (equals 0). The precedence of the logical operators is below that of the relational operators, so expressions such as this example can be written without parentheses.

The operators && and || are dyadic operators; they take two operands. The negation operator ! is monadic (i.e., unary); it takes only one operand. It produces a 1 when the operand is *false* (zero), and a 0 when the operand is *true* (non-zero). (This is the same semi-Boolean logic that we saw previously in the if, for, and while statements.) Thus,

```
!a
```

means the same as

```
a == 0
```

The *and* and *or* operators are "short-circuit" operators; evaluation proceeds left to right and stops when the result is determined. Thus in

```
d != 0 && n / d < 10
```

if the first comparison gives a *false* result, the second operation is not performed. In this example, this prevents a divide-by-zero problem. This property of logical operators is commonly used in C programs for situations in which the second operand should not be evaluated if the first comparison determines a case that should not be tested further.

Combining logical and relational operators allows us to test whether a character is a digit:

```
if ('0' <= c && c <= '9')
    printf("c is the digit %c\n", c);
```

Or to test for an uppercase letter:

```
if ('A' <= c && c <= 'Z')    /* ASCII only */
    printf("c is the uppercase letter %c\n", c);
```

Or to test for a printable character (refer to the code table in Section 1.2):

```
if (' ' <= c && c <= '~')    /* ASCII only */
    printf("c is the printable character '%c'\n", c);
```

(These latter tests assume the ASCII code set, which is not quite universal for C. We will shortly describe a technique that is better because it is portable — that is, it is not tied to a particular machine or compiler, but can be run in a variety of environments.)

Using several of these tests, we can create a program to generate a simple "code table":

```
codes1.c [3-8]:
    /* codes1 - print ASCII codes
     */
    main()
        {
        short c;

        for (c = 0; c <= 127; c = c + 1)
            {
            printf("%3d 0x%02x 0%03o", c, c, c);
            if (' ' <= c && c <= '~')
                printf(" '%c'", c);
            if ('0' <= c && c <= '9')
                printf(" digit");
            if ('A' <= c && c <= 'Z')
                printf(" uppercase");
            if ('a' <= c && c <= 'z')
                printf(" lowercase");
            printf("\n");
            }
        }
```

Question [3-9] When the variable c reaches the value 0x20 (ASCII blank, or ' ') how many of the relational expressions in codes1.c evaluate to a *true* (1) result? _____

How many evaluate to *true* for the value 126 (tilde, '~')? _____

Write the value of each expression (0 or 1):

    1 < 4 && 4 < 7   _____

    1 < 4 && 8 < 4   _____

    !(2 <= 5)   _____

    !(1 < 3) || (2 < 4)   _____

    !(4 <= 6 && 3 <= 7)   _____

3.4   Character Input/Output

All our programs so far have generated their own output, without any input at run time. Thus, none of them were interactive, that is, responsive to the keyboard. Input is required if a program is to be interactive, and as our first example of getting input to a program, we present getchar. Each time a program calls getchar like this

```
c = getchar()
```

getchar will wait for terminal input from the user, and return one character back to the program. At some point during the execution, the user may indicate "no more input," and the special value EOF will be returned from getchar. In our Standard Environment, "no more input" is indicated by hitting the <ctrl-d> key (the letter d with CONTROL shift); other environments have other equivalents **[3-10 os]**.

Both names, EOF and getchar, are defined in a *standard include-file* named stdio.h, which we will now wish to include into all our compilations. One common method is to begin each program with the line

```
#include <stdio.h>
```

but there is a more general approach. In the working environment, it is likely that your project or organization will have developed a local include-file for all its programs; our own include-file local.h plays this role for our book. When you do have a local include-file, put the

```
#include <stdio.h>
```

right into it, as we have done with our local.h **[3-11 cc]**.

An interactive version of our "codes" program looks like this:

codes2.c **[3-12]**:
```
/* codes2 - print ASCII codes
 */
#include "local.h"
main()
    {
    short c;

    while ((c = getchar()) != EOF)
        {
        printf("%3d 0x%02x 0%03o", c, c, c);
        if (' ' <= c && c <= '~')
            printf(" '%c'", c);
        if ('0' <= c && c <= '9')
            printf(" digit");
        if ('A' <= c && c <= 'Z')
            printf(" uppercase");
        if ('a' <= c && c <= 'z')
            printf(" lowercase");
        printf("\n");
        }
    }
```

In codes2.c, we have introduced a notational convenience of C, the *embedded assignment*, in the expression

```
(c = getchar()) != EOF
```

which combines two steps: First, getchar returns a value which is assigned to the variable c; next, this value is compared against EOF. If it is not equal, the loop continues; if it is equal, the loop terminates and the program stops. The parentheses around

```
(c = getchar())
```

are necessary, because assignment has lower precedence than all the other operators that we have seen so far.

Question [3-13] If you typed one line of input to the codes2.c program, consisting of the characters 1aA! followed by a newline, what would its output be? Compile the program and try it.

If you try the codes2 program at the keyboard, you will notice the typical *line-by-line buffering* provided by most environments: even though getchar returns one character at a time, you will see no output until you type an entire line and hit the RETURN, or NEWLINE, or the corresponding newline key on your terminal. This is because the codes2 program does not see the input characters until you hit the newline key. This line-by-line buffering allows you to correct typing mistakes at the terminal and is generally a useful behavior. Most environments will also provide you with a "raw keyboard" entry mode in which the buffering is turned off, but this is entirely different in each environment. For the rest of our book, we will continue to assume that input is buffered line-by-line.

You may be wondering why the variable c was declared to be a short integer. It must be bigger than any of the characters returned by getchar, because the EOF returned value must be distinguishable from any possible char value. In most environments, EOF is actually equal to the integer -1 and if assigned to a char variable, this could be confused with a possible char value.

To emphasize this last distinction, we introduce a made-up data type name for a variable which holds the returned value from getchar — such a variable will be declared as a metachar variable. The file local.h contains a definition of the name metachar to be short. With the inclusion of this metachar declaration, our program becomes codes3.c **[3-14]**:

```
/* codes3 - print ASCII codes
 */
#include "local.h"
main()
    {
    metachar c; /* return from getchar: char or EOF */

    while ((c = getchar()) != EOF)
        {
        printf("%3d 0x%02x 0%03o", c, c, c);
        if (' ' <= c && c <= '~')
            printf(" '%c'", c);
        if ('0' <= c && c <= '9')
            printf(" digit");
        if ('A' <= c && c <= 'Z')
            printf(" uppercase");
        if ('a' <= c && c <= 'z')
            printf(" lowercase");
        printf("\n");
        }
    }
```

Henceforth, we will use local.h in all our programs.

So far, we have used printf to print strings, even if they contain only one character, as in

```
printf("\n");
```

The same result is achieved by

```
putchar('\n');
```

with a smaller and faster program. The argument to putchar should be one individual character, either variable or constant. We can combine getchar and putchar to create a program that simply copies its input to its output:

copy.c **[3-15]**:

```
/* copy - copy input to output
 */
#include "local.h"
main()
    {
    metachar c;

    while ((c = getchar()) != EOF)
        putchar(c);
    exit(SUCCEED);
    }
```

Exercise 3-1. Write a program hex.c which will read characters from the terminal (until EOF), printing the code for each character in hexadecimal representation. (Use octal, if you prefer.) Each code should be printed with two numeric digits (with possible leading zero), one code per line of output.

Exercise 3-2. Write a program chksum.c which will compute the sum of all its input bytes.

Exercise 3-3. Write a program strip.c that will remove all characters from its input except for whitespace, letters, and digits.

Exercise 3-4. Write a program plot.c that will read characters from its input until EOF, printing a line of asterisks proportional in length to the binary value of the character that was read. In other words, the program functions as a simple plotter, treating the input line as a digital input signal. Apply a scaling factor, so that the largest ASCII character will fit onto an 80-character line.

3.5   Character-type Tests

Character-type tests occur frequently enough in programming that they have been incorporated into the Standard C Library. We can accomplish the same thing as

```
if ('0' <= c && c <= '9')
```

by saying

```
if (isdigit(c))
```

And we can replace

```
if ('A' <= c && c <= 'Z')
```

with

```
if (isupper(c))
```

Apropos the problem of portability to non-ASCII machines, these library tests will work for either ASCII or EBCDIC and thus give the advantage of portability.

In order to use these library tests, we need to add a new line to our programs:

```
#include <ctype.h>
```

This line is a command to the C preprocessor to include some standard definitions into our compilation so that names such as isdigit and isupper will be recognized. In contrast to the include-file stdio.h, the file ctype.h is not needed by the average program, and we will explicitly include it whenever it is needed. It will not be included by our standard local.h include-file.

These are the tests available from ctype.h:

isalpha(c)	c is a letter
isupper(c)	c is an uppercase letter
islower(c)	c is a lowercase letter
isdigit(c)	c is a digit
isalnum(c)	c is an alphanumeric character
isspace(c)	c is a "whitespace" (space, tab, carriage return, newline, or formfeed)
ispunct(c)	c is a punctuation character
isprint(c)	c is a printing character (including space)
iscntrl(c)	c is a non-printing character (less than ' ')
isascii(c)	c is an ASCII character (code less than 0200)

Returning to the version of codes that printed a complete table, we can add all these tests to obtain codes4.c, our latest version of the code table.

codes4.c [3-16]:
```
/* codes1 - print ASCII codes
 */
#include "local.h"
#include <ctype.h>
main()
    {
    metachar c;

    for (c = 0; c <= 127; c = c + 1)
        {
        printf("%3d 0x%02x 0%03o", c, c, c);
        if (isprint(c))
            printf(" '%c'", c);
        if (isdigit(c))
            printf(" D");
        if (isupper(c))
            printf(" UC");
        if (islower(c))
            printf(" LC");
        if (isalpha(c))
            printf(" L");
        if (isalnum(c))
            printf(" AN");
        if (isspace(c))
            printf(" S");
        if (ispunct(c))
            printf(" P");
        if (iscntrl(c))
            printf(" C");
        printf("\n");
        }
    }
```

See Appendix B for its output. If your printing terminal does not print the standard ASCII codes that we are showing, it would be useful for you to compile and run `codes4.c` to see the code correspondence for your terminal.

3.6   Bitwise Logical Operators

We return now to the three Boolean operators AND &, OR |, and NOT ~, and introduce a fourth operator, EXCLUSIVE-OR ^. The operators are defined by these tables:

```
     AND              OR              NOT            EXCLUSIVE-OR

     &   0   1        |   0   1        ~              ^   0   1
       --------         --------        ----            --------
   0 |  0   0      0 |  0   1      0 |  1         0 |  0   1
   |                |                |                |
   1 |  0   1      1 |  1   1      1 |  0         1 |  1   0
```

In C, these operators are applied in parallel to the individual bit positions. Hence they are called *"bitwise logical operators."* They must be carefully distinguished from the *logical* operators, && || !, which we saw in Section 3.3. The logical operators have similar names, but treat the entire operand as one single *true*-or-*false* value. We will avoid confusion over names by terming the bitwise operators *bit-and, bit-or, bit-negate,* and *exclusive-or.*

Taking *bit-not* ~ as the simplest example, consider the binary number

0000000000000111 (i.e., 0x0007 or 0000007 or just 7).

The *bitwise negation (bit-negate)* of this number would be written

~0x7 or ~07 or just ~7

and its value would be

1111111111111000 (written in C as 0xFFF8 or 0177770)

on a 16-bit-word computer, and

0xFFFFFFF8 or 037777777770

on a 32-bit-word computer. Bit-not is its own inverse;

~0x0007 equals 0xFFF8, and

~0xFFF8 equals 0x0007.

assuming a 16 bit word.

Question [3-17] Convert each number to 16-bit binary, and then negate it:

0x40 = _____   01 = _____

~0x40 = _____   ~01 = _____

The dyadic ("two-operand") bitwise operators are shown in the following table:

m   0001001100111111 (i.e., 0x137F or 011577), and

n   1111011100110001 (i.e., 0xF731 or 0173461).   .

m & n 0001001100110001 (i.e., 0x1331 or 011461).

m | n 1111011101111111 (i.e., 0xF77F or 0173577).

m ^ n 1110010001001110 (i.e., 0xE44E or 0162116).

In other words, the *bit-and* & of two numbers has a 1 bit in each position where both numbers have a 1 bit; all other positions are 0 bits. The *bit-or* | has a 0 bit in each position where both numbers have a 0 bit; all other positions are 1 bits. The *exclusive-or* ^ has a 1 bit in each position where both numbers have opposite bits; all other positions have 0 bits.

Question [3-18] Write the binary result of these operations:

```
  0000000001111111      0000000011000000      1111111111111100
& 0111010110011010    | 1000000000000100    & 1000000001111111
```

_____   _____   _____

Notice that the result of bit-and, bit-or, and exclusive-or does not depend on the word size of the computer, but the result of bit-negate does. If we want to write a binary value which consists of all 1-bits except for three low-order 0-bits, we should write this value as ~7, not as 0xFFF8 (its 16-bit value), nor as 0xFFFFFFF8 (its 32-bit value). When examining code for portability to other machines, give the bit-negation operations special attention.

The precedence of the bitwise operators is intrinsically confusing, and we recommend *always* fully parenthesizing any expression that involves the operators bit-and, bit-or, and exclusive-or. In other words, write

    n = ((a & b) | c);

not

    n = a & b | c;

The bitwise operations are not allowed upon floating-point numbers, but they may be used upon integer data of any size.

One last note about bitwise operations. The bitwise negation operator ~ is also known as the *ones complement* operator; and another way to accomplish the twos complement negation is to take the ones complement negation and add 1 to the unsigned result. For example, the ones complement negation of 0 is a word filled with 1-bits:

    1111111111111111   equals   ~0

The twos complement negation of 0 is simply 0, or

    0000000000000000

and we could have gotten this result by adding 1 to ~0, using unsigned arithmetic.

Question [3-19] Write the ones complement and twos complement of these numbers **[3-20 mach]**:

    9 = 0000000000001001   0xFF00 = 1111111100000000

    _____   _____
    (ones complement)   (ones complement)

    _____   _____
    (twos complement)   (twos complement)

3.7 Shift Operators

The *left shift* operator << takes two integer operands and produces an integer result. Let us look in detail at the operation

    0x10 << 3

The operation starts by placing the left operand (0x10 here) into an int sized temporary **[3-21 mach]**:

    | 0000000000010000 |
    |_____|

Next the bits within this temporary are all moved ("shifted") to the left by the number of places given by the right operand (3 here). The result looks like this **[3-22 mach]**:

    | 0000000010000000 |
    |_____|

Thus, 0x10 << 3 equals 0x80, or 108 in decimal.

An interesting arithmetic fact about shifting is that the left-shift operator is equivalent to a multiplication by a power of two. In this example, 3 places were shifted. Two to the third power is 8, 0x10 is 16, and 16 times 8 is 108.

The bits shifted into the number at the right-hand edge (the *low-order bits*) are always zero bits.

The *right-shift* operator >> works in similar fashion by shifting to the right. Thus, 0x10 >> 3 produces 2 as a result **[3-23 mach]**:

```
--------------------
| 0000000000010000 |
|_____|

        >> 3

--------------------
| 0000000000000010 |
|_____|
```

Notice that the bits shifted from the left-hand edge are filled with zeroes. If the number being shifted is a non-negative number, the fill bits are always zeroes. (And, of course, if the left operand is an *unsigned* variable, it is guaranteed to be non-negative.) Right-shift when applied to *negative* numbers can give different results in different environments, and we suggest never doing it, in the interests of portability.

Restricting ourselves, then, to right-shifting only non-negative numbers, the right-shift operation is equivalent to a division by a power of two. In this example, 0x10 >> 3 equals 0x10 / 8, or 2.

These examples have shown the shifting of int sized numbers. If the number being shifted is a long integer, the expression result is similarly a long.

For an example that uses shifts, consider this program which builds a binary number:

getbn.c **[3-24]**:
```
/* getbn - get a binary number and print it
 */
#include "local.h"
#include <ctype.h>
main()
    {
    metachar c;
    short n;

    n = 0;
    c = getchar();
    while (c != EOF && isspace(c))
        c = getchar();
    while (c == '0' || c == '1')
        {
        n = ((n << 1) | (c - '0'));
        c = getchar();
        }
    printf("%5u 0x%04x 0%06o\n", n, n, n);
    }
```

This program skips over any whitespace input characters. Then, as each '0' or '1' character is read, the previous value of n is doubled (shifted left by one bit) and a 0 or 1 is bit-or'ed into the low-order bit. Thus, if the input is

        1011

the program produces the value 11 (0x000B hex, 000013 octal).

Question [3-25] What output will the program produce for input 100001?

What output will the program produce for input 1111111111111111?

Exercise 3-5. Write a program wrdcnt.c that will tell how many bits there are in a "word" (int) on your computer.

3.8   Functions

Consider this C program which uses the previous section's binary conversion code:

getbn2.c [3-26]:

```
/* getbn2 - get and print binary numbers
 */
#include "local.h"
#include <ctype.h>
main()
    {
    short getbin();
    short number;

    while ((number = getbin()) != 0)
        printf("%5u 0x%04x 0%06o\n", number, number, number);
    }
/* getbin - get binary input number
 */
short getbin()
    {
    metachar c;
    short n;

    n = 0;
    c = getchar();
    while (c != EOF && isspace(c))
        c = getchar();
    while (c == '0' || c == '1')
        {
        n = ((n << 1) | (c - '0'));
        c = getchar();
        }
    return (n);
    }
```

We see here our first C program that contains a function other than main. From a practical point of view, functions save the programmer much work. Several new concepts must be explained:

1.   Call and return

2.   Returned type

3.   Local variables and scope of names

4.   Returned value

5.   Specification and manual page

6.   Arguments

(1) Call and return: The *function-call operator* consists of a left parenthesis appearing after an identifier;   the identifier is the name of the function
being called.   The left parenthesis must be matched by a subsequent right
parenthesis; between the parentheses may appear *argument* expressions.   The
simplest function call has no arguments at all, such as

```
getbin()
```

When our `getbn2` program reaches this expression, the `main` function *calls* the
`getbin` function. (Thus, `main` is the *calling function* and `getbin` is the *called
function*).   The calling location in `main` is memorized for later use.   The code
of the called function begins executing, starting with the statement

```
n = 0;
```

Statements from `getbin` keep executing until a `return` statement is executed.
(Reaching the function's closing brace, or "falling off the end," also causes a
return.)   At this point, control returns to the remembered place in the calling
function.

(2) Returned type: The `getbin` function produces a `short` result, so its
first line is

```
short getbin()
```

This declares to the compiler that the number coming back from `getbin` can
be properly assigned to a `short` variable, as is done in `main`.

(3) Local variables and scope of names: The open-brace { on the next
line means "BEGIN" — it marks the beginning of the function.   And the close-
brace } at the bottom marks the "END" of the function.   Between these mark-
ers, the function may have its own local variables.

At the top of the `getbin` function come declarations of variables:

```
metachar c;
short n;
```

These are *local* variables, meaning that any code outside this function has no
access to these names.   The *scope* of each name extends from the line where it
is declared, to the closing brace.   Thus, these names are not accessible in the
`main` function; only the variables declared in `main` can be used there.   This
means that two different programmers could write the two functions without
needing to coordinate their choice of names.

After the declarations comes a blank line — not a requirement of C, but
added for readability.   Then come the *executable statements,* which do the
work of the function.   The algorithm (or "precise method") is the same as we
saw in `getbn.c`: skip over whitespace and build the number bit by bit.

(4) Returned value: When control reaches this line

```
return (n);
```

control passes back to the calling program, and the value of n is delivered to the statement that called getbin. (Assembler programmers may be interested in knowing that on most machines this *returned value* is placed in a machine register, and the calling program knows to look in this register for the returned value **[3-27 cc]**.)

In this example, the calling program stores the returned value into the variable n and then compares this value to zero. As long as it is non-zero, the program prints the number in three formats: unsigned decimal, hexadecimal, and octal.

Question [3-28] If the input to getbn2 consists of these three lines

```
101
1111
00000
```

what does the output look like?

(5) Specification and manual page: We provide a concise description of the information needed to use the getbin function in the format introduced by UNIX manuals. The NAME entry gives a brief description of the function. The SYNOPSIS entry shows how the function is defined. The DESCRIPTION entry discusses how to use the function. The BUGS entry describes any quirks, "features," or actual errors in the existing implementation. (It is poor practice to distribute software with actual errors in it, but even poorer practice to distribute it with no warnings.)

---

getbin   USER MANUAL   getbin

NAME

getbin - get a binary-coded number from input

SYNOPSIS

```
short getbin( )
```

DESCRIPTION

Getbin first reads and ignores any whitespace input characters, then reads any number of '0' and '1' characters. This latter string is converted to a binary integer and returned as a `short` integer. If end-of-file is reached, 0 is returned.

BUGS

The end-of-file return is indistinguishable from actual 0 input.

Now is a good time to become familiar with the reference manual provided with the compiler that you are using. In the section where C functions are described, find the page describing `printf`. You will notice that it has more capabilities than we have described so far.

Question [3-29] (Using the `printf` manual page) How can the output be printed *left-adjusted* in its field width?

(6) Arguments: Data may be passed from the calling function to the called function via arguments. The values to be passed are listed, separated by commas, between the parentheses that follow the function name. In the called function, *parameter* names are declared to access these argument values, and the names are used thereafter as ordinary variables are. We need a new function to see the mechanism, since `getbin` had no arguments.

It is good programming practice to write the manual page first before you write the function; accordingly, here is the manual page for our new function.

NAME
putbin - print short integer in binary format

SYNOPSIS
```
void putbin(n)
short n;
```

DESCRIPTION
The parameter n is printed as a 16-bit binary number.

And now the function:

putbin **[3-30]**:
```
/* putbin - print number in binary format
 */
void putbin(n)
    short n;
    {
    short i;

    for (i = 15; i >= 0; i = i - 1)
        {
        if ((n & (1 << i)) == 0)
            printf("0");
        else
            printf("1");
        }
    }
```

This new function begins with

```
void putbin(n)
```

The type-name void is used here for the first time. It means that this is a function that does not return a value **[3-31 cc]**. Your compiler, like the cc of our Common Environment, may not yet support this type; for this reason, we have provided

```
#define void int
```

in our standard include-file local.h. In the calling program, putbin should be called without an assignment of result, as in

```
putbin(0xFF);
```

The following line

```
short n;
```

declares a short integer, n, as the parameter — the number to be printed.
putbin looks at the bits of n, printing a 0 or 1 for each one. Notice the new
embellishment, else, on the if statement; it means "if the previous condition
is *false*."

Here is a program which uses both the getbin and the putbin functions:

bdrill.c **[3-32]**:

```
/* bdrill - binary arithmetic practice
 */
#include "local.h"
#include <ctype.h>
main()
    {
    short a, b;
    short getbin();
    void putbin();

    while ((a = getbin()) != 0 && (b = getbin()) != 0)
        {
        printf("\n    a = ");
        putbin(a);
        printf("\n    b = ");
        putbin(b);
        printf("\na + b = ");
        putbin(a + b);
        printf("\na & b = ");
        putbin(a & b);
        printf("\na | b = ");
        putbin(a | b);
        printf("\na ^ b = ");
        putbin(a ^ b);
        printf("\n");
        }
    }
(getbin function goes here)
(putbin function goes here)
```

Question [3-33] What output will bdrill produce from this input? Compile it
and try it.

```
10101
11001
```

3.9   Lvalue, Rvalue, Increment, Decrement

The assignment statement

```
x = y;
```

typically produces assembler code that looks like this:

```
LOAD y
STORE x
```

On some machines, the value of **y** (the "right-hand side" of the assignment) is loaded into a temporary register and then placed into the storage of the variable **x** (the "left-hand side" of the assignment). On other machines, the assignment produces assembler code like

```
MOVE y TO x
```

with the same end result. Thus in C (as in most high-level languages), the left-hand side of the assignment must be an *lvalue* — an expression that references storage in the machine.

In contrast, the right-hand size of an an assignment may be an lvalue, or it may be an *rvalue,* which is any expression that is not an lvalue. A constant provides a simple example of an rvalue, such as the 0 in the statement

```
x = 0;
```

No machine memory is required to hold the zero. For example, the compiler might generate a "CLEAR x" instruction as the assembler code for this assignment statement.

Another way to describe the language's restriction is that rvalues are not allowed on the left-hand side of an assignment:

```
0 = x;
```

is illegal, as well as nonsensical.

We consider now some more operators that require lvalue operands: the *increment* ++ and *decrement* -- operators. In the statement

```
x = ++y;
```

the value of ++y is one greater than the original value of **y**. In addition, there is a *side-effect:* the storage of **y** is incremented sometime during the execution of the statement. The operator ++, when applied *to the left of* its operand, is known as a *prefix* operator.

Conversely, when ++ is written *to the right* of its operand, it is known as a *postfix* operator. The postfix form is different in that the value of **y++** is the value of **y** *prior* to the incrementation.

To use some concrete values, if **y** initially contains the value **99,** the statement

```
x = ++y;
```

will produce 100 in both **x** and **y**. If **y** now contains 100, the statement

```
x = y++;
```

will produce 100 in **x** and 101 in **y**.

Everything said about ++ applies to --, except that it *decrements* instead of incrementing. Thus if **y** is initially 99, the statement

```
x = --y;
```

will produce 98 in both **x** and **y**. If **y** now contains 98, the statement

```
x = y--;
```

will produce 98 in **x** and 97 in **y**.

Increment and decrement cannot be applied to rvalues. It is illegal to write --0 or 0++. In such cases, the compiler will complain "lvalue required," because the operator must have an lvalue operand.

These operators may be used for their side-effect alone, without forming part of a larger expression; for example, the statement

```
++x;
```

will increment **x**. When used solely for side-effects, the prefix and postfix forms are equivalent; the statement above is equivalent to this one:

```
x++;
```

For consistency, we suggest using the prefix form when using the operators for side-effects only. This make the operator more visible.

The precedence of these operators is higher than any others we have seen, except for parentheses, which have the highest precedence. Thus we can write

```
x = y + z++;
```

without parentheses, although it would be more straightforward to write simply

```
x = y + z;
++z;
```

As we will see in Section 3.15, C is not very precise about the exact moment that the side-effect takes place; tricky expressions such as

```
n++ + n++
```

can give different results in different environments.

These operators are often written as the *step* expression of a **for** statement. For example, in putbin.c, we wrote

```
        for (i = 15; i >= 0; i = i - 1)
```

whereas more fluent C would read

```
        for (i = 15; i >= 0; --i)
```

Or in codes4.c, where we wrote

```
        for (c = 0; c <= 127; c = c + 1)
```

we would now write

```
        for (c = 0; c <= 127; ++c)
```

There may be a small improvement in speed of execution from these changes.

3.10   Assignment Operators

"Add 2 to x" can be written as

      x = x + 2;

or as

      x += 2;

The *assignment operator* += is a combination of the + (add) and = (assignment) operators. All the arithmetic and bitwise operators have combined forms like this **[3-34 cc]**:

x += n	Add n to **x**
x -= n	Subtract n from **x**
x *= n	Multiply **x** by n
x /= n	Divide **x** by n
x %= n	x gets the remainder of dividing **x** by n
x <<= n	Shift **x** left by n
x >>= n	Shift **x** right by n
x &= n	x gets **x** bit-and'ed with n
x |= n	x gets **x** bit-or'ed with n
x ^= n	x gets the exclusive-or of x and n

The assembler code produced by

      x += n

is usually shorter and faster than the assembler code produced by

      x = x + n;

Many machines have an instruction like "ADD n TO x" which will do the job for +=.

Each of these operators produces a result equal to the new value of the left-hand side; it is legal to say

```
x = (y += z);
```

However, for readability we prefer

```
y += z;
x = y;
```

The precedence of these operators is the same as that of assignment — the lowest of all the operators we have seen so far. Thus, in order to say "divide x by y minus 1," we need no parentheses:

```
x /= y - 1;
```

3.11   Nesting of Operators

Each of the C operators produces a result that can be *nested* inside a larger expression. This is because C language accepts an expression anywhere a value is allowed. For example, we have often seen loops that start like this:

```
while ((c = getchar()) != EOF)
```

The assignment c = getchar() is *nested inside the comparison.* This is the sequence of events in evaluating the expression

```
(c = getchar()) != EOF
```

Call getchar, producing an int result.
Store the result in c.
Compare c with EOF, producing *true* or *false.*

When the assignment is nested like this, be sure to enclose it in parentheses; it is lower in precedence than most of the operators.

Another common form of nesting is the multiple assignment statement:

```
x = y = 0;
```

In this case, parentheses are not needed, because C interprets it properly:

STORE 0 IN y.
MOVE y TO x.

3.12   Address-of Operator and Scanf

C provides an operator which tells the *address* of its operand: &x gives the address of x. The operand of & must be an lvalue, something which has storage in the machine.

Our first use of & is to read numerical data with the *scanf* function. This function uses *formats,* just as *printf* does, to specify how input data is to be read. For example, the format "%hd" specifies a short (h for "halfword")

integer in d ("decimal") format. To read a short integer into the variable n, use

```
scanf("%hd", &n);
```

The argument &n tells scanf where to store the data that it reads. If, for example, n is located at address 8730 and contains the value 99,

```
n    8730      |      99 |
               |_____|
```

then the expression n has the value 99, and the expression &n has the value 8730. So if the program executes scanf("%hd", &n), after the user types "1000" (followed by newline), the storage of n will contain the numeric value 1000:

```
n    8730      |    1000 |
               |_____|
```

The scanf function knows to store the 1000 into location 8730 because that is the number that was passed as the value of &n. If instead we made the common mistake of calling scanf("%hd", n) the value passed to scanf would be 99, the *contents* of n. What happens next is unpredictable. On some machines, the attempt to store the 1000 into location 99 would cause a hardware error; on others, the memory at location 99 would suddenly receive the value 1000, leaving the value 99 unchanged in n.

Using scanf, several numbers can be read on the same line:

```
scanf("%hd %hd %hd", &n1, &n2, &n3);
```

When the user types

```
123      456      789 (NEWLINE)
```

the variables n1, n2, and n3 will contain 123, 456, and 789. The numbers typed on the input must be separated by whitespace (blanks, tabs, or newlines). Any whitespace in the format string itself will be disregarded; in this example, "%hd %hd %hd" reads three short integers, just as would "%hd%hd%hd".

The formats used by scanf are similar to those used by printf, but there are some differences. scanf needs a distinction between short data and int data [3-35 cc], and a similar distinction between float data and double data. These are the formats:

```
%c    char - reads one input character
%hd   short - reads one decimal number
%ho   short - reads one octal number
%hx   short - reads one hexadecimal number
%ld   long - reads one decimal number
%lo   long - reads one octal number
%lx   long - reads one hexadecimal number
%d    int - reads one decimal number
%o    int - reads one octal number
%x    int - reads one hexadecimal number
%f    float - reads one decimal number
%e    same as %f
%lf   double - reads one decimal number
%le   same as %lf
```

Question [3-36] Write a program, pr2a.c, to read two hexadecimal numbers into long variables, and print the two variables and their sum. Make another such program, pr2b.c, with double variables, using the proper formats.

3.13   Conditional Operator

The conditional operator produces a choice between two alternatives:

```
c ? x : y
```

produces the value of x if c is *true* (non-zero) and produces the value of y if c is *false* (zero). Thus,

```
a = n == 0 ? b : c;
```

does the same thing as

```
if (n == 0)
    a = b;
else
    a = c;
```

The conditional operator is sometimes useful in making a program shorter:

```
printf("%d\n", (a > b) ? a : b);
```

does the same thing as

```
if (a > b)
    printf("%d\n", a);
else
    printf("%d\n", b);
```

and usually generates less code.

The conditional operator is commonly used for such constructs as the *minimum (min)* of two numbers, the *maximum (max)* of two numbers, and the *absolute value* of a number:

```
minxy = x < y ? x : y;

maxxy = x < y ? y : x;

absx  = x < 0 ? -x : x;
```

Question [3-37] Modify your `pr2b.c` program to create `maxmin.c` which prints the max and min of the two input numbers.

One useful application of the conditional operator is in changing the case of letters. The function `toupper` converts lowercase to upper, and `tolower` does the reverse **[3-38 cc]**.

```
toupper [3-39]:
    /* toupper - convert lower-case letter to upper case
     */
    metachar toupper(c)
        metachar c;
        {
        return (islower(c) ? c + 'A' - 'a' : c);
        }


tolower [3-40]:
    /* tolower - convert upper-case letter to lower case
     */
    metachar tolower(c)
        metachar c;
        {
        return (isupper(c) ? c + 'a' - 'A' : c);
        }
```

The technique of changing case by adding a constant offset works in both ASCII and EBCDIC. The conditional operator ensures that only the desired letters are altered.

The conditional operator is *triadic (ternary)*, meaning that it requires three operands: the expression being tested, and the two alternative outcome expressions. It is the only triadic operator in C.

Precedence of conditional is slightly above assignment, which allows all the conditional expressions above to be written without parentheses.

3.14   Arrays and Subscripting

So far, we have looked at variables which are single items of data; these are called *scalars*. Now we will look at variables which contain multiple items of data; in C, such variables are known as *arrays*.

A variable is declared to be an array by putting a *subscript* after the variable name in the declaration. For example, to declare an array s which contains 512 char data items, we would write this declaration in C:

```
char s[512];
```

In the machine memory, s would look like this:

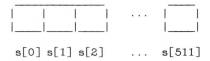

```
   s[0] s[1] s[2]    ...   s[511]
```

Each little box in the diagram represents the space to hold one char value; on all C machines, this amount of space is one byte. Thus, the variable s occupies 512 bytes of memory. Notice that the subscripts of the individual elements start at 0, and run upwards to 511 — one less than the declared number of elements. This scheme is known as *zero origin subscripting,* and it is the only scheme that C provides. By the way, we *strongly* suggest that you form a verbal habit of saying "*initial* element," not "first element," when referring to array element *sub* zero, such as s[0].

It is worth being precise about the *type* of an array variable. (Many problems that novices have with C can be traced to confusion about the types of the variables.) The data types of the scalar variables we have seen so far are all simple names, such as char or int. A very important rule can be given for determining the precise type of a C variable: the type is whatever is left by scratching out the name of the variable from its declaration statement. So for example, given the declaration statement

```
int i;
```

the type consists of whatever remains after scratching out the name i, namely the word int. And similarly, the type of our array variable s is just what is left after scratching out the name s, namely char[512]. To say this type out loud, one might say literally "char bracket five-twelve bracket", but the proper way to say it is "array of 512 chars". In other words, a declaration in C forms a "sandwich" of two things: the *type* is the "bread," and the name being declared is the "meat." (If the type is a simple type like int, the "sandwich" is "open-face.")

Another general rule is that the *memory size* of a variable is completely determined by its type. Thus, the size of s is the memory size for the type char [512], namely 512 bytes. C language even has an operator which will tell the size of a expression — the sizeof operator. And sizeof can also tell the size of a *type*, as well. Consider this little program:

```
sizes.c [3-41]:
    /* sizes - report the size of some types and expressions
     */
    #include "local.h"
    main()
        {
        char c;
        char s[512];
        short n;
        short m[40];

        printf("%3d %3d\n", sizeof(c), sizeof(char));
        printf("%3d %3d\n", sizeof(s), sizeof(char[512]));
        printf("%3d %3d\n", sizeof(n), sizeof(short));
        printf("%3d %3d\n", sizeof(m), sizeof(short[40]));
        }
```

Here we are simply asking the compiler to print out the sizes of our data, specified once by the variable name and once by its type name. And its output, as we expect, is **[3-42 cc] [3-43 mach]**

```
  1   1
512 512
  2   2
 80  80
```

The variable s is an array of 512 individual chars; each of its elements can be referenced using a *subscript*, which can be any expression that produces an integer. Thus, s[0], s[1], and s[511] are all elements of s, as is s[i], where i is an integer variable. (Strictly speaking, i must have a value between 0 and 511 if s[i] is to designate an element of this array s. The C compiler does *no checking* to determine if a subscript is indeed within the bounds of an array; it is entirely the programmer's responsibility to use legal subscripts.) Each of these elements of the array designates a piece of the memory in the machine; the determination of the *address* of an element is given by a formula known as the *subscripting formula*. In C, the subscripting formula is this:

address of i-th element =

address of 0-th element + i * (size of each element)

In this example, the size of each element is 1 byte. Therefore, if the array s is located at address 2000 in the machine, the address of s[101] is 2000 + 101, or 2101. So s[101] is a single char of storage which is located at 2101.

Let us look at another example:

```
short m[100];
```

According to our rules above, this declaration says that m has the type short[100], i.e., an array of 100 shorts. If each short occupies 2 bytes, then the size of m is 200 bytes. Suppose that m is located at address 4000 in the machine; then the address of m[40] is 4080 **[3-44 mach]**.

By the way, another common name for *subscripting* is *indexing* — the terms "zero-origin subscripting" and "zero-origin indexing" are equivalent.

Strings, in C language, are constant arrays of chars. The array contains the characters of the string, followed by the null terminator \0 which marks the end of the string in memory. Thus the string "april" looks like

```
|  97 | 112 | 114 | 105 | 108 |   0 |
| 'a' | 'p' | 'r' | 'i' | 'l' |'\0' |
```

in the memory. There is a useful function, strlen, in the standard library which will tell us the length of a string. *"Length,"* when applied to arrays of characters, refers to the number of non-null characters appearing before the null terminator. Thus, the length of the string "april" is 5 --

```
strlen("april")
```

would return the value 5 — whereas the *size* of "april" is 6 (including the null terminator).

An array of characters can be copied into another array with the strcpy function. For example, if s has the type char[512], we can safely copy "april" into s by writing

```
strcpy(s, "april");
```

One character array can be tacked onto the end of another ("catenated") with strcat(s1,s2)

```
strcpy(s, "april");
strcat(s, " fool");
```

will leave s containing the characters "april fool" plus a null terminator.

Two strings can be compared using strcmp(s1,s2) One by one, the string characters are compared until corresponding characters differ (or the null is reached). The returned value is negative, zero, or positive according to whether s1 sorts lower than, equal to, or greater than s2. (Note that the sorting order can be different using different character sets — one reason to use ASCII for all your C programming.) Thus,

```
strcmp("123", "124")
```

is negative.

```
strcmp("3", "12")
```

is positive, and

```
strcmp("ab", "ab")
```

is zero.

Each of these string functions is quite simple to write. The "string copy" function, strcpy, could look like this:

strcpy.c **[3-45]**:
```
/* strcpy - copy characters from s2 to s1
 */
void strcpy(s1, s2)
    char s1[], s2[];
    {
    unsigned i;

    i = 0;
    while (s2[i] != '\0')
        {
        s1[i] = s2[i];
        ++i;
        }
    s1[i] = '\0';
    }
```

(This version of strcpy is simpler than the one in our Common Library; it has no returned value.)

It is the programmer's responsibility to be sure that there is enough space in the receiving array for the operation of strcpy and strcat. The functions do no checking for length.

The simplest way to print a string is with the "%s" format of printf. If a1 is an array of characters, calling

```
printf("%s", a1);
```

will deliver each character of a1 to be output, up to the first '\0' null character. Any '\n' newline characters in a1 will be printed along with the others, but no extra newlines will be added. (If one or more newlines are desired besides whatever is in the array a1, they may be put into the format string, such as "%s\n".)

Question [3-46] What does the following program print? (The defined constant BUFSIZ comes from stdio.h; it is usually 512 or 1024, large enough for the largest line of input.)

```
string.c [3-47]:
    /* string - practice with character arrays
     */
    #include "local.h"
    main()
        {
        char a1[BUFSIZ];
        char a2[BUFSIZ];

        strcpy(a1, "every ");
        strcpy(a2, "good boy ");
        strcat(a2, "does ");
        if (strlen(a1) < strlen(a2))
            strcat(a2, "fine ");
        else
            strcat(a1, "very ");
        if (strcmp(a1, a2) < 0)
            {
            strcat(a1, a2);
            printf("%s\n", a1);
            }
        else
            {
            strcat(a2, a1);
            printf("%s\n", a2);
            }
        }
```

The "get line" function from Kernighan and Ritchie [1978] is an excellent way of reading one input line into a string. Unfortunately, this function is not included in most versions of the standard library, so we have provided a definition of the name getln in our local.h include-file. With this definition, the expression

```
getln(s, n)
```

will read one line (including the newline \n) into the string s. A null terminator will be put at the end of s. If the input is at end-of-file, the value EOF is returned; otherwise, the new length of s is returned. Thus, this program will copy lines of input onto the output:

```
copy2.c [3-48]:
    /* copy2 - copy input to output
     */
    #include "local.h"
    main()
        {
        char s[BUFSIZ];

        while (getln(s, BUFSIZ) != EOF)
            printf("%s", s);
        }
```

Exercise 3-6. Write a program byttab.c that reads an input file and tabulates the number of times it sees each one of the 128 legal ASCII characters. At the left margin, print the numeric code for the first tabulation on that line, followed by eight tabulations. But if all eight numbers are zero, do not print the line.

Exercise 3-7. Write a program words.c that reads an input file and prints each word on a separate line. (A word, in this context, is a sequence of non-whitespace characters.) Along with each word, print its hash-sum (the sum of the characters in the word), once as a four-digit hex number and once as a 5-digit decimal number. Print the hex number with leading zeroes, the decimal number with leading blanks.

3.15   Comma Operator

So far, we have seen two uses of the comma symbol in C. It serves to separate a list of variables in a declaration, as in

```
double a, b;
```

And it separates the arguments to a function, as in

```
printf("%d\n", n);
```

In both of these cases, the comma is a *separator* of C; it is part of the punctuation of declarations and function arguments.

But there is another use of comma in which it is an *operator*. Two expressions can be "spliced" together with the *comma operator*. For example, this line counts as one statement in C:

```
t = s[i], s[i] = s[j], s[j] = t;
```

The effect of this line is to "swap" two array elements s[i] and s[j], using a temporary variable t. One reason for using this "comma-spliced" construction is to indicate that the statement forms one "atomic" operation, in this case a "swap" operation. It alerts a maintenance programmer that these lines constitute one operation that should be kept together.

A second use of the comma is to perform more than one expression in the initialization or the step of a for loop. Both uses of comma are found in the following revers.c program, which reverses the lines of its input. An early use of the program was to create a "crossword-puzzle" dictionary of words sorted by their endings. Instead of creating a new sort program (which would be a big effort), it was easier to reverse the words, sort them, and reverse them again. The algorithm uses two indexes, i and j to point ⸍

left-hand and right-hand sides of the string that is to be reversed. Rather than artificially making one of them the "controlling" variable of the loop, we can give both variables equal status in the loop. Here is the program:

```
revers.c [3-49]:
    /* revers - print input lines reversed
     */
    #include "local.h"
    main()
        {
        char line[BUFSIZ];   /* the line of input text */
        short len;           /* length of line */

        while ((len = getln(line, BUFSIZ)) != EOF)
            {
            if (line[len - 1] == '\n')
                line[--len] = '\0';
            reverse(line);
            printf("%s\n", line);
            }
        }
    void reverse(s)
    char s[];
        {
        char t;
        short i, j;

        for (i = 0, j = strlen(s) - 1; i < j; ++i, --j)
            t = s[i], s[i] = s[j], s[j] = t;
        }
```

In the function **reverse** we see three different uses of the comma operator. The `for` loop is initialized with the single expression

```
i = 0, j = strlen(s) - 1
```

The *step* of the loop is the expression

```
++i, --j
```

And the "swap" is spliced together as we saw earlier.

It is considered poor style to string expressions together with commas just to save printout paper; it makes the programs harder to maintain later.

3.16   Order of Evaluation

The actual sequence in which operands are evaluated is left unspecified for most of the C operators. Consider these functions:

```
short f1()
    {
    printf("reached f1\n");
    return (1);
    }
short f2()
    {
    printf("reached f2\n");
    return (2);
    }
```

If we write

```
x = f1() * f2();
```

the result is guaranteed to be 2 (1 times 2), but in which order will the `printf` messages be printed? C does not say; either is possible.

Some operators, however, *do* guarantee sequence of evaluation:

1.   a, b   comma
2.   a && b   logical and
3.   a || b   logical or
4.   a ? b : c   conditional

In each case, the evaluation of a will take place before the evaluation of b (or c). Moreover, in case 4 exactly one of the two expressions b and c will be evaluated. To this list of four guarantees, C adds one more sequence guarantee:

5.   full expression

C guarantees that each "full expression" (the enclosing expression that is not a subexpression) will be evaluated completely before going further.

The four operators above, plus the "full expression", will be called the *sequence points* of C.

One vital reminder: each of the arguments in a function call is a full expression, but the comma that separates them is *not* a sequence point; the compiler is free to evaluate the arguments left-to-right or right-to-left, or randomly. Thus the function call

```
printf("%d %d\n", f1(), f2());
```

does not guarantee whether f1 will be called before or after f2.

Besides governing the sequence of evaluation, the sequence points are important for controlling *side-effects*. Any operation that affects an operand's storage is said to have a *side-effect*. These are the operators with side-effects:

```
++    --                        increment and decrement
=                               assignment
+=   -=  *=  /=  %=             arithmetic assignment operators
<<= >>= &=  |=  ^=              bitwise assignment operators
```

In addition, whenever a function-call appears in an expression, some side-effects might take place during the execution of the function.

   In C, the exact time at which the side-effect takes place is indeterminate. All that is guaranteed is that the side-effect will be complete by the time the next sequence point is reached. For example, this code cannot be guaranteed to produce a consistent result:

```
a[i] = i++;
```

If the side-effect of the increment takes place before the subscript is evaluated we get one result; if the side-effect takes place after the subscripting, we get a different result. Moral: do not write code which depends upon the timing of side-effects.

Question [3-50] Mark Y or N whether each of these statements is *vulnerable* to the timing of side-effects:

```
_____    n = n++;

_____    printf("%d %d\n", ++n, ++n);

_____    n = ++m;

_____    n = y *= 2;
```


3.17   Floating-point Computation

   Most of the operators that we have seen can be applied to floating-point data as well as to integers. (The exceptions are the bitwise operators: & | ~ ^ << and >>.) Several special considerations apply to floating-point computation.

   To begin with, because machines differ in their floating-point mechanisms, answers may be slightly different on different machines. And on any machine, answers are only approximate — accurate only to a limited number of decimal places. Comparing two floating-point results for exact equality is generally risky. Adding a long series of numbers can create a noticeable *roundoff error;* the more numbers in the series, the larger the error. Subtracting two nearly equal numbers can also create a roundoff error. A small roundoff error can also creep in when decimal input is converted to internal binary format or vice versa.

These considerations suggest two cautionary notes. First, before attempting serious scientific or engineering computations with long sequences of floating-point operations, you should first consult a text on numerical analysis, such as Hamming [1973]. Second, if you use floating-point numbers for dollars and cents computations, be aware that a printed result could be off by a penny.

A number of useful functions are available in the C library for floating-point computation. Some of the more common functions are

`cos(x)`	cosine of **x**
`exp(x)`	*e* raised to the **x**-th power
`log(x)`	natural logarithm of **x**
`log10(x)`	base-10 logarithm of **x**
`pow(x, y)`	**x** raised to the y-th power
`sin(x)`	sine of **x**
`sqrt(x)`	square root of **x**

All these functions accept `float` or `double` arguments, and return a `double` result. When you use these math functions, you should add the line

```
#include <math.h>
```

to your program, to ensure that all the names are understood as returning `double` values.

The following mortgage program, `mortg.c`, is an example of simple floating-point computation.

mortg.c **[3-51]**:

```
/* mortg - compute table of payments on mortgage
 */
#include "local.h"
#include <math.h>
main()
    {
    double intmo;    /* monthly interest */
    double intyr;    /* annual interest */
    double bal;      /* balance remaining */
    double pmt;      /* monthly payment */
    double prinpmt;  /* payment allocated to principal */
    double intpmt;   /* payment allocated to interest */
    double dnpmts;   /* number of payments, in double */
    short i;         /* loop index */
    short npmts;     /* number of payments */
    short nyears;    /* number of years */

    printf("Enter principal (e.g. 82500.00): ");
    scanf("%lf", &bal);
    printf("Enter annual interest rate (e.g. 16.25): ");
    scanf("%lf", &intyr);
    printf("Enter number of years: ");
    scanf("%hd", &nyears);
    printf("\nprincipal=%.2f  interest=%.4f%%  years=%d\n\n",
        bal, intyr, nyears);
    intyr /= 100.;
    intmo = intyr / 12.;
    npmts = nyears * 12;
    dnpmts = npmts;
    pmt = bal * (intmo / (1. - pow(1. + intmo, -dnpmts)));
    printf("%8s %10s %10s %10s %10s\n",
        "payment", "total", "interest", "principal", "balance");
    printf("%8s %10s %10s %10s\n",
        "number", "payment", "payment", "payment");
    printf("%8s %10s %10s %10s %10.2f\n",
        "", "", "", "", bal);
    for (i = 1; i <= npmts; ++i)
        {
        intpmt = bal * intmo;
        if (i < npmts)
            prinpmt = pmt - intpmt;
        else
            prinpmt = bal;
        bal -= prinpmt;
        printf("%8d %10.2f %10.2f %10.2f %10.2f\n",
            i, intpmt + prinpmt, intpmt, prinpmt, bal);
        }
    }
```

The most complicated part of the program is the computation of the monthly payment, pmt. Using the program's variable names in conventional mathematical notation, the standard formula looks like this:

$$pmt = bal \times \frac{intmo}{1 - (1 + intmo)^{-dnpmts}}$$

The rest of the program is just bookkeeping and printouts.

When compiling programs using the math library, add -lm to the command line **[3-52 cc]**:

```
cc -o mortg mortg.c -lm
```

This specifies a special math link-library.

The execution of mortg.c looks like this:

```
Enter principal (e.g. 82500.00): 10000.00
Enter annual interest rate (e.g. 16.25): 18.00
Enter number of years:  1

principal=10000.00  interest=18.0000%  years=1
```

payment number	total payment	interest payment	principal payment	balance
				10000.00
1	916.80	150.00	766.80	9233.20
2	916.80	138.50	778.30	8454.90
3	916.80	126.82	789.98	7664.92
4	916.80	114.97	801.83	6863.10
5	916.80	102.95	813.85	6049.24
6	916.80	90.74	826.06	5223.18
7	916.80	78.35	838.45	4384.73
8	916.80	65.77	851.03	3533.70
9	916.80	53.01	863.79	2669.91
10	916.80	40.05	876.75	1793.15
11	916.80	26.90	889.90	903.25
12	916.80	13.55	903.25	0.00

Notice that there are round-off errors; on payment numbers 4, 5, and 10, the subtraction of principal payment from balance is off by a penny.

Question [3-53] Revise the mortg.c program to make it correct to the penny. (Hint: forget the decimal points and use long arithmetic.)

Exercise 3-8. Revise mortg.c as above, with decimal points appearing properly in the printout.

One general environmental note: some machines have special hardware for floating-point operations, and your programs will run many times faster if it is used. If you are running on a time-sharing system like a large UNIX, the standard compile command will probably take advantage of any special hardware. If you have your own system, you should consult your compiler manual to determine how it handles floating-point operations.

3.18   Precedence and Associativity

In the individual sections on operators we have seen specific rules of precedence. Now we describe them all together in one table. (For completeness, we are showing the primary operators . and ->, and the monadic usage of *; their details will wait until Chapter 7.)

Operator Type	Precedence Level	Operators
Primary	15	() [] -> .
Monadic	14	! ~ ++ -- - (type) * & sizeof
Arith-	13	* / %
metic	12	+ -
Shift	11	>> <<
Rel-	10	< <= > >=
ational	9	== !=
Bitwise Logical	8	&
	7	^
	6	|
Logical	5	&&
	4	||
Cond.	3	?:
Asst.	2	= += -= *= /= %= |= ^= &= >>= <<=
Comma	1	,

As undigested information, this table is formidable and leads many programmers to cop-out attitudes like "when in doubt, use parentheses." However, the design of C embodies real insight and programming experience, and a few simple rules give full mastery of C precedence:

(1) Bitwise operators have intrinsically confusing precedence and should *always* be used with parentheses. The confusion comes from their dual nature — they are both quasi-arithmetic and quasi-logical. They are quasi-arithmetic in that n & 3, which gives the rightmost two bits of n, is prone to usage in

contexts such as

```
n & 3 == 2
```

which is wrong; it should be written

```
(n & 3) == 2.
```

But they are quasi-logical in that one could write

```
a == b & c == d
```

where the precedence is correct — but the logical operator && is generally preferred. Therefore, always parenthesize the operators

```
<<   >>   &   |   ^
```

(2) *Primary* operators ( ) [ ] -> . are naturally the strongest operators. In any scheme, parentheses must be the strongest. The other operators serve to describe the access to data and should be stronger than any other operators upon that data.

(3) *Monadic* (unary) operators are naturally stronger than other arithmetic operators. Otherwise

```
x = -5 + n;
```

would be taken as

```
x = -(5 + n);
```

contrary to intuition.

(4) *Arithmetic* operators should be higher than relational because

```
a + b < c + d
```

sounds natural (passes the "telephone test") when read aloud as *"a plus b is less than c plus d."* Within the arithmetic level, multiplicative operators * / % are traditionally stronger than additive operators + -.

(5) *Relational* operators should be, by the "telephone test" again, stronger than logical:

```
a < b && c < d
```

reads aloud properly as *"a is less than b and c is less than d."* In readable code, one never needs to remember that equality operators == != have slightly lower precedence than comparison operators < <= > >= and we therefore simply group them all under the category of *relational* operators. Within the logical operators, the Boolean multiplicative "and" && is stronger than the Boolean additive "or" ||.

(6) *Conditional* is higher than assignment, because a "choice" can be assigned to a variable:

```
x = n > 0 ? n : 0;
```

(7) *Assignment* is lower than all these operators, because expressions using these operators can be assigned to a variable:

```
n = a + b;
ready = able && willing;
```

(8) *Comma* is lowest of all, because assignments can be strung together with commas:

```
tmp = a, a = b, b = tmp;
```

Thus, by these rules there are really eight levels to remember:

1. primary
2. monadic
3. arithmetic
4. relational
5. logical
6. conditional
7. assignment
8. comma

plus the historical convention placing *multiplicative* above *additive*.

Question [3-54] Parenthesize to show the binding:

```
a    ==   b    &&   c    !=   d

y    =    3.14   *   -   d
```

Precedence rules by themselves do not answer all questions about grouping; there still are cases of adjacent operators all having the same precedence, such as

```
a - b - c - d
```

To most people, this would mean *"subtract b from a, then subtract c, then subtract d"* (a "left-to-right" reading), rather than *"subtract d from c, then subtract this from b, then this from a"* (a "right-to-left" reading). C therefore associates operators of equal precedence left-to-right, with these exceptions:

(1) *Assignment* groups right-to-left to allow multiple assignments:

```
x = y = 0;
```

which is indeed the "natural" grouping.

(2) *Monadic* operators are generally written to the left of their operand: `~~x` means `~(~x)` and therefore right-to-left association is more natural. It also hardly matters, except in the case of `*p++` which groups as `*(p++)` and is also beyond the scope of this chapter.

(3) *Conditional* `?:` groups right-to-left, but in readable programs conditionals are never nested inside each other, so the rule is irrelevant.

These rules can easily be memorized. They eliminate all uncertainty about precedence and associativity in C.

3.19   Conversion

C has a preference for certain data types when it evaluates expressions. On most C machines, there are machine registers that are big enough to hold an int result, and smaller data will be widened to int size when used in an expression. (That is, the storage for the variable does not expand; a temporary is created, usually in a register, and this temporary has int size.) Of course, if long numbers are bigger than int numbers on your machine, it would not work very well to shorten them down to int in calculations. Therefore, long is also a preferred type. Also, double is always a preferred type; any float operand will be widened into a double temporary.

These rules can be summarized like this: There are certain preferred sizes. Any data not already occupying one of these sizes will be widened to the next-largest preferred size when it appears in an expression. The more general technical name for this widening process is *promotion*.

A second rule concerns the dyadic and triadic operators: after any promotions to preferred size, if the operands are of different size, the smaller one will be promoted to the size of the larger one. The result will be of this larger size. This part of the process is known as *type balancing*.

A third rule concerns unsigned data. Whenever an unsigned item is promoted to a larger size, there is enough room to express it as a signed number in the wider size. But if after promotions to preferred size, one of the operands is signed and the other is unsigned, the signed operand is converted to unsigned data, and the result of the operation is unsigned.

The effect of these rules can be summarized in a table. Each of the preferred types is marked with an asterisk (*). Each operand will be promoted to the nearest larger preferred type, and if two operands are involved, the smaller will be promoted to the type of the larger **[3-55 cc]**.

2-byte machine	4-byte machine
* double	* double
float	float
* unsigned long	* unsigned int, unsigned long
* long	* int, long
* unsigned int, unsigned short	unsigned short
* int, short	short
unsigned char	unsigned char
char	char

Another set of conversion rules applies for *assignment* and the *assignment operators* (+= -= etc.). In such cases, the only conversion required is that the result value is converted to the type of the left-hand side of the assignment. Thus, in this code fragment

```
short i;
float f;

i = f;
f += i;
```

the first assignment truncates any fraction bits and loses any high-order bits that will not fit into a short variable. The second assignment operation directly adds i to f with no requirement for a promoted temporary. (This can give shorter and faster code on some small microprocessors.)

Some examples will illustrate these rules. In our first example, we will perform some arithmetic with short, long, and float data. Consider this code fragment:

```
short n;
long lnum;
float f;

n = n * lnum / f;
```

The product n * lnum involves a short variable n and a long variable lnum. The variable n will be promoted to long size, and the operation takes place in long arithmetic. Next, the float variable f is promoted to the preferred double size into a temporary. Then the long result is divided by the double temporary, so the long result is promoted to double, and the division takes place in double arithmetic. Finally, the double result is assigned back to a short variable, causing a loss of any fraction digits, and a truncation to the size of a short. (The example, admittedly far-fetched, is chosen only to illustrate the conversions.)

Conversion can be specified explicitly with the *cast* (or *coercion*) operation **[3-56 cc]**, which consists of a type enclosed in parentheses. For example, remembering that the square-root function, sqrt, requires a double argument, one could take the square root of a short variable i like this:

```
sqrti = sqrt((double)i)
```

This covers the rules for conversions between scalars in C. A different kind of conversion is needed to convert between scalars and numbers stored in strings. This kind of conversion has no built-in operator in C; one must call functions to do it. For example, if in the string s we have stored the character representation of a number such as 123, it might look like this in the memory:

```
s            |  49 |  50 |  51 |   0 |
             | '1' | '2' | '3' |'\0' |
```

To convert the contents of s into a char, short, or int number n, we could write

```
n = atoi(s);
```

The atoi ("ASCII to int") function takes a character array argument, and treats it as the decimal representation of an integer. Similarly, for a long number lnum, we could convert it from s via

```
lnum = atol(s);
```

using the atol ("ASCII to long") function. And for a double number d, there is atof for "ASCII to float." (This is a slight misnomer; the name should mean "ASCII to double.")

```
d = atof(s);
```

All these functions will skip over any leading whitespace in the string, and stop converting when they reach a character that cannot be part of the number they are converting.

The most general way to convert the other direction — from scalar numbers into printable representations in character arrays — is to use the sprintf ("string printf") function. This handy function formats its arguments just as printf does, but its output goes into a string instead. For example,

```
char s[BUFSIZ];
short n;

n = 246;
sprintf(s, "%d", n);
```

will leave s looking like this:

```
s        |  50 |  52 |  54 |   0 |
         | '2' | '4' | '6' |'\0' |
```

Of course, sprintf is much more powerful than this simple example suggests. We can format a whole list of scalars and other strings into one string:

```
sprintf(s, "%3s %3s %2d %2d:%02d:%02d %4d",
    weekday, mo, day, hh, mm, ss, yr);
```

could leave s looking like this:

```
"Fri Nov 11 15:47:04 1982"
```

The receiving array s must be long enough to hold all the generated characters, or they will run over into other storage.

The scanf function also has a "string" counterpart called sscanf. It "reads" from a string instead of from the input; if s looks like the result above, we could read from it a list of arrays and short integers like this:

```
sscanf(s, "%3s %3s %2hd %2hd:%02hd:%02hd %4hd",
    weekday, mo, &day, &hh, &mm, &ss, &yr);
```

After the conversion is complete,

weekday	contains	"Fri",
mo	contains	"Nov",
day	contains	12,
hh	contains	15,
mm	contains	47,
ss	contains	4, and
yr	contains	1982.

Just like scanf, sscanf returns the number of successful assignments performed (seven, in this case), and this returned value should be tested to be sure that sscanf succeeded. In Section 3.22, we will see some useful things that we can do if the returned value indicates a conversion failure.

3.20   Overflow

Overflow is what happens when when a value is computed which is too large for the space available to hold the result. You can see the phenomenon of overflow with a hand calculator. If the calculator holds six digits, you can enter the number 999,999:

```
| 999999 |
|_____|
```

If you then add 1 to this value, the calculator may overflow in a computer-like fashion:

```
  _____
 | 000000 |
 |_____|
```

Or, more likely it will complain about the result:

```
  _____
 | ERROR  |
 |_____|
```

Most C machines never complain about overflow **[3-57 mach]**. They just keep running with the portion of the overflowed number that fits the storage that is available.

The operators that can overflow are + - * ++ -- and <<. When you use these operators, be sure that the result is not marred by overflow problems. The responsibility for guarding against overflow rests entirely with the programmer.

Exercise 3-9. Another type of overflow occurs when a number that should be positive appears negative by overflowing into the high-order bit. Make use of this behavior (true for both twos complement and ones complement machines) to write a function `maxint` which returns the largest positive `int` value on whatever computer the program is compiled for. Include your `maxint` function in a program `maxi.c` which prints your result.

Exercise 3-10. Write a similar function `maxlng` which returns the largest positive `long` value on whatever computer the program is compiled for. Include your `maxlng` function in a program `maxl.c` which prints your result.

3.21   Defined Types and Defined Constants

In the preceding sections, we have occasionally used new type names from the file `local.h`. Now, here is the entire collection of these names, which are known as *defined types*. Each defined type is presented along with its usage, and the equivalent names to use if you are not using the file `local.h`.

tbool   A one-byte character (8 bits or more), tested only for zero (*false*) or non-zero (*true*). (`char`)

ushort   A two-byte integer (16 bits or more), used for unsigned arithmetic. (`unsigned short`, or `unsigned int` on a 2-byte machine)

bits   A two-byte integer (16 bits or more), used for bitwise operations. (`unsigned short`, or `unsigned int` on a 2-byte machine)

metachar   A variable used to receive the returned value from functions such as `getchar` which return either a `char` value or the EOF indication. (`short`)

bool   An `int`-sized integer (16 bits or more), for functions returning *true* or *false*. (`int`)

void   A type name for functions that return no value. (Available on some new compilers, otherwise `int`)

Using these types, we can present the preferred uses of type names in C, in the form of a table. Each row of the table specifies the size of the variable, and each column specifies the usage.

	Numbers (signed)	Numbers (unsigned)	Bit Masks	Text Characters	Boolean (0 or 1)
char	–	–	–	char	tbool
short	short	ushort	bits	metachar	–
long	long	–	–	–	–
float	float	–	–	–	–
double	double	–	–	–	–

Note that `int` is not specified for any uses in this table. The intent is to avoid careless dependence on the `int` size of the computer. A few specific uses of `int` size are proper:

Type	Usage
unsigned	Counting or indexing a number of bytes
bool	The returned value of a Boolean function
void	Type name for a function returning no value (if not provided by compiler)

It is possible to prepare a portable scheme of defined types for signed and unsigned arithmetic using all the integer sizes, but the details are beyond the scope of this book; see Plum [1981]. In the absence of such defined types, your most portable approach to unsigned arithmetic is to use the `ushort` defined type, being sure not to depend upon more than 16 bits of its size.

The `bits` defined type deserves special mention. It is intended to alert the maintenance programmer that bitwise operations are being performed upon the data. As we saw in Section 3.6, various machine differences require that one be very careful when mixing bitwise and arithmetic operations upon the same data. In particular, our rule about not right-shifting negative data can be made more specific: any time the right-shift operation appears on any expression of a size smaller than long, the right-shift operation should be accompanied by the (bits) cast on the left-hand operand. Some examples are shown in the following bits.c program.

bits.c **[3-58]**:
```
/* bits - examples of bitwise operations
 */
#include "local.h"
main()
    {
    bits b1, b2;

    b1 = 0xF0F0 & 0x1234;
    b2 = b1 | 0x60;
    printf("b1=0x%04x, b2=0x%04x\n", b1, b2);
    b1 = ~1 & 0307;
    b2 = (bits)b1 >> 2;
    printf("b1=0%03o, b2=0%03o\n", b1, b2);
    b1 = 0xF001 | 0x8801;
    b2 = b1 & 0xB800;
    printf("b1=0x%04x, b2=0x%04x\n", b1, b2);
    }
```

Question [3-59] What does bits.c print?

Will it give the same results on any C machine? _____

The file local.h also contains some *defined constants,* including YES and NO. As you might expect, YES is 1, and NO is 0. The defined constants FAIL, SUCCEED, STDIN, STDOUT, and STDERR will be explained in the next section.

In the file stdio.h are defined EOF (usually -1, the "end-of-file" returned value), and BUFSIZ (usually 512 or 1024, the most efficient size for input/output arrays using read or write).

C language provides an alternative method of defining new types, called typedef. A declaration prefaced by the keyword typedef will make the declared name synonymous with the declared type. Thus instead of writing

```
#define bool int
#define void int
```

we could write

```
typedef int bool, void;
```

In this book we are using #define in our local.h include-file solely for the simplicity of using only one method.

One final note on defined types: we are using lower-case names for these new type names. Our convention is that type names which are defined by organization-wide standard headers should be written as ordinary lower-case names, because these names acquire essentially the same immutable status as the reserved words of the language. As a rule, however, one should distinguish any other names created via #define or typedef by some typographical convention such as putting them into upper case.

3.22   More about Input/Output

So far, all your input and output has gone through the interactive terminal — input from the keyboard, output to the screen (or printer). The full treatment within C is much more general.

In our Common Environment, each program starts its execution with access to three streams of data, one for input and two for output [**3-60 os**]:

stdin   The "standard input," the usual source of input characters.

stdout   The "standard output," the usual destination for output characters.

stderr   The "standard error output," where error messages are sent.

It is often helpful to depict these connections with a simple diagram:

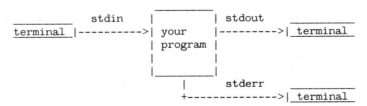

```
  _____     stdin     _____      _____
 | terminal |---------->| your    |-------->| terminal |
  ‾‾‾‾‾‾‾‾‾              | program |          ‾‾‾‾‾‾‾‾‾‾
                        |         |
                        |_____|
                         |    stderr        _____
                         +------------>| terminal |
                                         ‾‾‾‾‾‾‾‾‾‾
```

The same program can be made to put its standard output into a file instead of the terminal, simply by adding a *redirection* request to the command line when you execute the program [**3-61 os**]. Thus, using the codes4 program as a useful example, we could create a file containing the code-table output by executing

```
codes4 >table
```

Error messages, if any, will continue to come out on the screen, instead of being buried inside the output file:

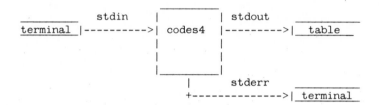

Exercise 3-11. Compile and run codes4.c on your system. Print the resulting file and compare it carefully to the output that was shown in Appendix B.3.5.

A similar redirection is possible for the standard input. If we wish to run our mortg2 program using data that we have stored in a file called house1, we can execute the program like this:

        mortg2 <house1

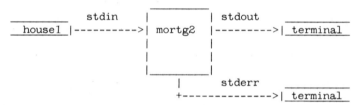

In this case, the output will come out to the terminal. If we wish instead to capture the output in a file, we can run

        mortg2 <house1 >house1.out

If we execute our copy program with both input and output redirection, we achieve a simple file-to-file copy:

        copy <filein >filout

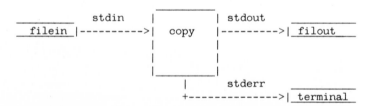

These streams of data — *stdin, stdout,* and *stderr* — have conventional *file numbers* (also known as *file descriptors*) in C, which we have defined in our local.h file **[3-62 os]**:

        #define STDIN   0
        #define STDOUT   1
        #define STDERR   2

We have seen the use of STDOUT in

```
write(STDOUT, "hello, world\n", 13);
```

which copies 13 characters to the standard output. It is equally possible to write

```
write(STDERR, "Please type one number\n", 23);
```

and send the characters to the standard error output instead. The need for such messages occurs frequently, and we can make a useful function to print them more easily **[3-63 cc]**:

```
remark [3-64]:
    /* remark - print non-fatal error message
     */
    #include "local.h"
    void remark(s1, s2)
        char s1[], s2[];
        {
        write(STDERR, s1, strlen(s1));
        write(STDERR, " ", 1);
        write(STDERR, s2, strlen(s2));
        write(STDERR, "\n", 1);
        }
```

Providing two different string arguments to the **remark** function allows us to print a message plus a character array variable, often useful in situations like this:

```
n = sscanf(s, "%lf", &x);
if (n != 1)
    remark("I cannot read x from ", s);
```

In this last example, once the error message has been printed, the program continues on its way. Often, we want it to stop in its tracks and give up. The function **exit** provides us the means to stop instantly, while providing the operating system with a "status code" reporting on the success or failure of our program. We have defined the conventional values SUCCEED and FAIL in our local.h include-file **[3-65 os]**. Now that we have described the SUCCEED value, every program should announce its successful completion with

```
exit(SUCCEED);
```

as a matter of good style.

Adding an error **exit** to our previous example gives

```
n = sscanf(s, "%lf", &x);
if (n != 1)
    {
    remark("I cannot read x from ", s);
    exit(FAIL);
    }
```

This combination of error message followed by exit occurs often enough to deserve its own function, error **[3-66 cc]**:

```
error [3-67]:
    /* error - print fatal error message
     */
    #include "local.h"
    void error(s1, s2)
        char s1[], s2[];
        {
        write(STDERR, s1, strlen(s1));
        write(STDERR, " ", 1);
        write(STDERR, s2, strlen(s2));
        write(STDERR, "\n", 1);
        exit(FAIL);
        }
```

And in the interests of encouraging "defensive programming" — preventing programs from going haywire when given bad input — we suggest attaching error calls at each unrecoverable error point:

```
if (sscanf(s, "%lf", &x) != 1)
    error("I cannot make x from", s);
```

(We have not followed our own prescription in several preceding programs; if you have entered them on your system, take a moment to add the error function to them and protect all calls upon scanf.)

And now the read function. Like write, this is a small and simple function.

```
n = read(STDIN, s, BUFSIZ);
```

will read at most BUFSIZ bytes from the standard input, returning the number of bytes that were read. A negative return indicates an error; a zero return means end-of-file. If the input comes from a terminal, read will return one line (including '\n' newline); from a file, read will read as many bytes as it can, up to BUFSIZ, in this case. The array s is *not* null-terminated. At this point in your learning of C, the read function will be useful only if your program is extremely limited by memory requirements.

Like the read function, write also returns the number of characters processed successfully. If this is not equal to the number requested to be written, an error has occurred. We can combine read and write into the most efficient form of file copying available from portable C:

```
copy3.c [3-68]:
    /* copy3 - most efficient file copy
     */
    #include "local.h"
    main()
        {
        char s[BUFSIZ]; /* array for characters */
        short i;         /* number of characters read */

        while (0 != (i = read(STDIN, s, BUFSIZ)))
            {
            if (i < 0)
                error("I/O error on read\n", "");
            else if (i != write(STDOUT, s, i))
                error("I/O error on write\n", "");
            }
        exit(SUCCEED);
        }
    /* error - print fatal error message
     */
    void error(s1, s2)
        char s1[], s2[];
        {
        write(STDERR, s1, strlen(s1));
        write(STDERR, " ", 1);
        write(STDERR, s2, strlen(s2));
        write(STDERR, "\n", 1);
        exit(FAIL);
        }
```

3.23   Timing a Program

On a small, single-user machine, you may be able to time the execution of your program just by using your stopwatch. On a multi-user time-sharing system, you will need to use some facility of the operating system, since your program is sharing the machine with other programs at the same time.

In our Common Environment, the simplest method of timing a program is the time command. For an example, to time the copy3 program, we create an input file of 100,000 characters (named 100KB) and execute this command [3-69 os]:

```
time copy3 <100KB >tmp
```

and obtain this timing summary (using Venix on a PDP-11/23):

```
real        5.0
user        0.2
sys         2.6
```

The "real" time is "wall-clock" time, the actual elapsed time in seconds. The CPU time — time actually used by the program — is the sum of "user" and "system" times: 2.8 seconds, in this case. Such timing measurements are generally dependent upon the total load on the system; several re-runs may be necessary for an accurate figure. To a rough approximation, we could conclude from this case that this system takes about 30 microseconds to read and write one character using copy3. (The Idris system on the same PDP-11/23 gives the same timing as this. On a PDP-11/70, the corresponding time is 20 microseconds per character.)

For an interesting account of program timing in different environments, see Gilbreath [1983].

CHAPTER 4: STATEMENTS AND CONTROL FLOW

The flow of execution through a program is controlled by statements such as `if`, `while`, and `for`. The convenience that they provide to the programmer and the clarity that they give to the program are major advantages of high-level languages like C over low-level assembler languages. There is also an important correspondence between these control structures and the structure of data, which we will examine after looking at each control structure in detail.

4.1 Statements and Blocks

C programs are built out of *statements,* which in turn may contain expressions. Indeed, one of the simplest statements is the *expression statement,* which consists of one expression followed by a semicolon. Most of the statements that we have seen in programs so far are in fact expression statements, such as these:

```
++i;
printf("hello, world\n");
n = 0;
```

Another simple statement is the *return statement,* which may appear with an expression, as in

```
return (n + 1);
```

or without an expression:

```
return;
```

Execution of the `return` statement causes a return of control to the calling function.

Also, C has a *null statement,* which consists of one lonely semicolon:

```
;
```

The null statement is the high-level equivalent of the "NO-OP" of assembler languages, except that the null statement generates no code at all. It is useful in contexts such as

```
while (getchar() != '\n')
    ;
```

which simply swallows characters until a newline is read.

C also has a *compound statement,* or *block,* formed by putting braces around any number of statements. Thus, in a C function, all the lines from the opening brace to its matching closing brace constitute a block, as in

```
hello.c [4-1]:
    main()
        {
        write(1, "hello, world\n", 13);
        }
```

A statement's *syntax* (or *grammar*) of a statement tells what form the statement must have so that the *compiler* understands it correctly. We will describe both the syntax rules and the *readability format,* the form required for humans to understand it correctly. For the *compound statement,* or *block,* the rules look like this:

```
SYNTAX (Simplified)
```
   { *stmt** }

```
READABILITY
```
   {
   stmt*
   }

In these rules, the large-type asterisk (*) means "repetition." Thus, the notation *stmt** means a *repetition* of zero or more *stmt*s (statements).

The compiler, of course, ignores extra whitespace, so the indentation does not show in the syntax rule, only in the readability rule. This is, of course, not the only possible readability rule for compound statements. Consistency within your project or organization is the most important readability rule, and if your project already uses another format, then so should you. The main advantage of the readability format shown here is that all the components of a block are at the same level of indentation. By the way, Plum Hall has surveyed more than two hundred programmers at a large organization that has used C for a number of years, and opinion is divided almost equally among three popular formats for blocks, with a slight plurality favoring the one that we show here.

4.2   If

The simplest control statement of C is the `if` statement, which executes a statement if a certain expression is *true*. For example, this statement sets **x** to the absolute value of **x**:

```
if (x < 0)
    x = -x;
```

The `if` statement, as we have described it here, has this syntax:

```
if (expr) stmt
```

which means "the word `if`, followed by an open-parenthesis, followed by an expression, followed by a close-parenthesis, followed by a statement." The compiler has no need for whitespace, so it is not mentioned in the syntax description. The corresponding readability format looks like this:

```
if (expr)
    stmt
```

This means "the word `if`, one blank, an open-parenthesis, an expression, a close-parenthesis, a new line with one further tab-stop indent, and a statement." The symbols are the same as the syntax description, but the indenting is important for readability, as is the blank following the word `if`.

Question [4-2] Which of these are legal `if` statements according to the syntax descriptions? Which are correct according to the readability format?

	LEGAL?	READABLE?
`if (x < 0)` `y = x;`	_____	_____
`if (n) ;`	_____	_____
`if(c == EOF)` `done = YES;`	_____	_____

The `if` statement can be understood as having three steps:

1. After the keyword `if` there is an expression in parentheses. Evaluate the expression, to produce a single number.

2. Interpret the resulting value of the expression, according to the *semi-Boolean* logic: zero means *false*, non-zero means *true*.

3. If the expression value is *true*, execute the statement that follows the expression. If the value is *false*, skip that statement.

When drawn as a flow-chart, the logic of the `if` statement looks like this:

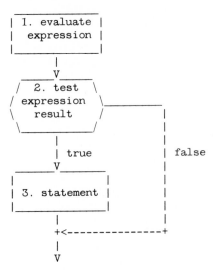

Side-effects are allowed inside the expression. It is good C style to use them this way to avoid creating otherwise useless "temporary" variables. Thus,

```
if (scanf("%hd", &n) != 1)
    printf("bad n\n");
```

is better than

```
nread = scanf("%hd", &n);
if (nread != 1)
    printf("bad n\n");
```

if the variable nread is not needed for anything further.

4.3   If-else

The if statement can include an alternative to be executed if the condition is *false*. The syntax in this case is

```
if (expr) stmt else stmt
```

or, according to our readability rules,

```
if (expr)
    stmt
else
    stmt
```

Combining this syntax form with the one from the previous section, we want to show that the else clause is *optional,* for which we use *square brackets [ ]* in our syntax rules. Thus, for the `if` statement we have these rules:

SYNTAX
    if (*expr*) *stmt* [else· *stmt*]

READABILITY
        if (*expr*)   if (*expr*)
            stmt   *stmt*
                            else
                                stmt

Since an `if` statement is a legal possibility for the *stmt* of our rules, one `if` statement can be nested inside another. Some care is needed. The `else` will be associated with the most recent "un-else'd" `if`; the compiler again pays no attention to the indenting. We suggest the following uniform rule to avoid the confusion.

> Whenever an `if` statement is nested inside another `if` statement, put braces around the nested statement.

Thus, this statement

```
/* nested if */
if (n > 0)
    {
    if (n % 2 == 0)
        printf("positive and even\n");
    }
else
    printf("not positive\n");
```

behaves differently from this statement

```
/* nested if-else */
if (n > 0)
    {
    if (n % 2 == 0)
        printf("positive and even\n");
    else
        printf("positive and odd\n");
    }
```

It would be a mistake to write

```
/* incorrect nesting */
if (n > 0)
    if (n % 2 == 0)
        printf("positive and even\n");
else
    printf("not positive\n");
```

because the compiler matches the `else` with the nearest "un-else'd" `if`.

Question [4-3] What does this `if` statement print, for each value of n:

```
if (n < 5)
    {
    if (n % 2 == 1)
        printf("A\n");
    else
        printf("B\n");
    }
else
    {
    if (n % 2 == 1)
        printf("C\n");
    else
        printf("D\n");
    }

n = 1   ____
n = 2   ____
n = 3   ____
n = 4   ____
n = 5   ____
n = 6   ____
n = 7   ____
```

4.4   Else-If

Whenever an `if` statement has nesting only inside its `else` clause, we can improve readability by formatting as though `else if` were one keyword. This emphasizes the *multiple choice* nature of the code. For example,

```
/* clear 3-way choice */
if (n > 0)
    printf("positive\n");
else if (n == 0)
    printf("zero\n");
else
    printf("negative\n");
```

This portrays the logic more clearly than slavish nesting with braces, such as this:

```
/* obscure 3-way choice */
if (n > 0)
    printf("positive\n");
else
    {
    if (n == 0)
        printf("zero\n");
    else
        printf("negative\n");
    }
```

Notice that we are not adding any new features to the syntax of the `if` statement; everything that follows the word `else` is syntactically one statement. We are just adding to the readability formats for `if` statement:

SYNTAX
    if (*expr*) *stmt* [else *stmt*]

READABILITY

```
if (expr)          if (expr)          if (expr)
    stmt               stmt               stmt
                   else               else if (expr)
                       stmt               stmt
                                      else if (expr)
                                          stmt
                                      else
                                          stmt
```

The `else-if` is an excellent format for an n-way choice, as in this children's game:

guess.c **[4-4]**:

```
/* guess - guess a hidden number between 1 and 15, in 3 guesses
 */
#include "local.h"
main()
    {
    char line[BUFSIZ];    /* input line */
    tbool found;          /* have I found it? */
    short n;              /* how many guesses left */
    short range;          /* how much to ajust next guess */
    short try;            /* next number to try */
    metachar reply;       /* the user's reply */

    found = NO;
    n = 3;
    range = 4;
    try = 8;
    printf("Each time I guess, please answer\n");
    printf(" H if I'm high\n L if I'm low\n E if I guessed it\n");
    while (n > 0 && !found)
        {
        printf("I guess %d\n", try);
        if (getln(line, BUFSIZ) == EOF)
            error("Bye!", "");
        reply = line[0];
        if (reply == 'H' || reply == 'h')
            {
            try -= range;
            range /= 2;
            --n;
            }
        else if (reply == 'L' || reply == 'l')
            {
            try += range;
            range /= 2;
            --n;
            }
        else if (reply == 'E' || reply == 'e')
            found = YES;
        else
            printf("Please type H, L, or E\n");
        }
    printf("Your number is %d\nThanks for the game\n", try);
    exit(SUCCEED);
    }
```

Since side-effects are allowable in each condition, the else-if allows a sequence of actions to be performed until one gets the right result:

```
/* a series of attempts */
if (try1() == YES)
    printf("success on the first try\n");
else if (try2() == YES)
    printf("success on the second try\n");
else if (try3() == YES)
    printf("third try is a charm\n");
else
    printf("some days, nothing works\n");
```

One of the advantages of this vertical alignment of the else-if is that modification is clear and simple: adding another case or removing one is easy.

Question [4-5] If the guesser had four tries, how big a range could it handle? ____ Five tries? ____

4.5 Switch

C provides a special form of multiple-choice control structure for the situation in which all the choices are specific alternative values· for one integer expression. This is the `switch` statement of C. It is constructed with the keyword `switch`, followed by an integer expression in parentheses, followed by a block (compound statement, enclosed in braces). Interspersed with the statements of the block are `case` labels, each of which precedes the statements to be executed when the expression has the value given by the label. At the end of each alternative section of code, there should be a `break` statement, which causes control to jump to the closing brace after the statements. Our previous example, `guess.c`, can be written equally well with `switch` or with `else-if`. We prefer `switch` in all such situations because it alerts the reader to a *mutually-exclusive* set of possibilities.

```
switch (reply)
    {
case 'H':
case 'h':
    try -= range;
    range /= 2;
    --n;
    break;
case 'L':
case 'l':
    try += range;
    range /= 2;
    --n;
    break;
case 'E':
case 'e':
    found = YES;
    break;
default:
    printf("Please type H, L, or E\n");
    break;
    }
```

There is a special case label — `default` — which stands for "none of the named cases." It is conventionally placed as the last case of the switch, but the compiler allows it to be placed anywhere. The order in which the cases appear does not matter, because the compiler ensures that they are all mutually-exclusive constant values. In other words, there cannot appear two instances of the same case label value.

After each case label, there may appear any number of statements, or *stmt**, in our syntax notation. Thus, these are the syntax and readability rules:

```
SYNTAX
    switch (expr) block

READABILITY
    switch (expr)
        {
    case const:
        stmt*
        break;
    case const:
    case const:
        stmt*
        break;
    default:
        stmt*
        break;
        }
```

It is common and proper to attach multiple case labels to one statement, as is done in the examples above. But a "flow-through" obtained by omitting a break is easily mistaken later for a careless (but common) bug. Therefore, if "flow-through" is really intended, insert a comment /* flow-through */ in place of the break. Avoid flow-through, except to prevent needless duplication of code lines.

4.6   While

The while statement repeats its statement body as long as the tested expression evaluates to a semi-Boolean *true* value, i.e., non-zero. The test is made each time before the body is executed, so that if it is *false*, the body is never executed.

The flow-chart of the while statement shows that the tested expression is always evaluated one time more than the body.

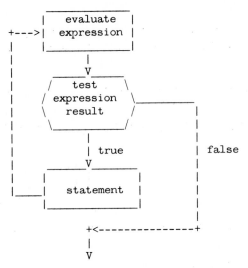

A loop of this form, where the first box is executed one time more than the second, is known in the programming-language literature as an $N + \frac{1}{2}$ time loop. In C, since the top box is only a single expression, whereas the second box can be a whole block of statements, the while loop might best be called an $N + \frac{1}{4}$ time loop. This form of loop is well suited to calling one function to get something, then executing a body which does something with it. For example, the simple input-to-output copy program:

copy.c **[4-6]**:

```
/* copy - copy input to output
 */
#include "local.h"
main()
    {
    metachar c;

    while ((c = getchar()) != EOF)
        putchar(c);
    exit(SUCCEED);
    }
```

If this program is applied to a file of 100 bytes, it will call getchar 101 times. The first 100 calls will return a data byte; the 101-st call will return the EOF value. Thus, the test is evaluated 101 times, and the body is done 100 times. Some academic authorities like to code this loop in a different way:

```
c = getchar();
while (c != EOF)
    {
    putchar(c);
    c = getchar();
    }
```

We prefer the first program, because the latter style forces the *duplication of code*. The objection is not so much that the resulting program is larger (although that is true), but rather that duplication of code is a problem during maintenance. It is all too easy to make a change to one of the duplicated instances while overlooking the other.

Summarizing syntax and readability:

> SYNTAX
> > while (*expr*) *stmt*

> READABILITY
> > while (*expr*)
> >   *stmt*

When coding a loop, you should be aware of a relationship known as the *loop invariant,* or the *typical picture of the loop.* This invariant is a relationship which

(a)   is always true, each time the loop is traversed; and

(b)   guarantees that the loop attains its goal when it terminates.

One can describe an invariant for any point during the execution of the loop, but the clearest place is just after evaluating the test and before executing the body, so we will henceforth assume this location. Thus, in the copy program, the invariant looks like this:

```
Already read:    __  __  __  __  ...  __
                                        c
Already written:__  __  __  __  ...
```

Or in words, "A series of one or more characters has already been read, and the last of them is in the variable c. The same series has been written, except for c, which has not been written."

To verify condition (a) above, that the invariant is always true, you can use *mathematical induction.* Prove that it is true the very first time, and then prove that if it was true for the first, second, ..., to n-th times, then it will be true after one more iteration to the n+1st time. In this case, our picture is obviously true the first time, when the series of characters contains only c. If it has been true for 1, 2, ..., n, then we have written a string of n characters. If the loop is then traversed one more time, c is now a new character, and the series of characters written is of length n+1. To write the induction out like this may seem tedious, but the mental processes that you go through in verifying a loop are really equivalent to this process.

Now, to verify condition (b) above, observe that when the loop terminates, c is equal to the EOF value. Thus the series of characters read and written contains every character of the input up to the EOF, which is the goal of the loop.

Strictly speaking, the invariant is required to be true only at one specific point. Programs are more readable, however, if the invariant is true throughout as much of the loop as possible. If we define the *domain of exceptions* as the portion of the loop in which the invariant does not hold true, our readability principle is to *minimize the domain of exceptions to the loop invariant.*

4.7   For

One way that C language assists you in achieving this readability principle is the for statement. This statement confines the primary manipulations of the loop invariant to one line of the listing. Consider this version of the function strscn, which searches a string s for the first occurrence of the character c. The function returns the subscript of this first occurrence, or the subscript of the terminating null character if there is no match. (The strscn function is not from the Common Library.)

```
strscn [4-7]:
    /* strscn - return the index of c in string s
     */
    unsigned strscn(s, c)
        char s[];    /* string to be scanned */
        char c;      /* char to be matched */
        {
        unsigned i;

        for (i = 0; s[i] != c && s[i] != '\0'; ++i)
            ;
        return (i);
        }
```

Compare the for loop above with this while loop:

```
i = 0;
while (s[i] != c && s[i] != '\0')
    ++i;
```

All those expressions which manipulate the loop variable are contained in the one line of the for controls, reducing the domain of exceptions.

The flow-chart of the for statement looks like this:

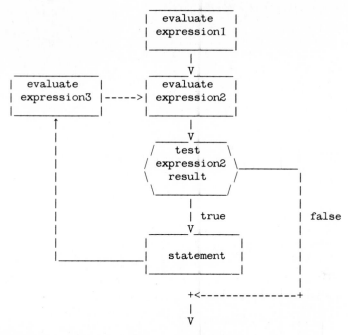

If the *expression1 (init)* is left blank, no initialization takes place. Similarly, if the *expression3 (step)* is left blank, no reinitialization takes place. And if the *expression2 (test)* is blank, the loop is executed "forever." In the standard include-file local.h, the symbol FOREVER is defined as

```
for (;;)
```

which is an "endless" loop. Thus, a "clock" program might have an outline like this:

```
FOREVER
    wait 1 second
    print the time
```

For a means of "breaking out" of an endless loop, there is the **break** statement. Execution of a **break** causes a jump to the next statement following the body of a **for**, **switch**, **while**, or **do-while**. Thus, in C, the true N + ½ time loop can be coded like this:

```
FOREVER
    {
    stmt*
    if (expr)
        break;
    stmt*
    }
```

Summarizing syntax and readability:

SYNTAX
        for (*expr*; *expr*; *expr*) *stmt*

READABILITY
        for (*expr*; *expr*; *expr*)   FOREVER
            stmt   {
                                                    *stmt**
                                                    if (*expr*)
                                                        break;
                                                    *stmt**
                                                    }

4.8   Do While

C provides a loop which tests *after* doing each iteration: the do-while
loop.   The flow-chart shows the unique form of this loop, which always performs its body of code at least once.

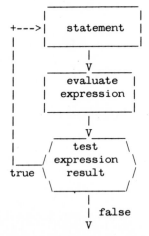

```
         _____
        |                |
+--->|    statement   |
    |   |_____|
    |            |
    |            V
    |    _____
    |   |   evaluate     |
    |   |   expression   |
    |   |_____|
    |            |
    |          __V_____
    |         /  test    \
    |_____/  expression  \
    true  \    result    /
           _____/
                |
                | false
                V
```

The do-while statement is desirable only if the problem dictates that the code
must be done at least once — for example, in testing for an interactive reply
to a prompt:

```
        do
            {
            printf("Answer y or n: ");
            ans = getchar();
            while (getchar() != '\n')
                ;
            } while (ans != 'y' && ans != 'n');
```

Good programs have the property that they "do nothing gracefully," that is, each body of code is performed only if there is something for it to do. A program should not do crazy things when inputs are missing. Use do-while sparingly.

Summarizing syntax and readability:

```
SYNTAX
    do stmt while (expr);

READABILITY
    do
        {
        stmt*
        } while (expr);
```

4.9   Design of Control Structures

Before tackling a programming problem, it is useful to sketch your approach to the program. Such sketching is known as *logic design,* or simply *design.* In our opinion, the simplest approach to logic design is based on the idea of *syntax.* We have seen how syntax is used in defining the legal structures of C. Now we will apply it to the programming problems themselves.

First, consider the syntactic structure of *repetition,* one thing repeated over and over. For example, we often treat an input file as a repetition of one single character after another. In our syntax notation, we write this as

   $c*$

where c stands for one character. Our sketching tool for logic design is a *program outline* or *pseudo-code,* written with a mixture of real C constructs and verbal phrases that stand for code to be written later. The program outline that corresponds to the syntax $c*$ is this:

   for each character c
      process c

This outline makes clear the structure of our program: do a certain processing for each character. If there are 100 characters to be processed, the body of the loop is done 100 times.

Further refinement of the outline is determined by the processing to be done. For example, if the characters are obtained by input from `getchar`, and if the processing consists of writing the character with `putchar`, the code for this outline becomes

```
while ((c = getchar()) != EOF)
    putchar(c);
```

Using the same program outline, if the characters are being taken from a string in memory, and the processing consists of printing their ASCII codes in decimal, we could translate the outline into this code:

```
for (i = 0; s[i] != '\0'; ++i)
    printf("%d\n", c);
```

You can see that these outlines are indeed just sketches. There is still some real programming work to the translation from outline to finished program. The outline simply serves to clarify the overall control structure of the program.

We thus have *Design Rule 1:*

1.   When the data being processed have the syntax of a *repetition* of things over and over, structure the program as a *loop,* whose body processes exactly one of the things.

One important point about loops: the simple $N + \frac{1}{4}$ time loop (which gets its data as part of the loop test) will not work in cases where a preceding part of the program has already read or produced the first data item for the loop. Often, a program must *read ahead* one item to know that the end of a loop is reached. Consider a simple tabulating program whose input consists of lines containing one account number and one entry for that account. The program's output is a series of lines which give the account number and the total of all entries for that account. The syntax of the input is

   { {*account entry*}* }*

This shows a repetition inside a repetition; the large braces { } are not C language braces, but a part of our syntax notation that *groups* everything inside them. An English translation of the syntax notation above is "a repetition of a repetition of *account*-followed-by-*entry*."

For those who like to work with a graphical notation, we can show the same information as a *syntax tree:*

The repetition inside another repetition means that the program will have the structure of one loop inside another:

> *for all account numbers*
> > *zero the sum*
> > *for all lines with the same account number*
> > > *add the entry to the sum*
> > *print the sum*

Or as a C program

```
nargs = scanf("%ld %lf", &account, &entry);
while (nargs == 2)
    {
    sum = 0.;
    this = account;
    while (nargs == 2 && this == account)
        {
        sum += entry;
        nargs = scanf("%ld %lf", &account, &entry);
        }
    printf("%ld %10.2f\n", this, sum);
    }
```

The inner loop must assume that the first line of each new account has already been read, because the new account number tells the program that all entries for the previous account have been processed — an example of "read-ahead logic."

Our second construct is a *sequence* of things, each being different in some way. In our syntax notation, a sequence is simply written as a list of the things one after another. Thus the syntax of *part1* followed by *part2* followed by *part3* is simply

> *part1 part2 part3*

and the syntax tree is

The corresponding program outline is the same list, written vertically:

process part1
process part2
process part2

For an example, consider the problem of reading a text file which is all in lower case and selectively capitalizing the first letter of each word. (We will be rather general here about a "letter": any non-whitespace character will be called a letter. We will just be sure that "capitalizing" a non-alphabetic character does not alter the character.) Since we will treat the initial letter of a word in a different way from the other letters, the relevant syntax for a *word* is

   a a*

and its syntax tree is

where *a* stands for one non-whitespace character. The input file consists of a series of words separated by whitespace, so its syntax is

   w* *{a a** *w**}*

and its syntax tree is

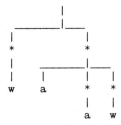

where *w* stands for one whitespace character. The corresponding program outline is this:

> *for each whitespace w*
>   *copy w*
> *for each word*
>   *capitalize the initial letter*
>   *for each succeeding letter a*
>   *copy a*
>   *for each whitespace w*
>   *copy w*

The body of our main loop is a *sequence* of three actions, some of which will themselves be loops. Since the program cannot know that it has reached the end of a word until a following whitespace is read, the loops must be coded with the read-ahead logic described above. That is, each loop must assume that its first case has already been read. The program thus looks like this:

```
while (isspace(c = getchar()))
    putchar(c);
while (c != EOF)
    {
    putchar(toupper(c));
    while (!isspace(c = getchar()))
        putchar(c);
    while (isspace(c))
        {
        putchar(c);
        c = getchar();
        }
    }
```

This program illustrates our *Design Rule 2:*

2. When the data being processed form a *sequence* of several different things, the program outline should contain a sequence of steps, each one of which processes one of the input items.

Our third design construct is a *choice* among several alternatives. Taking the same example as above, we might look at the file as containing two kinds of characters: those that should be capitalized and those that should not. Thus, the syntax of each character is simply

   $h \mid t$

where h is a "head" character to be capitalized, t is a "tail" character that should not be capitalized, and $\mid$ is a syntax notation for "choice." The syntax of the input file is thus

   $\{h \mid t\}*$

and the syntax tree is

The program outline that corresponds to a *choice* is an `if` statement or a `switch` statement. The outline to process this input file (which consists of a choice inside a repetition) is thus

> *for each input character c*
>   *if (c is a head character)*
>   *output capitalized c*
>   *else*
>   *output c*

The corresponding program looks like this:

```
for (waswhite = YES; (c = getchar()) != EOF; waswhite = isspace(c))
    {
    if (!isspace(c) && waswhite)
        putchar(toupper(c));
    else
        putchar(c);
    }
```

The handling of *choice* constructs is summarized by *Design Rule 3:*

3.   When the data form a *choice* among one or more alternatives, the program outline should contain an `if` or `switch` construct, each alternative processing one of the choices.

The capitalizing example has shown two different programs for the same problem, each arising from a different syntax view of the data. We prefer the second program, according to *Design Rule 4:*

4.   Choose the design which results in the simpler program.

This does not mean that *choice* always gives simpler programs than *sequence;* the extra variables (such as `waswhite`) can sometimes proliferate to an alarming extent. However, as a general rule, your first attempt should usually start by considering the data as a simple repetition of a single small thing: one character, one number, one line, etc. If the number of choices then looks overwhelming, look again at the data as being comprised of larger entities, and try again.

Exercise 4-1. Complete the first program fragment into a C program `accnt.c` and try it out.

Exercise 4-2. Complete the second or third program fragment into a C program cap.c and try it out.

4.10 Break and Continue

We have discussed the `break` statement in the context of the FOREVER loop, as a means of implementing the N + ½ time loop. Also, we have seen its use in the `switch` statement, where it terminates each of the alternative cases. The `break` statement is available within the `while`, `do-while`, `for`, and `switch`; it serves in each of these constructs as a jump to the end of the statement. Its effect is to immediately terminate execution of the loop (or `switch`).

Each time you code a `break`, you should question whether there is not a straightforward way to express the same logic without the `break`. Heavy use of `break` is often associated with the "step-at-a-time" thinking of beginning programmers. Consider this example, which looks for the first whitespace character in a string `s`:

```
/* misuse of break */
for (i = 0; i < BUFSIZ; ++i)
    {
    if (s[i] == ' ')
        break;
    else if (s[i] == '\n')
        break;
    else if (s[i] == '\t')
        break;
    }
```

A more professional approach is to state the looping condition in the test of the loop:

```
/* search for whitespace */
for (i = 0; s[i] != ' ' && s[i] != '\n' && s[i] != '\t'; ++i)
    ;
```

Or, generalizing the idea of whitespace,

```
/* search for whitespace */
for (i = 0; iswhite(s[i]); ++i)
    ;
```

Note the null statement that forms the body of the loop; the loop control itself contains all that is needed.

The `continue` statement is similar to `break`, in that it causes a jump in the execution of a loop. However, `continue` jumps to the *next iteration* of the loop. In the `for` loop, it jumps to the *step* of the loop, the third expression on the `for` line. In the `while` and `do-while` loop, it jumps to the *test*.

As with the `break`, the `continue` is prone to abuse by beginners. Whenever it can be replaced by a single `if` test, it should not be used. Consider this bad example, which skips the processing of whitespace characters:

```
/* bad use of continue */
for (i = 0; s[i] != '\0'; ++i)
    {
    if (s[i] == ' ' || s[i] == '\n' || s[i] == '\t')
        continue;
    process the character s[i]
    }
```

The example is better coded with an `if` which says when to *do* something, rather than saying when *not to do* something:

```
/* process only the non-whitespace characters */
for (i = 0; s[i] != '\0'; ++i)
    {
    if (s[i] != ' ' && s[i] != '\n' && s[i] != '\t')
        {
        process the character s[i]
        }
    }
```

Notice that `continue` has no relationship to the `switch` statement. A continue encountered inside a `switch` will jump to the next iteration of an enclosing loop, if there is one. Otherwise, the compiler will complain about the syntax error.

4.11   Goto

The `goto` statement, like the `break` and `continue`, is often associated with "one-step-at-a-time" thinking which misses the underlying syntax of the problem. Analyzing your problem into *repetition, sequence,* and *choice* structures will generally do away with the need for `goto`.

However, in some rare situations, the `goto` is the simplest solution to a programming problem. Furthermore, many C programs are themselves written by *other* programs, and `goto` is often needed by such program generators. The `goto` statement thus remains firmly entrenched in C language.

Syntactically, the `goto` statement is very simple, and the only readability rule is that it always deserves a comment explaining why it was necessary to use it:

```
SYNTAX
    goto label;
```

```
READABILITY
    goto label;      /* reason */
```

The label is an identifier followed by a colon, and it is prefixed to some statement inside the same function as the goto.

One situation commonly described as a candidate for goto is an error
that is detected inside a deeply nested loop. Why "deeply nested"? Because a
goto inside only one or two loops can easily be replaced by a new Boolean
variable, e.g. error, like this:

```
/* error-handling using goto */
for ( ... )
    for ( ... )
        {
        ...
        if (some error is detected)
            goto fixit;
        ...
        }
...
fixit: repair the damage
```

Compare this with

```
/* error-handling using Boolean variable */
for ( ...; !error && ...; ... )
    for ( ...; !error && ...; ... )
        {
        ...
        if (some error is detected)
            error = YES;
        else
            ...
        }
if (error)
    repair the damage
```

While we are describing the handling of errors, we should mention that
sometimes the responsibility for repairing the damage should rest with the
calling function, and all the called function should do is to pass back an error
indication:

```
if (some error is detected)
    return (-1);
```

And whenever a program is part of a real-time environment, errors must often
be handled by a system-wide recovery facility:

```
if (some error is detected)
     syserr(code);
```

Such a facility could, for example, re-initialize the devices being controlled, ring a bell for the operator, and prompt for further commands. This "global" handling of exception conditions can be accomplished in C, but the details are beyond the scope of this book. If you need such facilities, consult with a senior programmer or the library documentation for your system.

At any rate, the `goto` is hardly the universal answer to the problem of handling errors.

CHAPTER 5: FUNCTIONS

5.1   Syntax and Readability

A *function* is an independent set of statements for performing some computation.   Already you have seen many examples of the ways that you *use* functions;   now you will learn how to *create* your own functions.

Each function that you create should do one specific, nameable task. For example, from mathematics we have the *power* function, **x** raised to the power **y**:

$$x^y$$

As we saw in Section 3.17, in C the power function appears as

```
pow(x, y)
```

If we were going to write the pow function ourselves, we would need to attend to the *syntax* and *readability* rules for functions:

```
SYNTAX (Simplified)
    function:
        [type] name([params]) decl-list block

    params:
        name [, name]*

    decl-list:
        decl*

READABILITY
    /* comment                      /* comment
     */                              */
    type name()                     type name(a1, a2)
        {                               type a1;    /* describe a1 */
        decl*                           type a2;    /* describe a2 */
                                        {
        stmt*                           decl*
        }
                                        stmt*
                                        }
```

For example, a partial implementation of **pow** would look like this:

```
pow [5-1]:
    /* pow - return (positive) x to the power y
     */
    double pow(x, y)
        double x;    /* base */
        double y;    /* exponent */
        {
        double exp();    /* exponential function */
        double log();    /* natural log function */

        return (exp(log(x) * y));
        }
```

This function computes x^y by taking the natural log of **x**, multiplying the result by **y**, then taking the exponential function of the result. (If you are not familiar with the mathematical details, take our word for it, and continue undaunted.) We will address the components of the definition in the order they appear in the syntax:

1.   Type

2.   Name

3.   Parameters (optional)

4. Parameter declaration list (optional)

5. Block

(1) Type: If a function does not return any value, we have suggested that its type should be specified as void, in accordance with the most recent compilers **[5-2 cc]**. If it does return a value, standard C requires that this value must be a *scalar* — C does not allow a function to return an array, for example. The syntax shows that the *type* is optional; if none is specified, the compiler assumes int. In our readability rules, the *type* is mandatory, and we suggest being precise about the size of the data being returned **[5-3 cc]**. In the example of pow, the *type* being returned is double.

In Section 3.14, we saw precise rules for *type* in C. The same rules are important for function names. The type of the name pow is found by scratching the name off the definition line, leaving

        double ()

(with the understanding that any parameters, such as **x** and **y**, have no role in determining the function type.) Reading double () literally gives "double parenthesis parenthesis," but in more fluent C, this is read "function returning double." Just as with arrays, this shows the complementarity between declarations and usages:

        pow   has the type   double ()

        pow(**x**, **y**)   has the type   double

(2) Name: The name of the function can be any C identifier, but for maximum portability to non-UNIX systems, function names should contain no upper-case letters and no more than six characters. After the name is a mandatory left-parenthesis, whether or not any parameters follow.

(3) Parameters (optional): In Section 3.8, we saw that arguments are passed to a function in the *function-call* operation. In the definition of the called function, *parameters* are declared — these are local variables of the function which will contain the argument values when they are passed. In the C language literature, there is an unfortunate variety of names for arguments and parameters. In the *calling* program, within a function-call such as

        pow(2., 3.)

the values in parentheses are known as *arguments, actual arguments,* or *actual parameters.* In the definition of the function, such as

        double pow(**x**, **y**)

the names in parentheses are known as *parameters, formal parameters,* or *formal arguments.* We will try to refer consistently to *arguments* for the former, and *parameters* for the latter.

(4) Parameter declarations (optional): In C, it is the programmer's responsibility to be sure that the type of the arguments passed to a function is in agreement with the type declared for the parameters. If there are any parameters, they should be declared explicitly, even though C will default their type to `int` if they are not declared. If a parameter is declared to be `float`, C will change its declaration to `double`, since C widens any `float` arguments to its preferred size of `double` **[5-4 cc]**. (Simple conclusion: do not confuse the maintainers of your program by using `float` parameter declarations.)

(5) Block: A left-brace, zero or more declarations, zero or more statements, and a right-brace — these complete the function definition. Notice that if *this* function calls *other* functions, there should be a *declaration* for each of these called functions, such as `exp` and `log` shown above. This means that the type of a function is always declared in two separate places — once in the calling function, to say what type it expects from the called function, and once in the definition of the called function, to say what type it will indeed return.

There is, however, a default rule in C, whereby anywhere a program calls an undeclared function, the called function is assumed to return `int`. We suggest that you not rely on this default; any functions that are called by your program should have their returned type declared somewhere. (In Section 5.2, we shall see that "somewhere" is often an include-file.)

Question [5-5] What is the type of each expression:

The type of `log(x)`   is _____

The type of `log`   is _____

The type of `exp`   is _____

The type of `exp(log(y) * y)`   is _____

The "smallest" function — the one that contains the bare minimum components — has no *type*, no *parameter-list*, no parameter *declaration-list*, and nothing between the braces:

```
dummy ( )
    {
    }
```

Even though it does nothing except returning, it has its uses. For example, in building a large program it is sometimes useful to define dummy functions, or "stubs," to mark the place where further development will take place.

5.2   Argument Passing

As we saw earlier, function arguments are always passed *by value* in C. C compilers usually do this by copying the values into an *argument frame*, arranging for the called function to know where this argument frame is located in the memory. (By *argument frame*, we simply mean a sequence of the argument values, one after the other, in the memory.) This argument frame, although not a formal requirement of the language, is so universal that we will show it in our diagrams. The following program, powdem.c,

powdem.c **[5-6]**:
```
/* powdem - demonstrate power function
 */
#include "local.h"
#include <math.h>
main()
    {
    short i;

    for (i = 0; i < 10; ++i)
        printf("2 to the power %d equals %.0f\n",
            i, pow(2., (double)i));
    exit(SUCCEED);
    }
/* pow - return (positive) x to the power y
 */
double pow(x, y)
    double x;    /* base */
    double y;    /* exponent */
    {
    return (exp(log(x) * y));
    }
```

produces the following output:
```
2 to the power 0 equals 1
2 to the power 1 equals 2
2 to the power 2 equals 4
2 to the power 3 equals 8
2 to the power 4 equals 16
2 to the power 5 equals 32
2 to the power 6 equals 64
2 to the power 7 equals 128
2 to the power 8 equals 256
2 to the power 9 equals 512
```

Notice that the powdem.c file contains the line
```
#include <math.h>
```

This line brings declarations of the library functions into our program, including the lines

```
double exp();
double log();
```

Thus, the functions in the powdem.c file do not need to repeat these declarations. This, by the way, is the "modern" way to handle declarations for library functions; each library should be accompanied by its corresponding include-file with the necessary declarations.

In the powdem.c program, each time pow is called, the two values 2. and (double)i are copied into an argument frame (each occupying eight bytes of storage). The called function, pow, receives some indication of where the values are located, which we graphically indicate with "<- frame" [5-7 cc]. On the first iteration, when i equals zero, this looks like

```
 _____  <- frame
|                         |
|      2.                 |
|_____|
|                         |
|      0.                 |
|_____|
```

In this example, the arguments are double values; the cast operation (double)i was necessary to widen i into a double argument. In accordance with C language rules about widening to preferred types, if the arguments are float values, they are also widened into double-sized storage in the argument frame. If an argument is a long value, it is put into long-sized storage in the argument frame. If the argument is a char, short, or int value, it is put into int-sized storage in the argument frame. The called function must know, according to its own definition, what sizes to expect for each argument.

After the argument values are placed into the argument frame, the called function is then invoked, receiving an indication of where the argument frame is located.

Exercise 5-1. Remove the pow function from powdem.c so that the program will use the pow function from the standard math library. (You may need the -lm flag in order to access the standard math library [5-8 cc].) Compare its output with the output shown above.

5.3   Parameters and Automatic Variables

In the called function, the parameters are simply variables whose storage consists of the argument locations *in the argument frame*. In other words, the address of a parameter variable may be different each time the function is called — the address is determined by the "frame" indication received from the calling function. Thus, when our pow function is called as in the previous section, its parameter storage looks like this:

```
                    _____  <- frame
    x      |              2.       |
           |_____|
    y      |              0.       |
           |_____|
```

Notice that the names **x** and **y** have been added to the diagram. Parameter names are simply the names for specific locations in the argument frame that was passed by the calling function. Each machine and compiler may have their own method of accessing these locations, using the "frame" indication that was received from the calling function.

If the called function should *change* the value of a parameter, the calling program will never know it; once the called function returns, the argument frame is made available for re-use, or "trashed," in programmer vernacular. Thus, the called function can use the parameters just as it would use any other local variable.

Speaking of the local variables, let us look now at the way C language handles them. We will need a new example program, since powdem.c has no local variables other than its parameters. Consider, then, this version of the power function, named lpow, which accepts and returns long numbers. The algorithm is "brute-force": keep multiplying by lnum until n multiplications are complete.

```
lpow [5-9]:
    /* lpow - power function (for long data)
     */
    long lpow(lnum, n)
        long lnum;        /* base */
        long n;           /* exponent */
        {
        long p;        /* local ("auto") result */

        p = 1;
        for ( ; n > 0; --n)
            p *= lnum;
        return (p);
        }
```

Besides the parameters lnum and n, we see a local variable named p. In C, such local variables are known as auto ("automatic") variables, so named because C "automatically" creates storage for them each time their function is entered. Expanding our notion of "frame," our picture of the local storage for lpow looks like this **[5-10 cc] [5-11 mach]**:

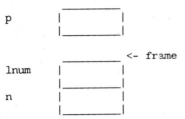

Thus, the storage for p is "private" storage for the lpow function, just as is the storage for the parameters lnum and n. It is given to lpow when the function is entered, and it is "trashed" when lpow returns.

Exercise 5-2. Write a demonstration program lpowd.c to exercise the lpow function. (Do not forget to declare

```
long lpow();
```

Unlike pow, the lpow function will not be found in any library; you must code it into your program.)

C language has a keyword for "automatic" variables — they can be explicitly declared as auto, as in

```
auto long p;
```

You will probably never see this keyword in an actual C program, since the compiler understands auto as the default for all local variables.

Returning for a moment to the parameters of a function, we have mentioned several times that it is the responsibility of the programmer to be sure that a function is called with arguments that are the proper data type for its parameters. There is a program named lint which can check this for you, if you are working in an environment that provides a lint command **[5-12 cc]**. To illustrate, consider

```
badpow.c [5-13]:
    /* badpow - demonstrate power function (argument mismatch error)
     */
    #include "local.h"
    #include <math.h>
    main()
        {
        short i;

        for (i = 0; i < 10; ++i)
            printf("2 to the power %d equals %.0f\n",
                i, pow(2, i));
        exit(SUCCEED);
        }
```

The pow function is being called with arguments that are integers, not the required double values. When we run lint upon this program, using the command

```
lint badpow.c -lm
```

we obtain a message like this:

```
pow, arg. 1 inconsistent "badpow.c"(11) :: "/usr/lib/llib-lm"(23)
pow, arg. 2 inconsistent "badpow.c"(11) :: "/usr/lib/llib-lm"(23)
```

The mismatch of arguments versus parameters has been diagnosed for us.

As a general rule, you should write programs about which lint gives no complaint. However, your project may define a list of "allowable" messages, because lint is sometimes overly fussy.

Exercise 5-3. If your environment provides lint, try it out on the programs that you have created so far.

5.4   Array Arguments

This simple picture of argument passing becomes more complicated when an argument is an array. Consider the string "hello", a constant of type char[6]. Supposing that it is located at address 1400, it looks like this in memory:

```
1400       | 104 | 101 | 108 | 108 | 111 |   0 |
           |_'h'_|_'e'_|_'l'_|_'l'_|_'o'_|_'\0'_|
```

When we pass "hello" as an argument, the argument frame does not receive the contents of the array. Instead, the *address* of the initial element of the array is passed. Thus, in order to call

```
strlen("hello");
```

the compiler will generate this argument frame:

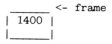

Now consider what happens in the strlen function:

strlen **[5-14]**:
```
/* strlen - return length of string s
 */
unsigned strlen(s)
    char s[];
    {
    unsigned i;

    for (i = 0; s[i] != '\0'; ++i)
        ;
    return (i);
    }
```

The crucial point to notice is that the parameter s is not really a character array; it is a variable that holds the *address* of the initial element of the array. The C terminology for such a variable is "character pointer," and s could equivalently be declared as

```
char *s;
```

(The type char * means "pointer to char.") When strlen runs through its loop, it will look successively at s[0], s[1], and so forth. Since s contains the value 1400, C understands that s[0] means "the character at address 1400," s[1] means "the character at address 1401," and so forth. In other words, the code performs with the same result as if s were in fact an array of characters; each one is tested for equality with the null character '\0' and the loop terminates when '\0' is found.

For a slightly larger example, consider the strncpy function:

strncpy **[5-15]**:
```
/* strncpy - copy n bytes from s2 to s1 (using while)
 */
void strncpy(s1, s2, n)
    char s1[], s2[];
    unsigned n;
    {
    unsigned i;

    i = 0;
    while (i < n && s2[i] != '\0')
        {
        s1[i] = s2[i];
        ++i;
        }
    while (i < n)
        {
        s1[i] = '\0';
        ++i;
        }
    }
```

The `strncpy` function copies a bounded number of characters from one string to another. (If the string being copied is shorter than the space available, the receiving string is "null-padded" — extended with null characters.)

The parameter storage for `strncpy` looks like this:

Question [5-16] Assume the following machine state just before calling

```
strncpy(save, line, 4)
```

VARIABLE	ADDRESS	STORAGE

| line | 800 | | 97 | 98 | 99 | 0 | |
| | | | 'a' | 'b' | 'c' | '\0' | |

| save | 1800 | | 119 | 120 | 121 | 118 | |
| | | | 'x' | 'y' | 'z' | 'w' | |

What does the parameter storage look like when `strncpy` is entered?

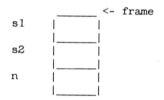

Question [5-17] At what address is `s1[0]` located? _____

Question [5-18] At what address is `s2[3]` located? _____

Question [5-19] What does the storage of `save` look like when `strncpy` returns?

| save | 1800 | | | | | | |
| | | | | | | | |

We have noted that when an unsubscripted array name appears in an expression such as `strncpy(save, line, 4)` the address of its initial element is used as the value. If you were to write `&save` or `&line` explicitly, this would be illegal, according to the standard given in Appendix A of Kernighan and Ritchie [1978] **[5-20 cc]**.

Exercise 5-4. The Standard Library provides a function

```
int strncmp(s1, s2, n)
```

which looks at no more than n characters of the strings to determine the comparison result. Write and test your own **strncmp** function.

C language has full access to all the data storage of your program — this allows it to *replace assembler code* in many engineering applications. But it also can lead to bugs and portability problems when the programmer does not understand what C is doing. For an example, consider the **dump** function, which prints n bytes of memory as hexadecimal numbers.

dmpdem.c **[5-21]**:

```
/* dump - print memory bytes
 *        (Warning - some usages may be non-portable)
 */
#include "local.h"
#define LINESIZE 16
#define BYTEMASK 0xFF
void dump(s, n)
    char s[];        /* byte address to be dumped */
    unsigned n;      /* number of bytes to dump */
    {
    unsigned i;      /* byte counter */

    for (i = 0; i < n; ++i)
        {
        if (i % LINESIZE == 0)
            printf("\n%08x: ", &s[i]);
        printf(" %02x", s[i] & BYTEMASK);
        }
    printf("\n");
    }
/* dmpdem - demonstrate dump function
 */
main()
    {
    char msg[16];
    double d = 100.;

    strncpy(msg, "testing 1 2 3\n", sizeof(msg));

    /* case 1 - quite proper */
    dump(msg, sizeof(msg));

    /* case 2 - ok, but output will vary with machine */
    dump(&d, sizeof(d));

    /* case 3 - non-portable, may cause hardware error */
    dump(0x40, 4);
    exit(SUCCEED);
    }
```

The parameter s is understood by dump to be the address of some byte (char) in the memory, and n is the number of bytes to be printed. The function blindly prints s[0], s[1], etc., using a format which will divide the printout into lines of sixteen bytes. (The bitwise-and with BYTEMASK prevents possible sign-extension.) The usages of dump can be divided into several cases, as the main program shows.

(1) When dump is applied to an array of characters no larger than the parameter n specifies, its usage is error-free and portable. The bytes of the array are printed one-by-one.

(2) When `dump` is applied to data other than `char` data, the internal representation of such data may be different on different machines, and the printouts could look different. The argument is not the same type as `dump` expects, and `lint` will complain about the mismatch.

(3) When `dump` is applied to an arbitrary *numerical address,* the program could "bomb out" with hardware errors on some machines (from trying to reference non-existent memory locations), and the usage is certainly *not portable.* This latter type of programming is only to be used when you are quite sure that a non-portable program is needed for one particular machine. The `lint` command will certainly complain, with good reason.

5.5   Recursive Functions

As we have seen, each function receives its own frame when it is entered, and this frame is given back when the function returns control. Thus it is easy for a function to *call itself,* thus becoming a *recursive* function.

The most familiar example of a recursive function is the factorial function:

```
n!  =   n × (n-1)!      if n > 0;

    =   1               otherwise.
```

Here is a program containing a factorial function:

```
fact.c [5-22]:
    /* factl - return n! (n factorial)
     */
    #include "local.h"
    long factl(n)
        long n;
        {
        if (n <= 1)
            return (1);
        else
            return (n * factl(n - 1));
        }
    /* fact - demonstrate factl function
     */
    main()
        {
        long factl();
        long result;

        result = factl((long)3);
        printf("3! = %ld\n", result);
        exit(SUCCEED);
        }
```

The function definition line

```
    long factl(n)
```

says that the function will return a `long` number, that its name is `factl`, and that it has one parameter, n. The crucial part of the function body is the expression

```
    factl(n - 1)
```

which calls the `factl` function from within itself, passing an argument which is one less than the value passed in the parameter n.

We will now trace the execution of the expression `factl(3)` in the main program. The value 3 is placed into an argument frame, and the function `factl` is called. Its parameter n has the value 3:

```
                    _____  <- frame for factl(3)
        n          |        3 |
                   |_____|
```

The function in turn executes the expression

```
    factl(n - 1)
```

thus placing 2 into another argument frame, and calling `factl` again.

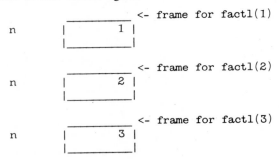

```
                      _____  <- frame for factl(2)
          n          |    2 |
                     |_____|

                      _____  <- frame for factl(3)
          n          |    3 |
                     |_____|
```

The process is repeated once again to place the value 1 into another argument frame and to call `factl` again.

```
                      _____  <- frame for factl(1)
          n          |    1 |
                     |_____|

                      _____  <- frame for factl(2)
          n          |    2 |
                     |_____|

                      _____  <- frame for factl(3)
          n          |    3 |
                     |_____|
```

This time, the function returns the value 1 and control returns to the computation of

```
    2 * factl(1)
```

giving the result 2. This result is returned into the computation of

```
    3 * factl(2)
```

giving the result 6, which is the last return from `factl`. The value 6 is thus assigned to `result`.

In mathematical terms, what has just transpired is the computation of 3! like this:

```
    3! = 3 * 2!
    2! = 2 * 1!
    1! = 1, so
    2! = 2, so
    3! = 6
```

Exercise 5-5. In Section 3.20, you wrote a function `maxlng` which returns the largest positive `long` number available on your machine. On the assumption that `double` variables can hold values much larger than `long` variables **[5-23 mach]**, write a program `facmax.c` to determine the largest value of n such that `factl(n)` is less than the largest `long` number on your machine.

Exercise 5-6. Using the result of the previous exercise, modify the `factl` function for "defensive programming." That is, the function should examine its parameter n, and return –1 if a meaningful result cannot be produced.

5.6   Initializing Automatic Scalars

In the declaration of a scalar automatic variable, each variable may have an initializer attached to it. The initializer is written with an equal-sign and a value which becomes the initial value of the variable. Consider the following simple program:

```
inits.c [5-24]:
    /* inits - initialization examples
     */
    #include "local.h"
    main( )
        {
        char c = 'x';
        short i = 1;
        short j = i * 2;

        printf("%d %d %c\n", i, j, c);
        exit(SUCCEED);
        }
```

Question [5-25] What does `inits` print?

Each initializer applies to only one variable. We suggest that initialized declarations should each have a line of their own; it is very easy to falsely interpret this declaration (which initializes only n2)

```
        long n1, n2 = 0;
```

to mean

```
        long n1 = 0;
        long n2 = 0;
```

The initialization is performed by instructions that are executed each time the function is entered. Furthermore, these instructions are performed in the same sequence that the declarations appear in the program. Consider this program:

```
recpt1.c [5-26]:
    /* recpt1 - receipt example #1
     */
    #include "local.h"
    main()
        {
        short receip();

        printf("First = %d\n", receip());
        printf("Second = %d\n", receip());
        exit(SUCCEED);
        }
    short receip()
        {
        short number = 1;

        return (number++);
        }
```

Question [5-27] What does recpt1 print?

Because the receip function initializes its number to 1 each time the function is entered, the function would not work very well as a "take-a-number" dispenser. Before we discuss how to correct this behavior, we must discuss the different *storage classes* of the C machine.

5.7 Storage Class and Internal Static

The memory of the computer is organized by C into three areas, conventionally known as the *text, data* and *dynamic segments*. The relative location of these segments may vary in different environments, but we can picture them like this **[5-28 mach]**:

```
 _____
|           |
|  text     |      contains the machine instructions
|           |      for the program
|_____|
|           |
|  data     |      contains variables which remain in
|           |      fixed locations -- the "static" storage
|_____|
|           |
|  dynamic  |      contains automatic variables, parameters, and
|           |      function-call bookkeeping; changes as
|_____|      functions are called and returned
```

So far, all the variables we have seen have lived in the dynamic segment: the automatic variables of the `main` function and of other functions, and the parameters of functions.

C language administers these variables as a *stack*. A stack, in computing parlance, is a data structure with a "top" and a "bottom." A data item can be added at the top, which is called *pushing* the item onto the stack, and makes the stack larger. Or an item can be removed from the top, which is called *popping* the stack, and makes the stack smaller. In most C implementations, when a function is called, the frame for that function is *pushed* into the next space in the stack area. Thus, in this little program

```
stack1.c [5-29]:
    /* stack1 - stack example 1
     */
    #include "local.h"
    main()
        {
        f1(1);
        }
    f1(n)
        short n;
        {
        f2(n + 1);
        }
    f2(n)
        short n;
        {
        printf("%d\n", n);
        }
```

by the time the `printf` function is called, the stack looks something like this:

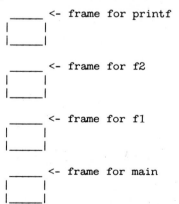

And each time a function returns, its frame is *popped* off the stack, thus made available for re-use in the next function call. These operations are done automatically by the code that C language generates; in other words, they are not anything that *you* have to program.

Now we want to consider the data segment, the location of variables which remain in fixed locations. These variables stay put while functions are called and return. Variables can be allocated into the (fixed-location) data segment by being declared as `static`. For example, the declaration

```
static short number;
```

will allocate the `short` integer named `number` into the (fixed-location) data segment. Syntactically, the keyword `static` is known as a *storage class*. (Another storage class keyword is `auto`, the default for local function variables, which we saw in Section 5.3.) The first variety of `static` variables is *internal* `static`. The internal `static` variables are declared inside a function block, just like the automatic variables. They are like automatic variables in that they are known only to the block in which they are declared, but they live in the data segment.

The initialization of `static` variables is different from that of automatic variables; initialization is done only once, when the program is loaded into the machine. Thus, in our `receipt` example from Section 5.6, we can place the receipt number in `static` storage and it will keep its value between calls upon the function. The program would look like this:

```
recpt2.c [5-30]:
    /* recpt2 - print two receipt numbers
     */
    #include "local.h"
    main()
        {
        short receip();

        printf("First = %d\n", receip());
        printf("Second = %d\n", receip());
        exit(SUCCEED);
        }
    short receip()
        {
        static short number = 1;

        return (number++);
        }
```

Question [5-31] What is the output of `recpt2`?

A note for the users of C on microprocessors: on small microprocessors such as 8080, Z80, and 6502, static memory is faster than automatic, and gives shorter code **[5-32 mach]**.

5.8   Separate Compilation and Linkage

So far, all our programs have been created as one source file. A source file may contain any number of separate functions, so it is certainly possible to write any C program this way. But there are several practical reasons for us programmers to create programs that are split into several source files:

1.   As we are debugging and revising a program, it is operationally easier if each re-compilation processes only one part of a large program.

2.   Once we have written and debugged a function, we do not need to keep re-compiling it as we work on other functions in the program.

We can compile a source file to produce *object code*, and by a process known as *linking*, we can combine its functions with other functions in other source files. The linking process is done by a tool known as a *linker*, or a *linkage editor*; the linker stitches together the code from several object-code files (or, "object files" for short) into a single executable program.

The linker also stitches our program together with functions whose object code has been collected into a *library* (or *object library*). This is the mechanism by which our programs are combined with the code for functions such as `strlen` or `printf`. The linker searches a pre-existing library (supplied with the compiler), looking for the names of any functions which are not found in our program itself.

Given this background, let us look in more detail at the steps the compiler goes through to compile a program such as our simple `receip` example. When we give the command

```
cc -o recpt2 recpt2.c
```

the compiler accomplishes five successive phases:

1.   The preprocessor is invoked, to do any #define or #include requests.

2.   The pre-processed program is compiled into a "parse tree," a relatively machine-independent representation of our program.

3.   The parse tree is converted into a human-readable assembler-code file, which specifies the actual machine instructions comprised by our program.

4.   An assembler is invoked to convert the assembler code **[5-33 cc]** into actual numeric machine instructions, and the result is an object file.

5.   The *linker* combines this object code with the object code in the compiler-provided libraries, to produce an executable program.

We can tell the compiler to stop after the production of object code with the flag `-c` **[5-34 cc]**. Suppose we break our `recpt2` program into two files. One file contains the main program:

```
recpt3.c [5-35]:
    /* recpt3 - print two receipt numbers
     */
    #include "local.h"
    main()
        {
        short receip();

        printf("First = %d\n", receip());
        printf("Second = %d\n", receip());
        }
```

And a second file contains the `receip` function:

```
receip [5-36]:
    /* receip - deliver a unique receipt number
     */
    #include "local.h"
    short receip()
        {
        static short number = 1;

        return (number++);
        }
```

Notice that *each* of the files must contain any #include statements that are needed; they are not remembered from any other files compiled.

A sequence of commands to compile these two files separately and then link them together would look like this:

```
cc -c recpt3.c
cc -c receip.c
cc -o recpt3 recpt3.o receip.o
```

Each of the first two commands compiles one source file into object code. On UNIX systems, the object file is given a name ending in the suffix .o [5-37 os].

The third command does nothing more than to *link* these two object files together, along with any library functions — printf, in this case — to produce an executable program called recpt2.

Now that we have separated the compilation of receip.c from the linking of it with the main program, we could make further changes to the main program recpt2.c, then re-compile and re-link without compiling receip.c again. In fact, we can combine the compile and link together like this:

```
cc -o recpt2 twonum.c receip.o
```

which will compile `recpt2.c` and link it together with `receip.o` (as well as with the library). The compiler determines which steps are necessary by looking at the suffix of the file name: files ending in `.c` are to be compiled, whereas files ending in `.o` are only to be linked **[5-38 cc]**.

A large program of hundreds or thousands of lines is typically written in a number of separate source files, with compile and link accomplished in the manner that we have just seen.

Now that you have seen these procedures for separate compilation of functions, when we show the code for a C function, we will portray it as it would look in a source file of its own, including its own `#include` and `#define` lines for whatever symbols it needs.

5.9   External Static Storage

If a C source file contains declarations of static variables appearing *before* any functions, then these variables will be known to all the functions in the file. Such variables are known as *external* `static` variables — external, because their declaration appears outside any function.

One common reason for using external static variables is to allow two or more functions in one file to share a variable, without requiring the programmers of other files to keep track of its name. A mundane reason for hiding its name from other files is simply to avoid the bookkeeping chore of remembering the name. In large programs another reason is more important: by *hiding* the name from other files, we can be sure that all accesses to this variable must go through the functions in its file — it becomes a *resource* administered by that file.

For a simple example of an external static variable, we introduce a *pseudo-random number generator*. This is a function which produces a series of numbers which appear to be chosen at random — they jump around randomly in value. Of course, they are not *really* random, and serious statistical analysis is beyond our scope. But for programs which roll dice, shuffle cards, or print unpredictable replies, a simple pseudo-random generator will serve. Here is a C source file containing an external static variable (named `rnum`) and two functions which access this variable.

rand **[5-39]**:
```
/* rand, srand - generate random numbers
 */
#include "local.h"
static long rnum = 0;
void srand(n)
    short n;
    {
    rnum = (long)n;
    }
short rand()
    {
    rnum = rnum * 0x41C64E6D + 0x3039;
    return ((short)(rnum >> 16) & 0x7FFF);
    }
```

These two functions, rand and srand, both access the external static variable rnum. The function rand uses it to generate a new random number. The function srand sets it to the new "seed" (initial random value). Only these two functions can see the variable rnum; any other functions will have to call rand or srand to have any effect on rnum.

Each time rand is called, it will return a new random number, which is a short integer greater than or equal to zero. Thus there are 32768 possible numbers that it can return. However, rand will produce 2^{32} numbers before it starts repeating itself; this measure is known as the *period* of the random number generator.

Most often, we do not actually want a number between 0 and 32767, but would rather choose the low and high limits ourselves. Here is another source file, nfrom.c, which contains one function, nfrom. This function returns a number between low and high, inclusive.

nfrom **[5-40]**:
```
/* nfrom - return a number between low and high, inclusive
 */
#include "local.h"
short nfrom(low, high)
    register short low, high;
    {
    short rand();
    register short nb = high - low + 1;

    return (rand() % nb + low);
    }
```

Question [5-41] Suppose a program were to call

```
nfrom(1, 10)
```

and rand( ) were to return 1003. What would nfrom return? _____

Question [5-42] Suppose a program were to call

      nfrom(1, 6)

and rand( ) were to return 3605. What would nfrom return? _____

        Now for a main program to exercise these functions. Let the numbers 0
through 51 stand for the different playing cards in a deck. For example, 0
could stand for "Ace of Spades," 1 could stand for "Two of Spades," and so
forth through Spades, Hearts, Diamonds, and Clubs. To shuffle a deck of 52
cards, we call nfrom once for each card, selecting the card randomly from the
remaining cards. The program looks like this:

```
shuf52.c [5-43]:
    /* shuf52 - shuffle a deck of 52 cards and print result
     */
    #include "local.h"
    #define NCARDS 52
    main()
        {
        short cards[NCARDS];
        short i;

        for (i = 0; i < NCARDS; ++i)
            cards[i] = i;
        shuffl(cards);
        for (i = 0; i < NCARDS; ++i)
            {
            printf("%2d ", cards[i]);
            if (i % 13 == 12)
                putchar('\n');
            }
        putchar('\n');
        }
    /* shuffl - permute the cards
     */
    void shuffl(deck)
        short deck[];
        {
        short t;         /* temporary for swap */
        short i;         /* index for loop over cards */
        short j;         /* index for swap */
        short nfrom();   /* fn to produce random no. */

        for (i = 0; i < NCARDS - 1; ++i)
            {
            j = nfrom(i, NCARDS - 1);
            t = deck[j], deck[j] = deck[i], deck[i] = t;
            }
        }
```

Here are some commands to compile and execute the program:

```
cc -c nfrom.c
cc -o shuf52 shuf52.c nfrom.o
shuf52
11 19 17 15  5 22 33 30 21 27 25 45 13    (output)
32 36  8 10 38 28 14 50 43 35 20 26 49
18  1  0 31 34 48 29 39 12 40 41 24 16
23 44  6 37 46 51  3 47 42  4  9  7  2
```

It is often convenient to make a *library* containing functions in object-code form. We could, for example, create a library to contain the functions nfrom, error, and remark like this **[5-44 os]**:

```
ar c mylib.a nfrom.o error.o remark.o
```

and we could then compile our shuf52.c program using this library:

```
cc -o shuf52 shuf52.c mylib.a
```

In general, the functions in a library should be ordered in "calling sequence" — that is, if function a calls function b, then a should appear before b in the library. If we wish to replace a function in a library, the command looks like this:

```
ar r mylib.a nfrom.o
```

5.10   Initializing Arrays in Static Storage

Arrays in static storage, unlike automatic arrays, may be initialized on their declaration. The initialization takes place when the program is loaded. There are no machine instructions in the object program to do the initialization; the object file contains the actual data values for the array. Here is an example:

```
static short digits[10] = {0, 1, 2, 3, 4, 5, 6, 7, 8, 9};
```

The list of initializers is enclosed in braces, and is separated by commas.

A shorthand is provided for initializers consisting of character values: the initializer may be written as a string of characters enclosed in double-quotes. Example:

```
static char msg[6] = "hello";
```

Remember, a character string always includes a \0 null terminator at the end. Thus, this last statement is completely equivalent to this one:

```
static char msg[6] = {'h', 'e', 'l', 'l', 'o', '\0'};
```

If the array bound is greater than the number of initializers, the extra elements are initialized to zero. If no bound is given, the bound is taken to be the number of initializers. A final convenience: the last initializer is allowed to have a trailing comma.

Question [5-45] What are the initial values?

```
static char st[5] = "std";
```

```
static char s[2] = "ab";
```

```
static short a[5] = {1, 2, 3};
```

```
static short b[] = {1, 3, 5, 7,};
```

Exercise 5-7. Write a program bingo.c which will randomly generate cards for the game of BINGO. The general format looks like this:

```
 _____
| B | I | N | G | O |
|___|___|___|___|___|
|   |   |   |   |   |
|___|___|___|___|___|
|   |   |   |   |   |
|___|___|___|___|___|
|   |   |X X|   |   |
|___|___|X X|___|___|
|   |   |   |   |   |
|___|___|___|___|___|
|   |   |   |   |   |
|___|___|___|___|___|
```

The B column contains non-duplicate numbers from 1 to 15; I, from 16 to 30; N, from 31 to 45; G, from 46 to 60; and O, from 61 to 75.

Exercise 5-8. Write a program dice.c which will roll two 6-sided dice ten thousand times and will tabulate how many times each result is obtained.

5.11   Two-dimensional Arrays

C language allows arrays of more than one dimension; we will describe here the two-dimensional form. These arrays are also known as *rectangular arrays,* because their contents form a rectangle:

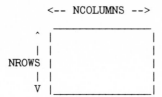

The following declaration statement creates space for a two-dimensional array of short integers:

```
short a[NROWS][NCOLUMNS];
```

The total storage space occupied by the array a is

```
NROWS × NCOLUMNS × sizeof(short)
```

i.e.,

```
NROWS × NCOLUMNS × 2
```

The declaration for a two-dimensional array of characters is similar, except that you must remember the extra space for a null terminator if each row is to be treated as a character string:

```
char s[NROWS][NCOLUMNS + 1];
```

The declaration can contain an initializer:

```
static char sampler[35][61] =
    {
    "LOVELOVELOVELOVELOVELOVELOVELOVELOVELOVELOVELOVELOVELOVELOVE",
    "L           OVELOVELOVELOVELOVELOV         LOVELOVELOVE",
    "LOV         ELOVELOVELOVELOVELOV              LOVELOVE",
    "LOVE        VELOVELOVELOVELOVEL                  VELOVE",
    "LOVE        VELOVELOVELOVELOVE          LOVEL    ELOVE",
    "LOVE        VELOVELOVELOVELOV         VELOVELO    LOVE",
    "LOVE        VELOVELOVELOVELOV          OVELOVOV   LOVE",
    "LOVE        VELOVELOVELOVELOV         LOVELOVOV   LOVE",
    "LOVE        VELOVELOVELOVELOV         ELOVELOVELO LOVE",
    "LOVE        VELOVELOVELOVELOV          VELOVELOVEL LOVE",
    "LOVE        VELOVELOVELOVELOV          OVELOVELOVE LOVE",
    "LOVE        VELOVELOVELOVELOVEL V    LOVELOVELOV   LOVE",
    "LOVE        VELOVELOVELOVELOVE  V    LOVELOVELO    LOVE",
    "LOVE        VELOVELOVELOVELOV   V     OVELOVEL     LOVE",
    "LOVE        VELOVELOVELOVELOVEL     VE            ELOVE",
    "L                           VELOV              LOVELOVE",
    "L                           VELOVELOV      LOVELOVELOVE",
    "L           VELOV                               E",
    "L           VELOV                               E",
    "LOVE        VELOVELOVELOV  VELOVELOVE     VELOVELOVELO    E",
    "LOVEL       ELOVELOVELO  OVELOVELOVE     VELOVELOVELOVE   E",
    "LOVEL       ELOVELOVELO  OVELOVELOVE     VELOVELOVELOVEL  E",
    "LOVELO      LOVELOVEL  LOVELOVELOVE      VELOVELOVELOVELO E",
    "LOVELO      LOVELOVEL  LOVELOVELOVE      VELOVELOVELOVELOVE",
    "LOVELOV     OVELOVE  ELOVELOVELOVE       VELOVEL VELOVELOVE",
    "LOVELOV     OVELOVE  ELOVELOVELOVE                VELOVELOVE",
    "LOVELOVE    VELOV  VELOVELOVELOVE        VELOVE   VELOVELOVE",
    "LOVELOVE    VELOV  VELOVELOVELOVE        VELOVEL  VELOVELOVE",
    "LOVELOVEL   ELO   OVELOVELOVELOVE        VELOVELOVELOVELO E",
    "LOVELOVEL   ELO   OVELOVELOVELOVE        VELOVELOVELOVEL  E",
    "LOVELOVELO  L   LOVELOVELOVELOVE         VELOVELOVELOVE   E",
    "LOVELOVELO      LOVELOVELOVELOVE         VELOVELOVELO     E",
    "LOVELOVELOV      ELOVELOVELOVE                           E",
    "LOVELOVELOV      ELOVELOVELOVE                           E",
    "LOVELOVELOVELOVELOVELOVELOVELOVELOVELOVELOVELOVELOVELOVELOVE"
    };
```

(Thanks to the artist Robert Indiana and the author David H. Ahl. Typing this initializer is truly a labor of love.)

We see that there are 35 rows in this array, each containing 60 data characters plus the null terminator that the compiler appends to each string.

The data is stored in *row-major order,* which means that each row forms an array of items in the memory. In C, each row is itself a one-dimensional array, and can be used in contexts where an array is allowed. For example, to print this array we could use this loop:

```
for (i = 0; i < 35; ++i)
    printf("%s\n", sampler[i]);
```

Each of the individual elements of a two-dimensional array is accessed using two subscripts like this

```
sampler[i][j]
```

The following program accepts an input string from the user, and substitutes each character of the string for a character of the sampler array, thus printing the sampler with the user's string.

prsam.c [5-46]:

```
/* prsam - print sampler
 */
#include "local.h"
#define NROWS 35
#define NCOLUMNS 60
main()
    {
    static char sampler[NROWS][NCOLUMNS + 1] =
        {
        "LOVELOVE ... LOVELOVE",
            /* et cetera, with the rest of the array */
        };
    short i;            /* row index for sampler */
    short j;            /* column index for sampler */
    short len;          /* length of s */
    char s[BUFSIZ];     /* user's message */

    printf("Enter a string:");
    if ((len = getln(s, BUFSIZ)) == EOF)
        error("Bye!", "");
    printf("\n");
    s[--len] = '\0';
    if (NCOLUMNS < len)
        len = NCOLUMNS;
    for (i = 0; i < NROWS; ++i)
        {
        for (j = 0; j < NCOLUMNS; ++j)
            if (sampler[i][j] != ' ')
                sampler[i][j] = s[j % len];
        printf("%s\n", sampler[i]);
        }
    }
```

Exercise 5-9. Enter and test the prsam.c program. (This may be the only program in the book that does useful things for your younger relatives.)

In Section 5.7, we saw that C maintains a "stack" for functions, in the "dynamic" memory segment. If you wish to create your own stack for use by a program, you cannot make use of C language's own stack mechanism.

However, it is easy to create your own stacks using external static storage. You need two functions — one to do the pushing and one to do the popping — and a shared data structure.

Consider the puzzle called "Towers of Hanoi." There are three vertical pegs onto which are slid disks of varying sizes — five such disks, for example. One may move a disk onto another peg only if all the disks on that peg are larger than it is. Initially, all the disks are on peg number one:

and the object is to move them to peg number three. Each stack of disks is like a programming "stack," as described above, since we can add or remove disks only on the top of each stack. We can represent the three pegs and the disks that are upon them by a two-dimensional array called **pegs**:

```
static short pegs[3][NDISKS] = 0;
```

This declaration makes use of the special property of C initializers which fills all uninitialized elements to zero; thus all the elements of **pegs** are initialized to zero. (Note that the puzzle may have any number of disks, specified by NDISKS but must have 3 pegs — the unmodifiable constant appears as is.) We also need an array **ndisks** to keep track of the number of disks on each peg:

```
static short ndisks[3] = 0;
```

Making provision for "defensive programming," we will include tests for the legality of requested push and pop operations. We also provide a dumppg ("dump pegs") function to show the state of our pegs. The real work of "pushing" takes place in one powerful statement:

```
pegs[peg][ndisks[peg]++] = disk;
```

"The next available space on **pegs[peg]**" is given by the element ndisks[peg], and the ++ postfix increment causes this number to be incremented after use; thus it is ready for the next operation. The entire statement therefore "pushes" the new **disk** number into the appropriate space. The "popping" operation is similarly performed by one powerful statement:

```
return (pegs[peg][--ndisks[peg]]);
```

In this case, the "next available space" number — ndisks[peg] — is decremented before use, to give us the subscript of the "most recently used space," while leaving the number ready for the next operation.

pegs.c [5-47]:
```
/* pegs.c - three functions (push, pop, dumppg) for Towers of Hanoi
 */
#include "local.h"
#include "pegs.h"
static short pegs[3][NDISKS] = 0;
static short ndisks[3] = 0;
/* push - put disk onto peg
 */
void push(peg, disk)
    short peg;    /* which peg: 0, 1, ... */
    short disk;   /* which disk: 1, 2, ... */
    {
    if (peg < 0 || 3 <= peg)
        {
        printf("Cannot push onto peg %d\n", peg);
        exit(FAIL);
        }
    else
        pegs[peg][ndisks[peg]++] = disk;
    }
/* pop - remove disk from peg
 */
short pop(peg)
    short peg;
    {
    if (peg < 0 || 3 <= peg)
        {
        printf("Cannot pop peg %d\n", peg);
        exit(FAIL);
        }
    else if (ndisks[peg] < 1)
        {
        printf("Cannot pop peg %d (it has %d disks)\n",
            peg, ndisks[peg]);
        exit(FAIL);
        }
    else
        return (pegs[peg][--ndisks[peg]]);
    }
/* dumppg - print status of disks and pegs
 */
void dumppg()
    {
    short i; /* index over pegs */
    short j; /* index over disks */

    for (i = 0; i < 3; ++i)
        {
        printf("Peg %d:", i);
        for (j = 0; j < ndisks[i]; ++j)
            printf(" %d", pegs[i][j]);
        printf("\n");
        }
    }
```

To go along with `pegs.c` we will also provide an include-file `pegs.h` which declares the functions available in `pegs.c` and any necessary defined constants (such as `NDISKS`). In modern programming terms, a set of one or more files such as `pegs.c` is known as a *resource monitor*, or *package*. And an accompanying include-file such as `pegs.h` is the *public interface* for the package — it defines what the user is allowed to see about the package.

`pegs.h` **[5-48]**:

```
/* pegs.h - interface for pegs package
 */
#define NDISKS 5
extern void push();
extern short pop();
extern void dumppg();
```

Exercise 5-10. Compile `pegs.c` to produce an object file `pegs.o`. Write a program `tower.c` which solves the Towers of Hanoi problem, for any specified number `NDISKS`. Compile `tower.c` separately from `pegs.c` and use the linker to combine them into an executable program. Hint: consider a recursive function

```
move(n, p0, p1)
```

which moves an entire heap of n disks from peg p0 to peg p1.

5.12   External Variables

External names are made known to any source file that references them; the linker arranges that all references to an external name will refer to the same location in storage. There are two kinds of external names: *external variables* and *external functions*.

The external variables all reside in the static storage (the data segment); automatic variables cannot be external.

External variables behave just like the external `static` variables that we saw in Section 5.9, except that they are known to all source files, not just the one in which they are declared.

The *definition* of an external variable initializes it with an initial value. External definitions should be placed at the front of the source file that they appear in, before any functions. For example, a `char` array named `screen` could be given an external definition like this:

```
char screen[24][80] = 0;

/*
 *  (now appear any functions in the file)
 */
```

This definition establishes the variable **screen**, initialized to all zeroes, and made known to any function that references it.

The *declaration* of an external variable is a request to link with the storage that is created by its *definition*. A declaration does not reserve any storage by itself; somewhere in one of the object files being linked together, there must be a definition of the variable. A declaration may appear either inside or outside a function, and it begins with the keyword **extern**, as in

```
void fn()
    {
    extern screen char[24][80];
```

Unlike a definition, an external declaration does *not* contain an initializer. Programs are easier to maintain if all external declarations are kept either inside functions or inside the public interfaces of packages.

We are deliberately showing no code examples of external variables. The techniques shown in the previous section eliminate all need that the introductory programmer might otherwise have for external variables. An excess of external variables has often been a feature of hard-to-maintain computer systems.

Turning now to external *functions*, we should point out that all the functions we have seen so far are, in fact, external. That is, their names are made known to the linker; there may be any number of declarations; but there may be only one definition. The *definition* of a function is just the technical name for the text of the function itself — this is what *defines* the function. The *declaration* of a function is like any other declaration — a "sandwich" of *type* and *name* — except that the keyword **extern** will be assumed if no storage class is given explicitly. Thus these two declarations are equivalent:

```
extern short pop();
```

```
short pop();
```

Both of them declare the name **pop** to have the type **short** ( ) (i.e., function returning **short**) and to have the storage class **extern**.

What other storage class might a function have? Although we did not mention it in Section 5.9, a function may have the storage class **static** attached to its definition. If so, the function can be called only by other functions *in the same source file* — it becomes a "private resource" of the "package" that it belongs to. Whatever its storage class, a function is always located in the *text* segment, referring back to the classification shown in Section 5.7.

5.13   Register Storage Class

We say good-bye for the moment to the static variables and take another look at the automatic variables and the function parameters. These are the variables that come into being when their function is entered and disappear when it returns. These variables can be placed in the actual hardware registers of the computer by declaring them to have register storage class. You simply put the keyword register on their declarations, and *voila*, they are placed in registers.

It sounds so simple — what is the catch? Well, to begin with, each machine is limited in the number of registers available for such variables. Many C machines have only three such registers available, but the number varies **[5-49 cc] [5-50 mach]**. Secondly, only certain data types can be placed in registers: char, short, int, with their unsigned versions, and the *pointer* variables that we have seen as array parameters. Finally, programs may not take the *address* (&) of a register variable — for example, we cannot read into a register with scanf.

Even with these three restrictions, register variables are useful for generating fast programs that take less space to run. Consider these two little programs that count to one million:

```
fast.c [5-51]:
    /* fast - count to one million
     */
    #include "local.h"
    main()
        {
        register short units;
        register short thous;

        thous = 0;
        while (++thous <= 1000)
            {
            units = 0;
            while (++units <= 1000)
                ;
            }
        }
```

```
slow.c [5-52]:
    /* slow - count to one million
     */
    #include "local.h"
    main( )
        {
        short units;
        short thous;

        thous = 0;
        while (++thous <= 1000)
            {
            units = 0;
            while (++units <= 1000)
                ;
            }
        }
```

On most machines, the **fast** version will take about one-half the time of the slow version **[5-53 cc]**.

One final note about **register** variables: on microprocessors such as 8080/Z80, register variables are usually *simulated* by special static variables administered by the compiler. They will otherwise behave the same as on bigger computers and will still be faster than ordinary automatic storage **[5-54 cc]**.

5.14   Scope Rules

The *scope* of a name consists of all those parts of the file which can "see" the name. In other words, it consists of all those places where the use of the name would produce a legal reference. There are four rules that determine the scope of names.

1.   *External variables:* for variables declared *outside* a function, the scope is the rest of the file — from the end of the declaration to the end of the file. If such external declarations are placed at the front of the file, as we have suggested, this allows all the functions in the file to see the variable.

2.   *Local variables:* for variables declared *inside a function,* the scope is the rest of the block — from the end of the declaration to the end of the block. This limited scope of local variables means that a programmer does not need to worry about inadvertently using a name that has been used inside some other function.

3.   *Visibility to the linker:* external variables declared as **static** will not be published to the linker; they will be known only within their source file. Other external variables will be published to the linker and linked together across source files. For an external variable to be known in a

source file other than the one containing its *definition,* that source file
must contain an **extern** declaration for the variable.

4.   *Function names:* the names of functions are *external* by default. It is
therefore not necessary to add the keyword **extern** to function declarations.

These four rules explain all the intricacies of variable scope, but an example is
still useful. Here are two source files containing three functions and declaring
six variables. The scope of each variable is indicated at the left of each line;
if a variable name appears on a line, it means that the line is in the scope of
that variable.

```
Scope
            x.c:
                #include "local.h"
                short a = 2;
a               static short b = 3;
ab              main()
ab                  {
ab                  short c = a + b;
abc
abc                 xsub(c);
abc                 }
ab          xsub(d)
ab              short d;
ab  d               {
ab  d               short e = 7 * d;
ab  de
ab  de              ysub(e);
ab  de              }


            ysub.c:
                #include "local.h"
                ysub(f)
                    short f;
    f                   {
    f                   extern short a;
a   f
a   f                   printf("%d\n", a + f);
a   f                   }
```

Question [5-55] What does the program **x** print?

5.15   Summary of Initialization

We have seen that there are two categories of data storage: "dynamic" storage for automatic, parameter, and register variables; and "static" storage for internal static, external static, and external variables. We have also seen two categories of variables: scalars and arrays.

To begin with, parameters can never have initializers. This leaves us with four rules for initialization of variables:

A.   *Automatic and register:*

A.1   *Scalars:* May be initialized to expressions, such as

```
short a = 10;
register short b = a + 1;
```

A.2   *Arrays:* These may not be initialized at all.

B.   *Internal static, external static, external:*

B.1   *Scalars:* May be initialized to constants, such as

```
static short a = 10;
```

B.2   *Arrays:* May be initialized to a list of constants (if needed, the compiler pads with zeroes):

```
static short ar[100] = {0};
static char msg[] = "help!";
```

Question [5-56] In this incorrect sample program, which lines have illegal initializers?

```
noinit.c:
    /* noinit - some illegal initializers
     */
    #include "local.h"
    short a = 0;
    short b = a + 1;
    short c[5] = {4, 3, 2, 1};
    main()
        {
        short d = a + 2;
        short e[3] = {1, 2, 3};
        static short f = d + 1;
        static short g[2] = {4, 5, 6};

        printf("initializers\n");
        }
```

5.16   Empty Brackets: Three Cases

There are three cases in which C allows the abbreviation of empty brackets on an array name, such as a[]. Unfortunately for the learner, this abbreviation means three completely different things in the three cases.

(1) When empty brackets appear on the declaration of a function parameter, they mean that the parameter contains the *address* of the initial element of the array which is passed to the function. (Indeed, C behaves the same way even if you do put a number inside the brackets; the number is just disregarded.) For example,

```
void fn(a)
short a[];
```

says that the parameter a contains the address of the initial element of an array of short integers.

(2) When empty brackets appear with an array initializer, they mean "take the array bound from the number of initializers." Thus in this example

```
short a[] = {012, 034, 056};
```

the size of array a is specified as three, by the compiler's counting the initializers.

(3) When empty brackets appear on an extern declaration, they mean "the array bound will be specified by the *definition* of the array (which appears elsewhere)." For example,

```
extern char msg[];
```

says that the size of msg will be specified by its definition, somewhere else.

There can never be any confusion about which rule is applicable to a specific instance of empty brackets because parameters can never be initialized and cannot be external variables, and extern declarations can never have initializers. (Only *definitions* have initializers.)

These three cases are worth memorizing.

5.17   Macros with Parameters

The C preprocessor provides for macro (i.e., #define) definitions with parameters. For example, in local.h we find these lines:

```
#define ABS(x)      (((x) < 0) ? -(x) : (x))
#define MAX(x, y)   (((x) < (y)) ? (y) : (x))
#define MIN(x, y)   (((x) < (y)) ? (x) : (y))
```

When a program has read these definitions, a line such as

```
    len = MIN(len, 10);
```

will be rewritten by the preprocessor into

```
    len = ((len) < (10)) ? (len) : (10));
```

This is known as "in-line replacement," because MIN has produced code directly in the program that invokes it — there is no function call-and-return overhead. Thus macros with parameters, or (as we shall refer to them) *macro functions,* can sometimes be used effectively to make a program run faster.

Macro functions have the advantage of being *generic* — they can accept data of any type. For example, ABS can be applied to any type of numeric data, integer or floating-point.

Macro functions, however, have an important restriction on their use: their arguments should in general not contain any side-effects. If we were to write ABS(++n) the generated code would look like

```
    (((++n) < 0) ? -(++n) : (++n))
```

thus incrementing n twice.

Macro functions are in general trickier to write correctly, relative to ordinary functions. In particular, each occurrence of a parameter in the replacement text needs to be parenthesized, as does the entire replacement text. If we wrote the following incorrect version of ABS,

```
    #define ABS(x) x < 0 ? -x : x
```

then the expansion of

```
    ABS(n + 1) + m
```

would be

```
    n + 1 ? -n + 1 : n + 1 + m
```

where the missing parentheses are sorely needed.

As a general rule, you should get your program working correctly first without defining any macro functions. Then introduce them later, if you need the speed advantage.

5.18   Conditional Compilation

The preprocessor can provide for parts of a program to be compiled *conditionally.* For example, our local.h include-file contains the lines

```
    #ifndef FAIL
    ...
    #endif
```

This says that if the symbol FAIL has *not* already been defined, then process all the lines up to the #endif line. If, on the other hand, the symbol already has been defined (presumably by previous inclusion of local.h), the following lines should be skipped. (With some C compilers, it is an error if an already-defined symbol is #defined again, although Kernighan and Ritchie [1978] imply otherwise **[5-57 cc]**.)

Another form uses #ifdef:

```
#ifdef TRYMAIN
    . . .
#endif
```

will compile the enclosed statements only if the symbol TRYMAIN has been defined. This provides a useful technique for attaching a simple test driver to each separately-compilable library function. Consider this packaging of our factl factorial function:

factl.c **[5-58]**:
```
/* factl - return n! (n factorial)
 */
#include "local.h"
long factl(n)
    long n;
    {
    if (n <= 1)
        return (1);
    else
        return (n * factl(n - 1));
    }
#ifdef TRYMAIN
main()
    {
    long factl();

    if (factl((long)3) != (long)6)
        error("failed 3", "");
    if (factl((long)13) != 1932053504)
        error("failed 13", "");
    exit(SUCCEED);
    }
#endif
```

We can cause the symbol TRYMAIN to be #defined by adding the flag -DTRYMAIN to our compile command **[5-59 cc]**:

```
cc -o factl.x -DTRYMAIN factl.c error.o
```

This will compile the main function as well as factl, producing an executable test program, factl.x. If factl.x runs successfully, it prints nothing and returns a SUCCEED code; if it fails, it prints a message and returns a FAIL code. This allows it to be used in an automated test procedure.

Other varieties of #if are available:

> #if   *constant-expression*

will evaluate the given constant expression and compile the following lines only if it is *true*.

   With all varieties of #if, the line #else may appear on a later line; in this case, the lines following #else will be compiled only if the #if, #ifdef, or #ifndef line evaluated *false*.

CHAPTER 6: SOFTWARE DEVELOPMENT

6.1 The Software Development Life Cycle

We now step back from the learning of C language to consider the overall process by which software comes into being. Each of our programming exercises has already been specified in enough detail that the intended program is clearly defined. This is not so in the typical real application. The coding of a program is only a small fraction of the total expense of software. The overall sequence of activities from birth to death of a program is known as the *software development life cycle,* and we now turn our attention to this sequence.

Weighty volumes have been written about this life cycle, and it is not our intention to supersede them. We wish merely to outline the process so that the beginner may have some appreciation of it. Here is our outline of the software development life cycle:

1. *Analysis:* getting enough information about the intended function of the software so that expected benefits can be compared with expected costs.

2. *Design:* outlining the approach to the problem in sufficient detail to verify that the software can achieve the expected benefits and can be produced within the expected costs.

3. *Implementation:* converting the design into working software.

4. *Maintenance:* (after release) enhancing the software's function and repairing previously undetected errors.

Unfortunately for pedagogic simplicity, these phases do not always follow one another so neatly as the outline implies. Often, information gained about the problem in one phase requires going back to an earlier phase and revising its product. This reality is known as the *iterative* approach to development. After we describe the work done in each phase we will discuss some approaches to iterative development. First, a look at each phase.

6.2   Analysis

The goal of analysis is to determine what function the software is to perform and to evaluate the economic viability of proceeding further.

In our discussion, we will assume that one individual is doing all the steps in the life cycle, an assumption that is true only in the smallest projects or cottage industries. As this individual proceeds through the phases, he or she will wear various "hats"; in this phase, the role is known as the *analyst* or *systems analyst*.

Some other individual plays the role of *user* or *system user* — the person who will ultimately make use of the software.

The first step in analysis is very important: establishing a good working relationship with the user. A cheerful, confident, empathetic analyst will succeed where a sullen, hesitant, self-centered person would fail. Studies have shown the the difficulty of the interface between the analyst and the user is *four times* more important in software productivity than *any* other single factor (Walston and Felix [1977]).

The analyst needs to get information from the user about what is wanted. As an analyst, you should be aware that the user will often have a *premature packaging* of the system, often based on a previous generation of technical knowledge. The important motto here is *"first what, then how."* This means, first determine what functions the software is supposed to perform (analysis), then determine how those functions will be implemented (design, implementation).

It may be important to *broaden the space of alternatives.* The user may start with only one specific idea, possibly including premature packaging. One strategy is to present a *menu of alternatives:* do not present just one approach to the problem, but rather a set of alternative approaches, each with its own benefits and costs.

Clarity of communication between analyst and user is important. Often the user's verbal formulations mean different things to user and analyst. One means of sharpening the communication is to present *specific examples,* small cases worked out in complete detail. There is almost always a small paper-and-pencil model that can be created to make the system tangible. Detailed pictures of sample inputs and outputs are necessary; sometimes similar small pictures are also needed for internal data.

The final product of the analysis phase is a *specification* (or *spec*) which is tangible, concise, useful documentation.

The spec should be the first in a series of documents which are useful in understanding what the software does. One useful strategy here is to cast the spec into the form of a *user manual,* which can serve as the rough outline for the eventual manual which will be delivered with the software. In addition, it may be useful to produce a rough draft of *training materials* as part of the spec — it is often during the process of training users that the problems of the software first become known. Since you are familiar by now with the library manual for your C compiler, we will use that format in·our discussions of specifications.

In this chapter, we will follow the development of a real program through all the phases of the life cycle. We have chosen a project that was a real-world undertaking for us recently — a portable Blackjack program that could be used no matter which operating system the office was using at the time **[6-1 os]**. The "menu of alternatives" can be described like this:

1. *Buy an existing package.* Estimated cost: $200 for video-game hardware using existing TV set. "Too expensive," says the user, "and it ties up my TV."

2. *Port existing software from one operating system.* "Cannot even present it to the user because of licensing restrictions," says the analyst, "and besides, it would not serve the purposes of a programming book!"

3. *Copy the design of existing software and re-program:* Estimated cost: 1 day design, 3 days programming. "Sounds good," says the user, "but the other program does not play Atlantic City rules."

4. *Use existing software as a guideline and design from scratch:* Estimated cost: 2 days design, 3 days programming. "That's my choice," says the user.

One advantage in programming something with an existing design or specification is that the uncertainties of analysis are drastically reduced. To be specific about this program, the structure of the game is given almost entirely by the rules of the game. Herewith, the rules:

> The object of this card game is to have the total point value of the cards dealt to you exceed the point value of the Dealer's hand without going over 21. If you draw cards that total more than 21, your hand is "busted" and you automatically lose. If your first *two* cards total 21, you have a Blackjack that automatically wins. If, however, both you and the Dealer have a Blackjack, it is a standoff.
>
> The dealer starts the game by dealing two cards face up to each Player. The Dealer takes one card face up. The Dealer's second card is dealt face down and placed underneath the first card. Each card assumes the value of the card shown. Kings, Queens, and Jacks count as 10. The Ace counts either as 1 or 11, whichever you choose. If you feel satisfied with your hand after receiving the first two cards, you "stand" and do not draw additional cards. If you feel you need additional cards to beat the Dealer, you gesture

one at a time for additional cards (called "hits") until you decide to stand. A Dealer must draw on any point total of 16 or less and must stand on any point total of 17 or more. If a Dealer busts, all Players win who have not busted. Otherwise, the Dealer pays all hands that exceed the Dealer's point total, takes all bets that are less and leaves ("pushes") all bets that equal the Dealer's point total. A Dealer's Blackjack (two-card point total of 21) beats a Player's three-card point total of 21. All winning bets are paid two-to-one, except a winning Blackjack which is paid 3 to 2.

SPLITTING PAIRS: If your first two cards are a pair with the same numerical value, you may split them into two hands provided that the bet on the second hand equals the original bet. Once the hands are split and the wager placed, you play out the first hand until satisfied. Only after the first hand is complete may you act on the second hand. A split hand may not be split again if another pair of cards with the same identical value is formed. Also, if the split pair are Aces, you are limited to a one card draw on each hand. In those instances where the Dealer subsequently gets a Blackjack, you lose the money wagered on the first bet only.

DOUBLING DOWN: After receiving the first two cards, you may elect to wager an additional amount not to exceed the value of the original bet. In any Double Down, you draw only one additional card. If the Dealer gets a Blackjack, the Dealer collects only the amount of the original wager.

INSURANCE: If the Dealer's first card is an Ace, you may elect to take insurance by placing a bet on the insurance line not greater than one-half of the original bet. The insurance bet is a wager that the Dealer will get a Blackjack with his second card. In other words, you are betting the Dealer will draw a 10, Jack, Queen, or King. Insurance pays 2 to 1 if the Dealer draws a Blackjack, but loses in all other instances.

SHUFFLING: The cards are dealt from a "shoe" containing four full decks. A yellow "shuffle" card is inserted towards the rear of the shoe, and when the shuffle card is reached, the cards are shuffled at the end of the current hand.

Further discussion produces a first draft of a manual page, which completes the analysis phase.

bj   USER MANUAL   bj

NAME
bj - play Blackjack

SYNOPSIS
bj

DESCRIPTION
Bj deals Blackjack for one player, according to Atlantic City rules. The
bet is specified by the player on each hand (since variable betting is essential to winning at Blackjack).

Summary of rules:

Player BJ (Blackjack, 21 in two cards) wins 3-for-2, except that player and
dealer both BJ is a "push" (no money exchanged). All other bets win
even money.

If dealer shows Ace, player may take "Insurance." If dealer subsequently
shows BJ, player wins even money, otherwise loses.

If player's first two cards are equal value, player may "Split Pair" into
two hands, placing a bet on the second hand that is equal to the original
bet. If the original pair were Aces, not further hits can be taken. Otherwise, the player takes hits on the first hand until satisfied (or "busted")
and then may take hits on the second hand. If the dealer subsequently
wins with BJ, only the original bet is lost.

After receiving the first two cards, player may "double down," wagering
an additional amount equal to the first bet. One hit is given at this time,
and no more may be taken.
- Player "busted" (over 21) loses.
- Dealer BJ beats anything but BJ.
- Dealer "busted" wins for every hand not busted.
Otherwise, dealer pays all hands exceeding dealer total, takes all bets
below dealer's total, and "pushes" all ties.

Dealer will announce each shuffle. The machine deals and keeps the
score.

The game can be terminated by typing the EOF character or the INTER-
RUPT character (both of which vary with operating system).

NOTE
Copyright © 1983, Plum Hall Inc. Permission is granted to reproduce this
manual page, provided copies include this notice.

6.3   Design

In the context of the software development life cycle, there are three aspects of software design: *logic design* (which we discussed in Section 4.9), *data design* (choosing the right data representations), and *packaging design* (selecting the overall package to be delivered). These three design processes proceed in parallel, or more accurately, in an iterative manner.

We will acknowledge right now that on a large project, an extra phase for *structural design* may be needed (Yourdon and Constantine [1978]). In such a case, the type of design we are describing here is known as *detail design,* or *logic design.* For the small problems that we are tackling now, no such distinction is needed.

Two important considerations will be addressed during the design process: *error-handling* (making sure the program behaves correctly in the face of errors outside of itself), *portability* (making sure that the program can be run in an appropriate variety of environments), and *documentation* (keeping a useful written record of what was produced).

The overall task of design is to refine the problem into pieces, each one of which is something that you are sure the programmer can implement.

The general strategy is known as *top-down design,* or *design by refinement.* We start with the specification — a general idea of what is needed — and proceed to refine the software into ever-smaller pieces. As was the case with our simple design examples in Section 4.9, our first step is to choose the basic repetition. We can consider a session to be a series of shuffles, a series of hands, or a series of transactions (bet, take card, etc.). Since a player may leave at the end of any hand, a "shuffle" is too big a unit. And a "transaction" is too small a unit — the structure of the game is lost. We will thus consider the game to be a repetition of hands, or

*hand**

Setting aside for a moment the complications of split pairs, shuffling, doubling down, and insurance, each hand is a sequence of events:

deal hit* hit-dealer* outcome

or in words, this sequence: dealing the cards, a repetition of hits, a repetition of hits for the dealer, and an outcome. Taking the bet from the player can be considered part of the major loop control — no bet, no game! (The repetition of hits for dealer could repeat *zero* times, because if dealer has 17 or more, or if all player hands are busted, the dealer takes no hits.) Thus, the whole game has the syntax

{ *deal hit* hit-dealer* outcome* } *

or as a syntax tree,

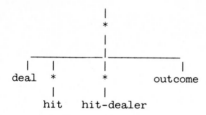

The program outline so far looks like this:

> *for each hand*
> > *deal the cards*
> > *while (player can hit and player asks for hits)*
> > > *hit player*
> > *while (dealer can hit)*
> > > *hit dealer*
> > *score the outcome*

    Shuffling is easy to add to this structure: as the first step of each hand before dealing, shuffling takes place if the shuffle point has been reached. Insurance is easy to add: after the deal, insurance bets are taken if the dealer shows an Ace. Adding shuffling and insurance to our syntax, the syntax now reads

$$\{[\textit{shuffle}] \;\; \textit{deal} \;\; [\textit{insur}] \;\; \textit{hit}^* \;\; \textit{hit--dealer}^* \;\; \textit{outcome}\} *$$

or as a tree,

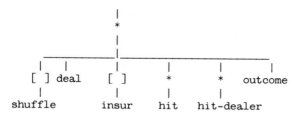

Question [6-2] Write the program outline of this revised syntax.

We look next at "doubling down." After insurance, our first query to the player must allow for more alternatives than simply "yes" or "no" to the first hit; it must allow for him to ask to double down. We will add a *query* just after the optional insurance.

Splitting pairs adds a loop around the taking of hits; two hands are played separately if player asks to split pairs. The syntax thus becomes:

$$\{ [shuffle]\ deal\ [insur]\ query\ \{ hit* \}*\ hit\text{-}dealer*\ outcome \}*$$

or as a tree,

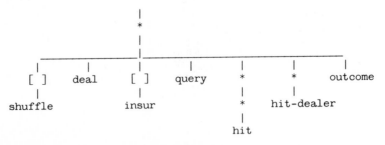

Our final program outline looks like this:

> *for each hand*
> > *if (deck is low on cards)*
> > > *shuffle cards*
> >
> > *deal the cards*
> > *if (dealer shows Ace)*
> > > *offer insurance*
> >
> > *query — split pair, double down?*
> > *for each hand of player*
> > > *while (player can hit and asks for hit)*
> > > > *hit player*
> > >
> > > *while (dealer can hit)*
> > > > *hit dealer*
> > >
> > > *score the outcome*

Question [6-3] Using this syntactic approach, it is fairly easy to modify the design to accommodate multiple players. Do so.

Exercise 6-1. Use your modified design to program `bj` for multiple players.

We now turn to the question of *error-handling*. There are several general strategies for handling errors:

1. *Ignore errors.* Simply proceed as if no error had happened. This strategy can only be used when errors do not affect the integrity of the program or its results.

2. *Complain about the error and quit.* This strategy can be used only in an interactive environment where the user is available on-line to re-enter the command.

3. *Complain and prompt for correct values.* This strategy also assumes an interactive user, but is more "friendly" in that the program does not exit.

4. *Change the erroneous values to acceptable values, and proceed.* An error message may also be produced.

In our `bj` program, we can assume an interactive user as the almost universal environment, so method 3 will be our choice in general.

Our next concern is *portability*. In this problem, we could lose portability if we succumbed to the temptation to use "bells and whistles" (fancy features of marginal usefulness) such as reverse-video or cursor-control characters. If we stick to simple line-by-line printing of ordinary characters we can maximize the range of target environments.

With regard to *documentation*, there are many formats to choose from. The ones that we will use are useful for a wide variety of problems:

1. *Manual pages* for each separately-callable function, or package of functions. These give the information necessary for a programmer to make use of the functions.

2.   *Internals-manual pages* for each function or package. These give the information that a maintenance programmer would need to understand and modify the code. A program outline (pseudo-code) should be given for the high-level functions.

After the design of the main program flow, we look for the capabilities that will be required at the next level — the "vice-president" functions of our program tree. Wherever possible, we will collect them into "packages," as described in Section 5.11. We prefer for the main program not to concern itself with the implementation details of the data.

Some details must nonetheless be attended to. We will at various times refer to the Dealer, or Player's first hand, or Player's second hand. Our solution will be no less general if we simply assign numbers to the different hands:

```
0   dealer
1   player's first hand
2   player's second hand
```

Within a hand, the cards must also be numbered. We will follow zero-origin conventions by starting the numbers with 0.

We also have a basic question to answer regarding data type. "Cash" is of the essence in this problem, but should it be recorded in double, long, or short data? To be sure, double is the only convenient way to handle 3-for-2 splits of $1 bets, but our audience may be forgiving if we round everything to even dollars — particularly if we make the minimum bet $2. And short may run faster on small processors, but when a user can play $1000 as cheaply as $2, the action can exceed $32767 very quickly. Our choice is to defer the question by defining our own data type, CASH, which we will define as long, but you can change it to another type if you desire. We must also be sure to #define two strings CASHIN and CASHOUT with the formats for scanf and printf.

A first pass through the pseudo-code suggests this set of functions:

```
bool deklow()       /* is deck low on cards */
void shuffl()       /* shuffle cards */
void deal()         /* deal the cards */
short val(h, n)     /* tell value of hand h, card n */
bool takes(s)       /* prompt message s, return YES or NO */
short query()       /* query -- split pair, double down? */
bool hit(h)         /* hit hand h, return "can hit again?" */
CASH outcom(...)    /* score the outcome, return net result */
```

In grouping these functions into packages, we consider the information to which they need access. Some of them are concerned with the deck of cards, some of them with the hands of the dealer and player, and some with the terminal interaction. We thus have our first draft for the packages. The "deck manager," dekmgr.c:

```
bool deklow()        /* is deck low on cards */
void shuffl()        /* shuffle cards */
```

The "hand manager," hndmgr.c:

```
void deal()          /* deal the cards */
short val(h, n)      /* tell value of hand h, card n */
bool hit(h)          /* hit hand h, return "can hit again?" */
CASH outcom(...)     /* score the outcome, return net result */
```

And the "terminal manager," ttymgr.c:

```
bool takes(s)        /* prompt message s, return YES or NO */
short query()        /* query -- split pair, double down? */
```

One final packaging observation: if you are working on a system that has directories, this is probably a good time for you to collect all files relating to bj into a directory devoted to that purpose **[6-4 os]**. On UNIX, the name of a file in that directory — bj.c, for example — would look like bj/bj.c. All our further work on the problem will be in the bj directory. For simplicity of access, we will copy into the new directory all the files that we will need:

```
mkdir bj
cp local.h nfrom.c error.c bj
```

With these first-level interfaces determined, we are ready for another draft of the top-level outline; it appears here in the form of a question.

Question [6-5] Write a more detailed outline for the main program, bj.c. Note any new functions that you discover in the process, and note all data that the top-level program needs to administer. Hand-simulate some simple cases for each function to determine if it has the information it needs. Do not include any miscellaneous printf calls that may be needed, but consider whether new functions are needed for printing results.

After this re-draft, we discover that we need to revise our package definitions: To the "deck manager," dekmgr.c, we add

```
void opndek()        /* initialize the deck */
```

To the "hand manager," hndmgr.c, we add

```
bool allbst()        /* are all player's hands busted */
short score(h)       /* tell point value of hand */
short split()        /* split the player's pair if allowed */
```

Now we want to iterate on the design once more, to determine other functions that may be needed, as one package may need hitherto undiscovered functions within another package. The outcom function, for example, still needs a determination of its interface. It will need to know the scores of the various hands, of course, but that information is available directly from the hndmgr package. In addition to the numerical scores, it needs to know if each hand is a "natural" Blackjack, for which we add another function to the hndmgr package:

```
bool isbj(h)          /* is hand a "natural" 2-card blackjack? */
```

It also needs to know the amount of the bet, whether player took insurance or doubled down, and the number of hands in play, all of which is known by the main function. Its interface thus looks like this:

```
CASH outcom(bet, tophand, isinsur, isdbl)
```

No further changes to the interfaces are needed. This set of notes defining each of our "managers" (packages) will serve as the rough draft for the manual page for each package. Now we are ready for implementation.

6.4   Implementation: Writing the Programs

Since we have already completed an analysis and a design for our problem, we are now left with the tasks that belong strictly to the implementation phase. These are the issues we will deal with:

1.   Translation into code: this should be easy, given a good design.

2.   Efficiency of execution time and space: wherever possible without compromising a clean design, we want the program to be as fast and as small as possible.

3.   Desk-checking (hand-simulation): details that were previously overlooked can show up at this stage.

4.   Editing the program (using correct layout from the start): do not rely on automatic formatters or "beautifiers."

5.   Creating test cases: some rules for thorough but economical testing.

6.   Documenting: leaving an understandable record of what was done.

7.   Packaging: converting a program into a product.

8.   Demonstration and acceptance test: clearly showing the user what was accomplished.

9.   Delivery and celebration: satisfaction in a job well done.

In this section, we will discuss the first step; the other steps will wait for the following section.

(1) Translation into code. Often, while training programmers to write readable code, we have remarked that the examples that programmers see in programming textbooks are vastly undercommented, since the *book text* surrounding the programs is, in fact, one large set of comments. We depart from the practice here, in an attempt to give a realistic example of how a program like this might be documented in practice. Our preference is for documentation

in the separate *internals-manual pages* mentioned in Section 6.1, and the description of the bj program will be given in this form. Thus, the remainder of this discussion on "Translation into Code" will be presented in the form of a set of manual pages to describe the external interface, and internals-manual pages to give information useful to the maintainer. The listings of the programs themselves are given on removable pages in Appendix B.6.4, so that they can be read along with the appropriate manual page.

Pretend, then, that your first working assignment as a maintainer of al-ready-written C programs is to understand this program that has just been presented to you. Sit back, relax, and enjoy.

dekmgr   USER MANUAL   dekmgr

NAME
dekmgr - deck manager: deklow, opndek, shuffl, tkcard

SYNOPSIS
```
#include "local.h"
#include "bj.h"
#include "dekmgr.h"

bool deklow()
void opndek()
void shuffl()
short tkcard()
```

DESCRIPTION
Deklow returns YES if the deck has reached the point for shuffling, otherwise returns NO.

Opndek initializes the deck and shuffles once.

Shuffl shuffles the cards and prints the message "Shuffle".

Tkcard returns, as a short integer, the next card from the deck.

These functions make no interpretation of the cards in the deck; any scheme of assigning short integers to cards will work equally well with these functions. Thus, they could deal Bridge, Pinochle, or Blackjack equally well.

BUGS
The size of the deck is compiled into dekmgr.c, which must therefore be recompiled to change deck size.

NAME

hndmgr - hand manager: allbst, deal, hit, isbj, outcom, score, show, split, val

SYNOPSIS

```
#include "local.h"
#include "bj.h"
#include "hndmgr.h"

bool allbst()
void deal()
bool hit(h)
bool isbj(h)
CASH outcom(bet, tophand, isinsur, isdbl)
void show(h, n)
short score(h)
short split()
short val(h, n)

bool isinsur, isdbl;
CASH bet;
short h, tophand, n;
```

DESCRIPTION

Allbst returns YES if all player hands are "busted," and NO otherwise.

Deal gives two cards to player and two to dealer. It produces a message in this format:

```
The dealer shows 5H
You have 2D + 9S
```

Hit gives another card to hand h , and prints a message (without new-line) in this format:

```
+ KD
```

Isbj returns YES if hand h is a "natural," or "Blackjack" — 21 in two cards, and NO otherwise. Player's hand can never be BJ if player has taken "double down" or "split pair."

Outcom determines the outcome of the hand and computes the net cash result; positive result is a win for player, negative is a loss. In all cases except "Bust," the outcome is announced by one or more messages.

Score tells the Blackjack value of hand n. Since val always reports 11 for Aces, score must keep track of the number of Aces found in the hand. If the score exceeds 21 and the hand contains Aces, the score is lowered by 10 for each Ace, as many times as necessary.

Show prints the two- or three-letter representation of a card. The current implementation maps integers and cards as follows:

AS – 0	AH – 13	AD – 26	AC – 39
2S – 1	2H – 14	2D – 27	2C – 40
3S – 2	3H – 15	3D – 28	3C – 41
4S – 3	4H – 16	4D – 29	4C – 42
5S – 4	5H – 17	5D – 30	5C – 43
6S – 5	6H – 18	6D – 31	6C – 44
7S – 6	7H – 19	7D – 32	7C – 45
8S – 7	8H – 20	8D – 33	8C – 46
9S – 8	9H – 21	9D – 34	9C – 47
10S – 9	10H – 22	10D – 35	10C – 48
JS – 10	JH – 23	JD – 36	JC – 49
QS – 11	QH – 24	QD – 37	QC – 50
KS – 12	KH – 25	KD – 38	KC – 51

In other words, for a given card value v, the spots are given by v % 13 and the suit is given by v / 13.

Split splits hand n into two hands if possible, and prints a message in this format:

```
Hand 1: 4S + 2D
Hand 2: 4H + 7C
```

If the hand cannot be split, split returns 1, otherwise 2.

Val reports the value of card n from hand h, according to Blackjack interpretation:

```
Ace     = 11
2-10    = card-spot value
J,Q,K   = 10
```

ttymgr   USER MANUAL   ttymgr

NAME
ttymgr - tty (terminal) manager: getbet, query, takes

SYNOPSIS
```
#include "local.h"
#include "bj.h"
#include "ttymgr.h"

CASH getbet()
short query()
bool takes(s)

char s[];
```

DESCRIPTION
Getbet prompts the user for a bet and reads one line of input. On EOF, getbet returns 0. If the input forms a valid number between MINBET and MAXBET, inclusive, the numerical result is returned as a CASH data item. Otherwise, a more explicit prompt is printed, and the process is repeated by reading another line of input. This protocol is more long-winded than a simple scanf, but the extra logic is important for avoiding unpleasant surprises for the user.

Query prompts the user for a variety of choices, currently

```
d         Double down
s         Split pair (if appropriate)
h         Hit
RETURN    None
```

One line of input is read, and if the initial character matches one of these possibilities, the coded value of the reply is returned:

```
NONE     = no selection, empty line
DBLDN    = double down
SPLIT    = split pair
HIT      = hit
```

If input is EOF, query takes an immediate exit via error("Bye!", "").

Takes prints the prompt for one designated action — either

```
i         Insurance
```

or

```
h         Hit
```

and returns YES if the user selects the prompted action; otherwise the return is NO. On EOF, takes exits via error("See you later", "").

NAME
bj - Blackjack internals overview

SYNOPSIS
```
#include "local.h"
#include "bj.h"
#include "dekmgr.h"
#include "hndmgr.h"
#include "ttymgr.h"
main()   /* bj program */
```

DESCRIPTION
The include-file `bj.h` specifies the CASH defined type `long`, in this implementation. The defined constants CASHIN and CASHOUT specify how it should be read by `scanf` and written by `printf`.

The constant DEALER is defined as 0, and its value cannot be altered. The player's hands appear herein by the actual values 1 and 2.

The program outline for `bj.c` is as follows:

>*for each hand*
>   *if (deck is low on cards)*
>   *shuffle cards*
>   *deal the cards*
>   *if (dealer shows Ace)*
>   *offer insurance*
>   *query — split pair, double down, first hit?*
>   *for each hand of player*
>   *while (player can hit and asks for hit)*
>   *hit player*
>   *while (dealer can hit)*
>   *hit dealer*
>   *score the outcome*

The main loop continues until a bet of zero dollars is received from `getbet`. Query combines the query for "hit," "split," and "double down," because the repetitive prompting for separate responses can become tiresome. The main program takes an appropriate action to each response.

The loop over player hands is actually traversed only once unless the player has split. If he has split, a message announces which hand is in play.

The determination of `canhit` is a somewhat complicated but straightforward consequence of the rules. If player doubled down, his hand has already been hit once and player can receive no further hits. If player split Aces, no hits are allowed. Hit will tell whether further hits are allowed.

The "Bust" message is printed immediately instead of waiting for the outcome because it must be made clear to player that first hand has busted before proceeding to second hand. All other outcome messages are printed by outcom.

To achieve consistency in formatting of messages, the convention throughout is that each function that prints a message will ensure that it is terminated with a newline. Show and hit functions are an exception to this convention, so that the dealer's hand can be printed all on one line.

After all hands are completed, outcom prints a description of the outcome and returns the net CASH outcome to the main program. The action and standing are printed after each hand.

Getbet returns 0 on EOF; if EOF is received at any other time during the hand, the game ends abruptly by error exits in the takes and query functions.

dekmgr   INTERNALS MANUAL   dekmgr

NAME
dekmgr - deck manager: deklow, opndek, shuffl, tkcard, varnum

SYNOPSIS
```
#include "local.h"
#include "bj.h"
#include "dekmgr.h"

bool deklow()
void opndek()
void shuffl()
short tkcard()
static short varnum()
```

DESCRIPTION
The include-file dekmgr.h simply declares the public functions in the dekmgr.c package. No defined constants are needed for use with dekmgr.c.

Deklow reports whether it is time to shuffle.

Opndek calls shuffl, to get ready for the first hand.

Shuffl permutes the deck as shown in Section 5.9 of Plum [1983]. The placement of the "yellow shuffle card," shufpt, is quite generous to card-counting players — somewhere in the first half of the last 52 cards. (If the number of decks or number of players is changed, be sure to revise shufpt so that enough cards are assured to be available for the last hand.) The variable nc always gives the index of the next available card.

Tkcard silently deals the next card from the deck. (It cannot print directly, because the dealer's hole card must stay hidden.) The test for the shuffle point is "defensive programming"; if the main function works properly, it will never be needed, but this cannot be determined just from the code for the deck manager.

Opndek initializes the deck. As programmed, the deck contains 4 full decks of 52 cards — NCARDS is defined internally as 4 * 52 and can be modified to any other multiple of 52.

ENVIRONMENTAL DEPENDENCY
Initialization of the deck contains the only known environmental dependency of the program — the varnum function calls the UNIX (or Idris) time function to set the random "seed" to a time-of-day value, to prevent dealing the same game every time. If you have a clock, any form of

varying result will do for this purpose. On systems with no real-time clock, creative methods are needed. If you are working on a small machine, you may have access to locations in memory whose contents are unpredictable and varying.. Such locations may be accessed using *pointers* in C; see Chapter 7 of Plum [1983].

SEE

Thomas Plum, *Learning to Program in C,* Cardiff, NJ, Plum Hall Inc, 1983.

hndmgr   INTERNALS MANUAL   hndmgr

NAME

hndmgr - hand manager: allbst, deal, hit, isbj, outcom, score, show, split, val

SYNOPSIS

```
#include "local.h"
#include "bj.h"
#include "hndmgr.h"

bool allbst()
void deal()
bool hit(h)
bool isbj(h)
CASH outcom(bet, tophand, isinsur, isdbl)
short score(h)
short split()
short val(h, n)

bool isinsur, isdbl;
CASH bet;
short h, tophand, n;
```

DESCRIPTION

The include-file hndmgr.h contains no defined constants, merely the declarations of the functions in this package.

The arrays **spots** and **suits** are chosen to make the printing of card values convenient. The array **hands** has three rows — one for dealer and two for player — of 12 cards each. The value 12 depends upon the number of decks in play; with 4 decks, the longest hand possible would be 4 Aces (score 4), 4 twos (score 12, so far), and 3 threes (makes 21, the maximum), so one further hit would invariably bust. Notice that **tophand** (how many player hands active) is maintained internally by hndmgr and also reported to bj.

Allbst returns NO if hand 1 has not busted, or (if two hands are in play) if hand 2 has not busted.

Deal deals one player hand and one dealer hand, printing the result.

Hit assumes on entry that the hand can be hit; it should not be called unless hand is hittable. It hits the designated hand and prints the new card (with no newline). It returns NO if the hand has busted, or (if the hand is Dealer's) if the hand reached or exceeded a score of 17.

Isbj returns YES if hand is Dealer's and has reached 21. Otherwise, for player's hand to be BJ, only one hand may be in play, it must have only

2 cards, and the score must be 21.

Outcom does not need to see the hands directly, and therefore is in a source file of its own, outcom.c. Outcom makes use of a static (i.e., internal to the file outcom.c) function, prmsg, to print the outcome messages, and add the delta (change) to value. If player has two hands in play, prmsg reports which hand is being announced. The "insurance" bet is scored separately from the other outcomes. The "Blackjack" outcomes can be scored without reference to the number of hands in play, since Dealer BJ wins the same amount regardless and player BJ can only take place with one hand in play. (A score of 21 on a split pair does not count as a BJ.) The other outcomes require looking at each of player's possible two hands. Each outcome prints the appropriate message and computes the result. Exception: the "Bust" message has already been printed, because with two hands in play, the player must be notified immediately if hand 1 has busted.

Score would be a simple total of the point value of the hand, except that Aces may count either 1 or 11, so an apparently busted hand may be reduced in score if it contains Aces. This function yields the maximum allowable score for the hand; i.e., if Dealer has Ace plus six ("soft 17") score reports 17, forcing Dealer to stand (no further hits).

Show prints a two- or three-character representation of the designated card from the designated hand.

Split determines whether the hand is splittable; thus it can be called without prior checking. If splittable, it splits the cards and draws two new cards, printing a message and updating tophand. It returns the current value of tophand.

Val tells the spot value of the card. It always reports Ace as 11.

ttymgr   INTERNALS MANUAL   ttymgr

NAME
ttymgr - tty (terminal) manager: getbet, query, takes

SYNOPSIS
```
#include "local.h"
#include "bj.h"
#include "ttymgr.h"

CASH getbet()
short query()
bool takes(s)

char s[];
```

DESCRIPTION
The include-file `ttymgr.h` contains no defined constants, merely function declarations.

Getbet persists in prompting for a reply until EOF is entered (return 0), or a valid number is read. It does not call `scanf` directly; since `scanf` will read across multiple lines seeking input, if the user mistakenly hits a RETURN, the terminal dumbly waits for more input. Another problem with getting input directly via `scanf` is that `scanf` does not consume the newline after the last data item, so input sequences can too easily become unsynchronized. The defined constants MINBET and MAXBET can be altered, within limits. MINBET must be greater than zero, and MAXBET should be at least 10 to 100 times smaller than the largest value that a CASH variable can hold.

Getbet is in its own source file; it does not need to share any data with the other functions in the package.

Query prompts the user for each of the allowable choices. "Hit" and "double down" are always allowable; "split" is allowed if player's cards are equal in value. If each of the prompts in this message have already been seen several times by the user, an abbreviated form of the prompt is produced. Like `getbet`, `query` persists in prompting until a valid reply is received, or EOF is reached. Both functions take an `error` exit at EOF, since the main program could not do anything useful with the reply. This means, of course, that the player is allowed to simply leave the table in the middle of the hand — hardly casino rules. On the other hand, player gets no report of the standing in this case either.

Takes follows the same protocol as `query`, except that only one option is available: `'i'` for "Insurance", or `'h'` for "Hit." The return from `takes` is therefore either YES or NO. On EOF, an `error` exit is taken. To simplify the logic of the main program, `query` will remember internally if player asked for "hit," and will return NONE as the reply. The takes function will deliver this remembered reply on its first invocation after query returns.

6.5   Implementation: The Latter Phases

In the previous section, we saw the full program documentation for the case study program, `bj.c`. The writing of the program was item (1) on our list of implementation phases. The other phases continue below.

(2) Efficiency of execution time and space: In most environments, the execution time of the program will be determined by the output speed of the terminal. Saving a microsecond here or there would give no real payoff. On the other hand, if one wanted to adapt this program into a totally automated player — for example, to use in testing an automated strategy for Blackjack — time efficiency could become more important. The UNIX "profiler" reveals that this program spends about two-thirds of its CPU time doing output. Of the remaining time, about half is spent calling, executing, and returning from the `val` function.

Exercise 6-2. Modify `hndmgr.c` and `hndmgr.h` so that `val` is implemented as a macro. Hint: you will need to add an **extern** declaration of **hands**, which must be made external in `hndmgr.c`.

Regarding space efficiency, the size of the program is often determined by how much of the function library it calls. In this case, the function `printf` would be the first to examine. With its code space of 3000 to 5000 bytes on most systems, this would be the first candidate for replacement. The simple conversions done here could be accomplished by a much simpler function. However, we will leave the program as is, in the interests of simplicity.

(3) Desk-checking (hand-simulation): In the normal course of producing a program, you should write it first on paper before entering at the terminal. Very few people can sit at a terminal and create a perfect program at the keyboard. And before entering it, check it first with a little hand-simulation. As you are reading this, take a small test case and simulate the computer's handling of it.

(4) Editing the program (using correct layout from the start): Having completed our desk-checking, we are ready to enter the program. At this point, it is important to be clear about the standard that we are using for the layout of the code. All the examples in this book have been presented in a certain layout format that we recommend. However, what is most important is that you adhere closely to whatever standard is followed by the other people on your project. Uniformity within a project is often a more attainable goal than uniformity within an entire organization, especially as programmers gain familiarity with the language and the problems of maintaining it. Naturally, we recommend Plum [1981] *C Programming Standards and Guidelines,* but in any case, get layout right when you enter the code. Do not rely on beautifiers or formatters to do the work for you. Good layout is a visible sign of clear thinking, and the discipline is useful.

After we enter the program, we are ready to compile. If we can document our compilation process with an automated facility such as a `make` file (Feldman [1979]) or a `shell` script, it will be easier for maintainers to follow in our footsteps.

(5) Creating test cases: There are good books on the subject of testing, such as Myers [1979], and we will only summarize some of the important methods.

Having spent all this time working to make the program correct, we now play devil's advocate and try to determine data cases which have the best probability of finding errors in it. Even if our current program passes all these tests successfully, they still remain useful as a *regression test,* a collection of cases which should be tried whenever a change is made to the program or to its environment (such as compiling it for another computer). To allow convenient regression testing, we should package our tests as commands which can be run without interaction with the terminal.

Our first technique for choosing test cases is *equivalence partitioning —* finding which classes of input are treated equivalently by the program. For example, if the `hit` function were to give incorrect results for a score of 20 in hand number 1, there would be no point testing it upon a score of 19, since the program behaves equivalently in both cases. To determine the equivalence classes, we use the specs from analysis and design, as well as the program itself. Each time a choice is specified (in C, an `if`, `switch`, `for`, or `while`) there is some value that is typical of a *true* test, and one typical of a *false* test. If we have done our work right, any particular data values that we choose for each of these cases will be as good as any other representative value. In other words, supplying two different tests for each case will be wasted effort. We will therefore usually prefer the least amount of data for each alternative.

Before we choose specific test cases, however, we should turn to our second testing method: *boundary-value analysis —* choosing data values which bracket each limit of the program. Each case that we choose by this method will also belong to one of the equivalence classes that we identified previously so such cases will do double duty in our testing. Applying this analysis to `outcom`, we identify one case for

```
score(1) == 21
```

This will serve as a specific value for one equivalence class. Choosing the bracketing value that is numerically closest to our first case gives

```
score(1) == 22
```

We can use this as part of another equivalence class. In similar fashion, the bracketing values for `score(2)` are also 21 and 22. Thus, our boundary-value analysis has supplied us with specific values to satisfy several of the equivalence classes that we determined earlier. Any other boundary-value cases we find will also be added to the test set, increasing the total number of cases.

A third testing criterion is *every-expression coverage* — being sure that all the code is executed by some test. This coverage should be assured by the combination of methods that we have already employed. Notice, however, that the converse is not true — just because each piece of the code is executed does not mean that our test coverage exercises all the limits of the program.

Question [6-6] Apply these three methods to designing test cases for the outcom function in bj/outcom.c.

	bet	toph	ins	dbl	bj[0]	bj[1]	sc[0]	sc[1]	sc[2]
1	___	___	___	___	___	___	___	___	___
2	___	___	___	___	___	___	___	___	___
3	___	___	___	___	___	___	___	___	___
4	___	___	___	___	___	___	___	___	___
5	___	___	___	___	___	___	___	___	___
6	___	___	___	___	___	___	___	___	___
7	___	___	___	___	___	___	___	___	___
8	___	___	___	___	___	___	___	___	___
9	___	___	___	___	___	___	___	___	___
10	___	___	___	___	___	___	___	___	___

Question [6-7] Predict what values outcom should give for each of your test cases. Compile outcom.c with the symbol TRYMAIN defined, to obtain the test driver for outcom. Run the driver, using your file of test cases as input. Compare the output with your predictions.

(6) Documentation: Since we have emphasized documentation as we worked through each phase, very little is left to be done. Our criteria for detailed documentation are determined largely by our expectations for the maintenance environment. In the typical industrial situation, the program will eventually be maintained by novice programmers who have little familiarity with the intricacies of the program. Thus, any points which required extra care or scrutiny in the implementation deserve a note somewhere for the benefit of the maintainers. Whenever an internals manual is part of standard procedure, it is probably better to keep all such comments there, as we have done. Otherwise, the code itself deserves much more liberal commenting than we have employed.

(7) Packaging: Since we have proceeded so far according to a very careful recipe, little more remains in the way of packaging.

Our program is split into separate source files. We did not blindly create one file per package; functions have been combined into a single source file only when there is data that they must share.

Our compiling procedures are captured in a UNIX make file (Feldman [1979]) or similar automated procedure **[6-8 os]**.

And finally, the manual pages are completed.

If the project were larger, an entire library, directory, tape, or diskette might be required. The collection presented here would be appropriate for a small to medium sized internal project.

The package is ready.

(8) Demonstration and acceptance test: A test case should be chosen which is representative of the function that the program is expected to perform. Our testing methodology did not require such a case; it was directed only to the revealing of errors, and many of the cases generated may be rather oddball examples. In the case of the Blackjack program, demonstration is easy — sit down and try it. But for some other systems, it must be carefully attended to.

(9) Delivery and celebration: No further lessons should be needed for the last phase!

6.6 Maintenance

Under the category of "maintenance," we are grouping both "enhancement" (adding new features and changing old ones) and "bug-fixing" (correcting errors in the original product).

In our case study, each of you who use this case-study problem will be playing the role of maintainers, so a few suggestions may be of use.

An important technique in maintenance is the discipline of *versions.* When changes are being made daily, it becomes hard to know what new symptoms have been created by recent work. Develop a regular cycle of version integration, so that you always have a system with known behavior to fall back on. At the very least, this implies that you will preserve one copy of the original product that you are maintaining.

A second technique is *regression testing.* Set up whatever programs and procedures you need so that the testing of a version can be totally automated from stored test data. Then, when changes are made, you have a procedure to insure that the new changes have not broken something which was previously working. With regard to the Blackjack program, this implies that you will create a "deterministic" version of the game, in which the "unpredictable value" returned by varnum is in fact a known constant. This ensures that you can receive the same predictable behavior each time the program is run (as well as whatever delight there may be in a "rigged" version of the game to astound your friends when you always guess the right decision).

Under the earlier topic of "packaging," we suggested the importance of *automating your compilation procedures.* The value is even greater during maintenance. If you have make, use it always. If not, create your own automated procedures. Running the regression test should be part of the automated procedures also.

An organized procedure for *tracking user feedback* is often helpful. Any "modification request" (or "MR," for short) can be given an identifying number and logged in a record-keeping system. (Apropos of user feedback, in the back of this book you will find a form for sending your comments to the publisher of this book, to assist in our own maintenance procedures.)

And finally, if you have lint, make use of it after each modification.

CHAPTER 7: POINTERS

7.1 Basics

We have already brushed up against pointers in their disguise as array parameters. In the general case, a 'pointer variable' holds the *address* of another variable. This implies that all pointer variables are exactly the same size on any given machine — they are big enough to hold one address, 2 or 4 bytes, as we have seen.

For example, consider this portion of a program:

```
short i, j;     /* i, j are both short integers */
short *p;       /* p is a pointer-to-short */

i = 123;
p = &i;
j = *p;
```

In a declaration, the symbol * means "pointer to" —

```
short *p;
```

means that p has the type **short** * (English translation -- "pointer to **short**"). A variable with the type **short** * can be assigned the address of a **short**, as in

```
p = &i;
```

Continuing with this example, let us assume that the storage of the three variables looks like this **[7-1 mach]**:

	BCPL	*C*
'take address of'	@	&
'use storage pointed to'	!	*

```
i    1200  |_____|
           |       |
j    1202  |_____|
           |       |
p    1204  |       |
           |_____|
```

After the two assignments,

```
i = 123;
p = &i;
```

the storage will look like this **[7-2 mach]**:

```
i    1200  |  123  |
           |_____|
j    1202  |       |
           |_____|
p    1204  | 1200  |
           |_____|
```

Now, if we look at the contents of p, we will find the value 1200, which is the address of i.

In an expression, * means "indirect" — i.e., "use the storage pointed-to." Thus,

```
j = *p;
```

means "copy a short integer from location 1200 into j — from 1200 because that is the *value* of the pointer variable p.

Thus, we obtain the same net result from saying

```
p = &i, j = *p;
```

as from saying

```
j = i;
```

The address-of operator can only be applied to *lvalues*, things that have an address in the memory.

Question [7-3] Which of the following are *illegal?*

```
_____     p = &i;

_____     p = &(i + 1);

_____     p = &++i;
```

7.2   Declaring and Using Pointers

In C, each pointer variable is declared to point to a particular type of data, and this type pointed-to is part of the type of the pointer. In these declarations,

```
short *pi;
short *pj;
short t;
long *pl;
double *pd;
```

we are declaring the following types:

pi	has the type	short *.
pj	has the type	short *.
t	has the type	short.
pl	has the type	long *.
pd	has the type	double *.

In declarations (such as these) the symbol * means "pointer-to"; in an expression, such as

```
j = *p
```

the symbol * means "indirect," or "the thing pointed to." Each pointer is pointing to its own kind of data, but the size of all the pointers is the same — the amount of memory needed to hold one address. A pointer variable is itself an lvalue — it has a location in the memory and can be assigned to. But the *indirect value (or "the thing pointed to")* of a pointer is also an lvalue — *pi is a short integer somewhere in the machine. The *type* of the indirect value can be determined several ways, equivalently. One way is to remove one asterisk from the type of the pointer — if pi has the type short *, then the indirect value, *pi, has the type short. Alternatively, we can read directly from the declaration of pi: scratch out the expression *pi from the declaration

```
short *pi;
```

and what do you have? Simply, short. Thus, a pointer declaration makes two statements simultaneously.

```
short *pi;
```

says that pi has the type short * (pointer to short), and that *pi has the type short. This is not accidental — the complementarity between the declaration type modifiers and the corresponding expression operators is one of the fundamental principles of C.

C language allows several declarations in the same statement, so long as all the variables have the same "base type." Thus,

```
short *pi, *pj, t;
long *pl;
double *pd;
```

means the same as the five declarations given earlier.

Since the indirect value of a pointer is an lvalue, it can be assigned into and incremented just like a variable. All these statements are legal and sensible for the variables declared above:

```
*pd += (double)*pi;
pi = &t;
*pi = (short)*pl;
pj = pi;
*pj /= 3;
++pj;
++*pj;
```

Question [7-4] Assuming the following initial configuration of memory, after this series of statements is executed, what is the resulting configuration of memory?

7.3   Pointers as Function Parameters

We have seen that C functions are always called by passing the *value* of each argument, making C a *"call-by-value"* language. The one apparent exception to this rule concerned arguments which are arrays, but as will be explained shortly, the *value* of an unsubscripted array name is the *address of the initial element*. Thus, for an array argument, what is passed is the address of something.

Using pointer values, it is also possible to pass the address of any scalar item of data also.

In the discussion of scanf, we have seen how to pass the address: simply add the & address-of operator to the name, as in

        scanf("%lf", &x);

What has not yet been shown is how you can write a function which will accept such an argument.

The function which receives the address argument will need to declare its parameter as a *pointer* variable. For example, a swap function for interchanging two short integers would look like this:

```
swap [7-5]:
    /* swap - interchange two short integers
    */
    #include "local.h"
    void swap(pi, pj)
        short *pi, *pj;
        {
        short t;

        t = *pi, *pi = *pj, *pj = t;
        }
```

In the calling program, if we wished to swap the values of n (located at address 800, say) and m (located at address 900), we would write

        swap(&n, &m);

At the time that swap is entered, the memory would look like this:

```
n    800   |   5  |
          |_____|


m    900   |  10  |
          |_____|


          _____  <- frame for swap
pi        |  800 |
          |_____|
pj        |  900 |
          |_____|
```

Question [7-6] At the time that **swap** is entered, what is the value of *pi? _____ What is the value of *pj? _____

Question [7-7] At the time the **swap** returns, what is the value of *pi? _____ What is the value of *pj? _____

7.4   Pointers and Arrays

C language has a very close relation between arrays and pointers. There is one important difference between them to bear in mind at all times. An *array* always consists of a "fat" amount of memory, enough space to hold all the elements of the array. The array q declared like this

```
short q[100];
```

reserves several hundred bytes of memory — 100 times the size of a **short** integer. On the other hand, a *pointer* always has a "skinny" storage — only enough storage to hold one address. So the pointer variable pq declared like this

```
short *pq;
```

itself only contains a few bytes.

If pq should be assigned the address of the initial element of some array, however, then we can access the array storage using the pointer variable. Thus, after we execute

```
pq = &q[0];
```

the initial element of the array can be accessed as *pq — the "thing pointed to" by pq. A picture may help:

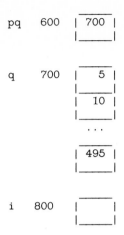

Question [7-8] If we now write

        i = *pq;

what value will i be given? _____

Hold your hats now, because we come to one of the fundamental secrets of C language. Mastering the rest of this section entitles you to consider yourself a *real* C programmer.

One convenience that C provides is that when an integer is added to a pointer, the language automatically *scales* the integer, multiplying it by the number of bytes in the indirect value of the pointer (by the "size of the thing pointed to"). Thus, if short integers are two-byte integers on our machine, and pq contains 700 as it does above, then pq + 3 equals 706. And pq + 10 is actually 720.

Therefore, in C, if one puts a subscript on a pointer, as in pq[n], it is defined to mean the same thing as *(pq + n). In other words, any reference to pq[n] means the same thing as "the value located at address pq + n." This formula is true for any pointer, and is worth memorizing:

        pq[n]   *means*   *(pq + n)

We have hinted several times at a related fact of C language, and state it outright — the *value* of an unsubscripted array name is the *address of the initial element of the array*. Thus, earlier where we wrote

        pq = &q[0];

we could equally well have written

        pq = q;

Why? Because q (with no subscript) *means* &q[0] — the two expressions are equivalent. Furthermore, since addresses are *pointer values*, any time we add an integer to an address value, C will scale the integer just as we saw above. To be specific for the example picture above, &q[0] has the value 700, and the expression q + 5 has the value 710. Since addition is scaled in this case, we can write the "indexing formula" like this:

&q[n] *means* &q[0] + n *means* q + n

Obviously, if the addresses are equal, then the things at the addresses are the same thing. Therefore,

*(&q[n]) *means* *(q + n)

But this roundabout expression *(&q[n]) is simply q[n] — "the thing at the address of q[n] is simply q[n]. Thus we finally have the important identity

q[n] *means* *(q + n)

We have derived, for any array q, the same relationship that we showed earlier for the pointer pq. Thus, we can use the subscription operator on either arrays or pointers, and equally well use the indirection operator * on either. If we (somewhat loosely) use the "equal sign" for "means the same as," we can write these identities as simple formulas:

q[n] = *(q + n)

pq[n] = *(pq + n)

Work this through until you understand it, and then memorize it. You will need to know it.

7.5   Functions using Pointers

If a pointer contains the value 0 (the actual number zero), it is understood to be a *null pointer* — i.e., not pointing at any valid data. In the file stdio.h, the name NULL is defined as 0, and we will use the name NULL for null-pointer values, rather than an actual 0. The C compiler makes sure that no variables will be allocated into machine location 0, so there is no chance that the address of some variable would be mistaken for the null pointer. If a function is defined to return a pointer value, it can return a null pointer to mean "there is no returned value." Consider, for example, the index function.

The function index searches a string to find the first occurrence of a specific character, and returns the address of that occurrence. (The function index is in the Standard Library, and is known as strchr in some versions.) If the character is nowhere to be found in the string, index returns a NULL value. Here is index written with subscripts:

```
index0 [7-9]:
    /* index0 - return index of first occurrence of char c in string s
     *  subscripted version
     */
    #include "local.h"
    char *index0(s, c)
        char s[], c;
        {
        unsigned i = 0;

        while (s[i] != '\0' && s[i] != c)
            ++i;
        return (s[i] == c ? &s[i] : NULL);
        }
```

And here is the corresponding version using pointers:

```
index [7-10]:
    /* index - return index of first occurrence of char c in string s
     *  pointer version
     */
    #include "local.h"
    char *index(s, c)
        char s[], c;
        {
        while (*s != '\0' && *s != c)
            ++s;
        return (*s == c ? s : NULL);
        }
```

Notice that both functions are declared to return data of type char *; this means that the function will return the address of a char. Both functions declare that the parameter s has the type char []. As we saw in Section 5.4, this means the same thing as char *, namely "pointer to char." Since the two types mean the same thing, many people declare all pointer parameters with the * form, but we prefer a different convention — use char * to mean a pointer to a *single* char, and char [] to mean a pointer to the initial element of an *array* of char.

In index0, the value returned is &s[i] if the character is found. If the character is not found, NULL (defined as 0 in stdio.h) is returned.

Turning now to index, the parameter s is again declared as char [], but we will be processing it explicitly as a pointer. The while loop keeps running as long as *s (the indirect value of s, "the thing that s points to"). The body of the loop consists simply of ++s; which increments s by the size of the data that it points to — namely, one byte. The function returns either the current value of s or else NULL, depending whether *s is equal to c.

Exercise 7-1. Write and test the function

```
char *rindex(s, c)
```

which returns a pointer to the *rightmost* occurrence of c in string s. (The function rindex is in the Standard Library, and is known as strrchr in some versions.)

Consider now the file strcpy2.c, which contains a version of strcpy closer to that in the Common Library — it passes back its first argument as the returned value.

strcpy2 [7-11]:

```
/* strcpy2 - copy characters from s2 to s1
 */
#include "local.h"
char *strcpy2(s1, s2)
    register char s1[], s2[];
    {
    char *s0 = s1;

    while ((*s1++ = *s2++) != '\0')
        ;
    return (s0);
    }
```

Note first that the parameters s1 and s2 are pointers that are allocated into registers, for speed. Let us next unpack the declaration

```
char *s0 = s1;
```

The *type* of s0 is char *, and s1 is the *initial value* of s0. In other words, the address contained in s1 is copied into s0 when the function is entered. The function would behave the same if the initialization were performed by an assignment:

```
char *s0;
s0 = s1;
```

In other words, it is s0 that is being initialized, not *s0. The while loop assigns one character (*s2) into the location pointed-to by s1, incrementing both pointers in the process. The loop stops when the null character has been copied. The value returned is s0, which was created solely to be returned.

7.6   Pointer Arithmetic

We have seen that when adding a pointer and an integer, C will *scale* the integer by the size of the pointer's indirect value. To be consistent with this scaled version of arithmetic, when a pointer is subtracted from another pointer, the difference is *divided by* the size of the indirect value. Thus, the pointers should be of the same data type, and if the results are to mean anything, both pointers should reference data within the same array. For example:

```
double x[10];
double *pa, *pb;

pa = x;
pb = pa + 3;
printf("%d", pb - pa);
```

will print the value 3.

Two pointers (of the same type) may be compared with each other. If the comparison is done by <, <=, >, or >=, the results are portable only if the two pointers are referencing data within the same array. Any pointer may be meaningfully compared for "equal" or "not equal" to NULL (i.e., zero).

7.7   Arrays of Pointers

We can declare an *array of pointers;* the array will contain nothing but address-size pointers. For example,

```
short *aptr[10];
```

declares that aptr is an array of 10 pointers to short integers. Take a moment to unpack the type of aptr directly from the declaration. Since [] binds more tightly than *, the declaration says that aptr[...] (aptr *sub* anything) has the type short *. Thus, aptr[0], aptr[1], etc., all have the type short *. And therefore, aptr is an array of pointers.

An array of char pointers is a handy way to represent a *table*. For example,

```
static char *cities[] =
    {"NY", "PHILA", "BOS", "LA", NULL};
```

creates an array of five char pointers, declared to be static so that it can be initialized. Its representation in memory might look like this:

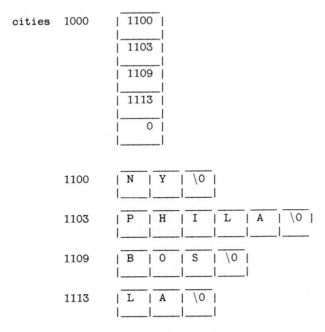

Question [7-12] Write the *type* and *value* of each expression:

	type	value
cities[1][1]	_____	_____
&cities[1][1]	_____	_____
*cities[1]	_____	_____

An array of pointers is sometimes known as a "ragged array," because each row may be of different size. (Contrast this with the "rectangular array" described in Section 5.11, where each row is of the same size.) A ragged array is useful in cases where a table contains data of widely varying sizes.

7.8   Command Line Arguments

One common use of ragged arrays is to provide arguments to the main function. So far, we have only seen main defined as a function with no arguments:

```
main( )
```

but it is more generally defined with two arguments:

```
main(ac, av)
    unsigned ac;
    char *av[];
```

An "argument count" is passed in ac, and av is a pointer to a "ragged array" of strings. (Kernighan and Ritchie [1978] use the names argc and argv, but we prefer the shorter names.)

If, for example, our program is named cmd, to execute it from the keyboard we could type

```
cmd a1 a2
```

and the program might receive some data looking like this **[7-13 mach]**:

```
ac      1400        |    3   |
                    |_____|
av      1402        | 1440   |
                    |_____|


av[0]   1440        | 1662 |      1662    |  c  |  m  |  d  | \0 |
                    |_____|              |_____|_____|_____|____|
av[1]   1442        | 1666 |      1666    |  a  |  1  | \0 |
                    |_____|              |_____|_____|____|
av[2]   1444        | 1669 |      1669    |  a  |  2  | \0 |
                    |_____|              |_____|_____|____|
av[3]   1446        |   0  |
                    |_____|
```

The declaration of av deserves some attention. First, notice that

```
char *av[];
```

means the same as

```
char **av;
```

namely, "pointer to pointer to char." We prefer the [] form, to indicate that the pointer is to the initial element of an array. In any case, if we look at the storage pointed to by àv, we will find an array of char pointers, each one pointing to a null-terminated string. By convention, av[0] is the name of the command itself. Thus, av[1] points to the first argument string, av[2] points to the second argument string, and so forth. The last element of the av array — av[ac] — is always a null pointer (value 0) **[7-14 cc]**.

In any operating system, the work of creating this argument vector must be done by the operating system itself and any start-up instructions executed before main is called. In our Common Environment, most of this work is done by the operating system; in other environments, the program may contain several hundred bytes of instructions to set up av before main is called **[7-15 os]**.

The simplest example program for command arguments is the echo program, which simply prints out its arguments. The last argument to be printed is followed by a newline; each of the others is followed by a space.

echo.c [7-16]:

```
/* echo - print command-line arguments
 */
#include "local.h"
main(ac, av)
    unsigned ac;
    char *av[];
    {
    unsigned i;

    for (i = 1; i < ac; ++i)
        printf(i < ac-1 ? "%s " : "%s\n", av[i]);
    exit(SUCCEED);
    }
```

Question [7-17] If we execute echo with the command

echo abc xyz 123

how many pointers are passed in the array that av points to? _____ What is the value of ac? _____

Exercise 7-2. A common convention for command-line arguments is that an argument whose initial character is + or − is called a *flag argument* (or *flag*, for short) and is optional. We have seen such flags earlier as the −c option of the cc command. Generally, such flags must appear before any non-flag arguments, so the common form for invoking a command is

cmd **[**flags**]** args

Modify the program echo.c to produce echo2.c which accepts an optional flag −n. If this flag appears, the output line should not have a newline at its end.

Exercise 7-3. Write program echo3.c which accepts no flags, but if the last argument ends with the two characters \c, the output line will not have a newline at its end.

CHAPTER 8: STRUCTURES

8.1 Basics

A structure is a collection of data items, whose types may vary, grouped together for ease of manipulation. There are several forms of structure declaration, but the format that we describe here is recommended, based upon our consulting experience.

First, we declare a structure *template* — a representation of memory layout, which will be named by a structure *tag* name. For an application example, consider the definition of some "task" to be done. We give it a character-string description, and specify the time that the task is planned to start, the time that it actually does start, and the time that it finishes. We will represent "time" values as long integers, being noncommittal for now as to whether the units are years, days, sixtieths of a second, or whatever.

```
#define TIME long

struct task
    {
    char *desc;
    TIME plan;
    TIME start;
    TIME finish;
    };
```

The keyword **struct** is followed by a *tag* name (**task**, in this case) which can be used later to *declare* a variable to have this template —

```
    struct task t;
```

declares one instance of the structure. Thus, **t** is a variable that has storage in the memory, whereas the tag **task** has no storage. The tag serves merely to name the "shape" or template for a structure. After declaring the template named **task**, the words **struct task** constitute a data type that can be used analogously with any other data type. Thus,

```
struct task ti, tj, tk;
```

declares three variables, each having the type `struct task`.

Question [8-1] What is the size of `ti` on a machine with 2-byte addresses? With 4-byte addresses?

```
            2-byte      4-byte
            machine     machine

sizeof(ti)  _____      _____
```

From this example, you see that the actual memory layout of a specific structure may be different on different machines. Portable code should never depend upon the actual numeric values of the offsets of structure members — let the compiler keep track of them.

Another issue for portability is the possibility of "holes" within a structure, a consequence of *alignment requirements* of computer hardware. On many machines, multi-byte data must be located at an address that is divisible by two, or divisible by four. If such data appears in a structure, and the previous structure member has not occupied all the space to the next evenly-divisible address, the structure will contain a "hole" — an unused, unoccupied space of one or more bytes. All the more reason not to write programs that embody assumptions about the actual numeric values of member offsets.

We generally prefer to put the declarations of templates into include-files and to give each template a name in capital letters:

task.h **[8-2]**:
```
/* task.h - include-file for TASK structure
 */
#define TIME long
#define TASK struct task
TASK
    {
    char *desc;
    TIME plan;
    TIME start;
    TIME finish;
    };
```

This creates the same template as before, but we can now use the name TASK as a data type, as in

```
TASK ti, tj, tk;
```

8.2   Members

The individual components of a structure can be referenced using the "dot," or *member*, operator:

```
ti.desc      has the type   char *,
ti.plan      has the type   TIME,
ti.start     has the type   TIME, and
ti.finish    has the type   TIME.
```

The expression structure.member is an *lvalue* — it can be used anywhere that a variable name is allowed. Thus we can write

```
ti.start = 0;
```

or

```
tj.desc = "Write manuals";
```

The member names of each structure are unique to that structure; they may be used in other structures, or as variable names, without any conflict between the uses **[8-3 cc]**. Each member name defines a *type* and an *offset*:

```
Members of struct task:
```

Name	Type	Offset (2-byte machine)	Offset (4-byte machine)
desc	char *	0	0
plan	TIME (long)	2	4
start	TIME (long)	6	8
finish	TIME (long)	10	12

8.3   Initialization

Structure initialization is similar to array initialization, except that the data types being initialized may be different for each member. We could, for example, write

```
static TASK vacation = {"leave for Hawaii", 1984, 0, 0};
```

(presumably treating the **plan** member as a "years" variable). Like arrays, structures must be in static storage in order to have an initializer. Also like arrays, if there are fewer initializers than members, the remaining members are initialized to zero.

Question [8-4] Write a short program **vacat.c** containing the above declaration for **vacation**. In the program, assign the value 1983 to the members **start** and **finish**. Print the resulting values of all members, using **printf**.

8.4   Nested Structures

One structure may be "nested" inside another. If, for example, we wished to record our TIME values as days and minutes, we could create a new template like this:

```
task2.h [8-5]:
    /* task2.h - include-file for TASK structure (using days and mins)
     */
    #define TIME struct time
    TIME
        {
        short days;
        short mins;
        };
    #define TASK struct task
    TASK
        {
        char *desc;
        TIME plan;
        TIME start;
        TIME finish;
        };
```

Now each of the TIME variables in a TASK is itself a structure, containing the members days and mins. If we declare a variable to be a TASK, as in

```
    TASK t2;
```

we can now reference t2.plan.days, t2.plan.mins, and so forth.

8.5   Arrays of Structures

We could reserve storage for five TASK structures with a declaration like this:

```
    TASK tt[5];
```

which, when the name TASK is expanded by the preprocessor, would look to the compiler like

```
    struct task tt[5];
```

The following program will read input values for the structures in tt and then print the resulting contents.

```
loadtt.c [8-6]:
    /* loadtt - read data into the task table
     */
    #include "local.h"
    #include "task.h"    /* the original include-file: TIME == long */
    #define TSIZE 5
    main()
        {
        TASK tt[TSIZE];              /* task table */
        char tstring[TSIZE][21];     /* string storage */
        short i;                     /* index for printing */
        short n;                     /* number of successful reads */
        short ret;                   /* returned value from scanf */

        n = 0;
        FOREVER
            {
            tt[n].desc = tstring[n];
            ret = scanf("%20s%ld%ld%ld",
                tt[n].desc, &tt[n].plan, &tt[n].start, &tt[n].finish);
            if (ret == EOF)
                break;
            else if (ret != 4)
                error("Data error", "");
            else if (++n >= TSIZE)
                break;
            }
        for (i = 0; i < n; ++i)
            printf("%20s %8ld %8ld %8ld\n",
                tt[i].desc, tt[i].plan, tt[i].start, tt[i].finish);
        }
```

Exercise 8-1. The following include-file `task3.h` has revised the declaration of a TASK such that the storage for each `desc` member is a character array included in the structure tt.

```
task3.h [8-7]:
    /* task3.h - include-file for TASK structure
     */
    #define TIME long
    #define DSIZE 20
    #define TASK struct task
    TASK
        {
        char desc[DSIZE+1];
        TIME plan;
        TIME start;
        TIME finish;
        };
```

Revise the `loadtt.c` program to use this revised declaration.

8.6   Pointers to Structures

A C language structure is an lvalue, in that one may take the address of a structure: &t will tell the address of the structure t. However, only a few operators are defined on structures, in the standard C defined by Kernighan and Ritchie [1978]:

&t   *address of* t
t.plan   *member* plan *of structure* t
sizeof(t)   *size of* t

In particular, in standard C one cannot pass a structure as an argument to a function, but one may give its *address* as an argument. In the called function, the argument needs to be declared as a pointer to a structure. For example, the declaration

        TASK *ptask;

declares that **ptask** has the type **TASK** * ("pointer to TASK"). To access the members of the structure that **ptask** points to, we use the "arrow" -> operator, as in

        ptask->start

The "dot" and "arrow" operators can each be written in terms of the other:

        ptask->start   *is the same as*   (*ptask).start

        t.start   *is the same as*   (&t)->start

Using structure pointers, we can write a function **gettask** and revise our **loadtt** program to use this function.

```
gettt.c [8-8]:
    /* gettt - read data into the task table (using gettask function)
     */
    #include "local.h"
    #include "task3.h"   /* revised to include storage for desc */
    #define TSIZE 5
    main()
        {
        TASK tt[TSIZE];              /* task table */
        short gettask();             /* function to get one TASK */
        short i;                     /* index for printing */
        short n;                     /* number of successful reads */

        n = 0;
        while (n < TSIZE && gettask(&tt[n]) == 4)
            ++n;
        for (i = 0; i < n; ++i)
            printf("%20s %8ld %8ld %8ld\n",
                tt[i].desc, tt[i].plan, tt[i].start, tt[i].finish);
        }
    /* gettask - get one TASK
     */
    short gettask(ptask)
        TASK *ptask;
        {
        short ret;                   /* returned value from scanf */

        ret = scanf("%20s%ld%ld%ld",
            ptask->desc, &ptask->plan, &ptask->start, &ptask->finish);
        return (ret);
        }
```

Exercise 8-2. Write a program runtt.c which will accept lines of data like those read by gettt but if the desc agrees with an existing TASK, the various TIME members are updated in place. The resulting structure should be printed out in sequence by the plan member of each entry.

In the UNIX compilers of Version 7 and later versions, one structure may be *assigned* to a structure of like type; for example,

```
    TASK t1, t2;

    t1 = t2;
```

Furthermore, a structure may be passed as an argument to a function, and the entire structure will be copied into the argument frame. (One then has the choice of passing structures as pointer values with the & address-of operator, or passing the entire structure, with no & operator.) Finally, a function may return a structure value [8-9 cc]. Thus, with these compilers one could define a data type COMPLEX as a structure (in an include-file complex.h):

```
complex.h [8-10]:
    #define COMPLEX struct complex
    COMPLEX
        {
        double real;
        double imag;
        };
```

and produce a library of functions such as cadd ("complex add"):

```
cadd [8-11]:
    /* cadd - add two COMPLEX numbers
     */
    #include "complex.h"
    COMPLEX cadd(x, y)
        COMPLEX x, y;
        {
        COMPLEX z;

        z.real = x.real + y.real;
        z.imag = x.imag + y.imag;
        return (z);
        }
```

Each time cadd is called, the two members of the first argument and the two members of the second argument are copied into the argument frame, where they are known by the names **x** and **y**. The resulting structure, **z**, is passed back to the calling program.

CHAPTER 9: EPILOG

As this book goes to press, a committee to standardize C is being formed by ANSI (the American National Standards Institute). An interesting observation from our consulting experience is that C programs are, in general, more easily ported to new environments than programs written in some other languages with a formal standard, such as Pascal. We have a possible explanation: C has a *concrete underlying model* — the common architectural scheme of modern processors — that may actually be a more reliable model than formal abstractions provide. The prospects are favorable, therefore, for a concise standardization of C language. We await the results with great interest.

Some people, of course, turn to the end of a book just to see how it came out. If, however, you have completed the previous chapters and done the questions and exercises, you now have the power of C language at your command. In particular, you have access to the entire data space available to your running program, which is essential in many engineering and systems programming applications.

As for the instructions that you prepare for the computer, the control structures of C language provide just the facilities that are needed for readable programs. Well-constructed C programs will be easily understood by the people who will maintain your programs in years to come.

To do operations beyond the repertory of C's operators and control structures, you can make use of the libraries provided by your vendor or your organization. Now is a good time for a detailed study of your manuals. Many projects will have special libraries for input/output functions more specialized than the simple "standard input" and "standard output" that we have used in this book. You now know enough C to make full use of these capabilities; the time you spend with the manuals will be well repaid in programming skill.

And when you begin to dream C programs, you will know you have made the language your own.

APPENDIX A: C LANGUAGE REFERENCE

The following pages constitute a "pocket guide" to C. They are not meant to replace the syntax reference that came with your compiler, but rather to serve as a guide to writing readable C programs according to the rules described in this book. Some of the more baroque possibilities of C syntax are deliberately omitted.

Each rule in Appendix A cites the appropriate section in the book; turn to that section for greater detail on syntax and usage.

The rules shown here use this syntax notation:

Symbol	Meaning	Usage
*	repetition	*stmt** means "zero or more *stmt*s"
[]	option	*[stor-cl]* means "an optional *stor-cl*"
|	choice	*h* | *t* means "either *h* or *t*"
{ }	grouping	{*h* | *t*}* means "a repetition of choices between *h* and *t*"

A.1   Programs

SECTION   READABILITY

A source file IS:

5.   program   /* comment
                           */
                          #include <std-file>
                          #include "local-file"
                          #define *ID const*
                          *data-definition**
                          *function**

A *data-definition* IS:

5.12   external *decl* (with initializer)

A *function* IS:

5.1   *function*   /* comment
        with   */
        params   *type name*(a1, a2)
                              type a1;   /* describe a1 */
                              type a2;   /* describe a2 */
                              {
                              *decl**

                              *stmt**
                              }

5.1   *function*   /* comment
        without   */
        params   *type name*( )
                              {
                              *decl**

                              *stmt**
                              }

A.2   Declarations

SECTION   READABILITY

A *decl* IS:

2.1   scalar   *[stor-cl] type name[, name]*;
       (uninitialized)

2.1   scalar   *[stor-cl] type name = expr;*
       (initialized)

3.14   array   *[stor-cl] type name[const];*
       (uninitialized)

5.15   array   *[stor-cl] type name[const]* =
       (initialized)   {

                        *const, [const,]**
                        };

5.13   *function*   *[stor-cl] type name( );*
       declaration

7.5   array param   *type name[ ];*
       (pointer)

7.1   pointer   *type *name;*

7.7   array of   *type *name[const];*
       pointers

8.1   structure   #define *STRUCTYP* struct *structyp*
       template   *STRUCTYP*
                            {
                        *decl**
                        };

8.1   structure   *STRUCTYP name;*
       (uninitialized)

8.3   structure   *STRUCTYP name* =
       (initialized)   {

                        *const, [const,]**
                        };

8.5   array of   *STRUCTYP name[const];*
       structures

8.6   pointer to   *STRUCTYP *name;*
       structure

A.3   Types

```
SECTION              READABILITY

        A type IS:

2.2     integer      char
                     short
                     int
                     long
                     unsigned char    (from some compilers)
                     unsigned short   (from some compilers)
                     unsigned long    (from some compilers)
                     unsigned
                     unsigned int

2.3     floating-    float
        point        double

8.1     structure    struct structyp

8.1     structure    STRUCTYP
        (#defined)


        A stor-cl IS:

3.21                 typedef

5.3                  auto

5.7                  static

5.12                 extern

5.13                 register
```

A.4   Statements

SECTION		READABILITY
	A *stmt* IS:	
4.1	*expression statement*	`expr;`
4.1	`null` *statement*	`;`
4.1	`return` *statement*	`return;` `return (`*expr*`);`
4.1	*block* (*compound statement*)	`{` *stmt*`*` `}`
4.2	`if` *statement*	`if (`*expr*`)` *stmt*
4.3	`if` *statement*	`if (`*expr*`)` *stmt* `else` *stmt*
4.4	`if` *statement*	`if (`*expr*`)` *stmt* `else if (`*expr*`)` *stmt* `else if (`*expr*`)` *stmt* `else` *stmt*

4.5	switch
	statement
		switch (*expr*)
		    {
		case *const*:
		    stmt*
		    break;
		case *const*:
		case *const*:
		    stmt*
		    break;
		default:
		    stmt*
		    break;
		    }

4.6	while *statement*	while (*expr*) *stmt*
4.7	for *statement*	for (*expr*; *expr*; *expr*) *stmt*

4.7	for
	statement
	(N + 1/2)
		FOREVER
		    {
		    stmt*
		    if (*expr*)
		        break;
		    stmt*
		    }

4.8	do-while
	statement
		do
		    {
		    stmt*
		    } while (*expr*);

4.10	break *statement*	break;
4.10	continue *statement*	continue;
4.11	goto *statement*	goto *label*; /* reason */

A.5 Expressions

SECTION   READABILITY

    AN *expr* IS:

3.	monadic *expr*	*monadic-op* (NO SPACE) *expr*
3.9	postfix *expr*	*expr* (NO SPACE) *inc-dec-op*
3.	dyadic *expr*	*expr dyadic-op expr*
3.13	conditional	*expr ? expr : expr*
3.8	*function* call	*name([expr[, expr]*])*
3.14	subscript	*name[expr]*
5.11	two subs	*name[expr][expr]*
7.1	indirect	**name*
8.2	dot (*member*)	*name.member*
8.6	arrow (*member*)	*name->member*

Operator Type	Precedence Level	Operators	Associativity
Primary	15	() [] ->	Left->Right
Monadic	14	! ~ ++ -- - (type) * & sizeof	Right->Left
Arith-metic	13	* / %	Left->Right
	12	+ -	Left->Right
Shift	11	>> <<	Left->Right
Rel-ational	10	< <= > >=	Left->Right
	9	== !=	Left->Right
Bitwise Logical	8	&	Left->Right
	7	^	Left->Right
	6	|	Left->Right
Logical	5	&&	Left->Right
	4	||	Left->Right
Cond.	3	?:	
Asst.	2	= += -= *= /= %= |= ^= &= >>= <<=	Right->Left
Comma	1	,	Left->Right

A.6   Common C Library

BOOK SEC.	UNIX MAN.	FORMAT	
3.17	3M	double	atan(x)
3.19	3	double	atof(s)
3.19	3	int	atoi(s)
3.19	3	long	atol(s)
-	3	char	*calloc(n, size)
-	3S	void	clearerr(fp)
-	2	int	close(fd)
3.17	3M	double	cos(x)
-	2	int	creat(s, perm)
3.22	2	void	exit(n)
3.17	3M	double	exp(x)
-	3S	int	fclose(fp)
-	3S	FILE	*fdopen(fd, mode)
-	3S	int	feof(fp)
-	3S	bool	ferror(fp)
-	3S	int	fflush(fp)
-	3S	metachar	fgetc(fp)
-	3S	char	*fgets(s, size, fp)
-	3S	int	fileno(fp)
-	3S	FILE	*fopen(s, mode)
-	3S	void	fprintf(fp, fmt, args)
-	3S	metachar	fputc(c, fp)
-	3S	int	fputs(s, fp)
-	3S	int	fread(p, size, n, fp)
-	3	void	free(p)
-	3S	FILE	*freopen(s, mode, fp)
-	3S	int	fscanf(fp, fmt, args)
-	3S	int	fseek(fp, lnum, n)
-	3S	long	ftell(fp)
-	3S	int	fwrite(p, size, n, fp)
-	3S	metachar	getc(fp)
3.4	3S	metachar	getchar()
3.14	-	int	getln(s, n)
-	3S	char	*gets(s)
6.3	3	char	*index(s, c)
3.5	3C	bool	isalnum(c)
3.5	3C	bool	isalpha(c)
3.5	3C	bool	isascii(c)
3.5	3C	bool	iscntrl(c)
3.5	3C	bool	isdigit(c)
3.5	3C	bool	islower(c)
3.5	3C	bool	isprint(c)
3.5	3C	bool	ispunct(c)
3.5	3C	bool	isspace(c)
3.5	3C	bool	isupper(c)

3.17	3M	double	log(x)
3.17	3M	double	log10(x)
-	2	long	lseek(fd, lnum, n)
-	3	char	*malloc(size)
-	2	int	open(s, size, n)
3.17	3M	double	pow(x, y)
2.8	3S	void	printf(fmt, args)
-	3S	metachar	putc(c, fp)
3.4	3S	metachar	putchar()
-	3S	int	puts(s)
5.8	3	short	rand()
3.22	2	int	read(fd, p, size)
-	3S	int	rewind(fp)
-	3	void	qsort(p, n, size, pf)
6.3	3	char	*rindex(s, c)
-	2	char	*sbrk(n)
3.12	3S	int	scanf(fmt, args)
3.17	3M	double	sin(x)
3.19	3S	char	*sprintf(s, fmt, args)
3.17	3M	double	sqrt(x)
5.8	3	void	srand(n)
3.19	3S	int	sscanf(s, fmt, args)
3.14	3	char	*strcat(s1, s2)
6.3	3	char	*strchr(s1, c)
3.14	3	int	strcmp(s1, s2)
3.14	3	char	*strcpy(s1, s2)
3.14	3	unsigned	strlen(s)
5.4	3	char	*strncat(s1, s2, size)
5.4	3	int	strncmp(s1, s2, size)
4.7	3	char	*strncpy(s1, s2, size)
6.3	3	char	*strrchr(s, c)
-	3S	FILE	*tmpfile()
3.13	3C	char	tolower(c)
3.13	3C	char	toupper(c)
-	3S	metachar	ungetc(c, fp)
-	2	int	unlink(s)
3.22	2	int	write(fd, p, size)

2.2		char	c;	/* character */
3.22		int	fd;	/* file descrip */
5.4		char	*fmt;	/* format */
-		FILE	*fp;	/* FILE ptr */
2.2		long	lnum;	/* long number */
-		char	*mode;	/* r, w, a */
2.2		int	n;	/* signed num */
5.4		char	*p;	/* pointer */
-		int	perm;	/* permission */
-		int	(*pf)();	/* ptr to fn */
5.4		char	*s;	/* string */
2.2		unsigned	size;	/* byte count */
2.3		double	x, y;	/* math args */

A.7   Formats for Printf

format-string:
> *item**

item:

non-%	ordinary character
%%	print single %
specification	format for one data *item*

specification:

%*[-][0][w][1]*c	ASCII character
%*[-][0][w][1]*d	decimal integer
%*[-][0][w][1]*u	unsigned integer
%*[-][0][w][1]*o	octal integer
%*[-][0][w][1]*x	hexadecimal integer
%*[-][0][w][.p]*f	fixed-point
%*[-][0][w][.p]*e	E-format
%*[-][0][w][.p]*s	string

w (*width*):
> *digit digit**

p (*precision*):
> *digit digit**

(In each *specification*, 0 specifies leading zeroes.)

A.8   Formats for Scanf

format–string:
    *item**

item:
whitespace	ignored
non-%	matches ordinary character
%%	matches %
specification	format for one input data *item*

specification:
%*[*]*[w]*c	char - reads one input character
%*[*]*[w]*hd	short - reads one decimal number
%*[*]*[w]*ho	short - reads one octal number
%*[*]*[w]*hx	short - reads one hexadecimal number
%*[*]*[w]*ld	long - reads one decimal number
%*[*]*[w]*lo	long - reads one octal number
%*[*]*[w]*lx	long - reads one hexadecimal number
%*[*]*[w]*d	int - reads one decimal number
%*[*]*[w]*o	int - reads one octal number
%*[*]*[w]*x	int - reads one hexadecimal number
%*[*]*[w]*[f | e]	float - reads one decimal number
%*[*]*[w]*[lf | le]	double - reads one decimal number
%*[*]*[w]*s	string - reads array of characters

(In each *specification*, * suppresses assignment)

A.9   Common C Bugs

General

Uninitalized variables. □ Off-by-one errors. □ Treating an array as though it were 1-origin (instead of 0-origin). □ Unclosed comments. □ Forgetting semicolons. □ Misplaced braces.

Types, Operators, and Expressions

Using `char` for the returned value from `getchar`. □ "Backslash" typed as "slash"; e.g., `'/n'` instead of `'\n'`. □ Declaring function arguments after the function brace, creating spurious local variables. □ Arithmetic overflow. □ Using relational operators on strings; e.g. `s == "end"` instead of `strcmp(s, "end")`. □ Using = instead of ==. □ Depending upon the order of side-effects in an expression e.g., `a[n] = n++`; □ Off-by-one errors in loops with increment. □ Precedence of bitwise logical operators. (Always parenthesize them.) □ Right-shifting negative numbers (not equivalent to division). □ Assuming the order of evaluation of expressions. □ Forgetting null-terminator on strings.

Control flow

Misplaced `else` □ Missing `break` in `switch`. □ Loop with first or last case abnormal in some way. □ Loop mistakenly never entered. □ Indexing an array with `for (i = 0; i <= NELEMENTS; ++i)`, which goes one step too far. □ Putting semicolon on the control line of `for`, `while`, `if`, etc.

Functions and program structure

Wrong type of arguments (relying on memory instead of manual). □ Wrong order of arguments. □ Omitting `static` on function's abiding storage. □ Assuming that `static` storage is re-initialized at each re-entry.

Pointers and arrays

Passing pointer instead of value — or value instead of pointer. □ Confusing `char` with `char *`. □ Using pointers for strings without allocating storage for the string. □ Dangling pointer references — references to storage no longer used. □ Confusing single quotes (`'\n'`) with double quotes (`"\n"`).

A.10   Table of ASCII Characters

Table of ASCII characters: ASCII, decimal, octal, hexadecimal

nul	0 0000 0x00	sp	32 0040 0x20	@	64 0100 0x40	`	96 0140 0x60
soh	1 0001 0x01	!	33 0041 0x21	A	65 0101 0x41	a	97 0141 0x61
stx	2 0002 0x02	"	34 0042 0x22	B	66 0102 0x42	b	98 0142 0x62
etx	3 0003 0x03	#	35 0043 0x23	C	67 0103 0x43	c	99 0143 0x63
eot	4 0004 0x04	$	36 0044 0x24	D	68 0104 0x44	d	100 0144 0x64
enq	5 0005 0x05	%	37 0045 0x25	E	69 0105 0x45	e	101 0145 0x65
ack	6 0006 0x06	&	38 0046 0x26	F	70 0106 0x46	f	102 0146 0x66
bel	7 0007 0x07	'	39 0047 0x27	G	71 0107 0x47	g	103 0147 0x67
bs	8 0010 0x08	(	40 0050 0x28	H	72 0110 0x48	h	104 0150 0x68
ht	9 0011 0x09	)	41 0051 0x29	I	73 0111 0x49	i	105 0151 0x69
nl	10 0012 0x0a	*	42 0052 0x2a	J	74 0112 0x4a	j	106 0152 0x6a
vt	11 0013 0x0b	+	43 0053 0x2b	K	75 0113 0x4b	k	107 0153 0x6b
np	12 0014 0x0c	,	44 0054 0x2c	L	76 0114 0x4c	l	108 0154 0x6c
cr	13 0015 0x0d	-	45 0055 0x2d	M	77 0115 0x4d	m	109 0155 0x6d
so	14 0016 0x0e	.	46 0056 0x2e	N	78 0116 0x4e	n	110 0156 0x6e
si	15 0017 0x0f	/	47 0057 0x2f	O	79 0117 0x4f	o	111 0157 0x6f
dle	16 0020 0x10	0	48 0060 0x30	P	80 0120 0x50	p	112 0160 0x70
dc1	17 0021 0x11	1	49 0061 0x31	Q	81 0121 0x51	q	113 0161 0x71
dc2	18 0022 0x12	2	50 0062 0x32	R	82 0122 0x52	r	114 0162 0x72
dc3	19 0023 0x13	3	51 0063 0x33	S	83 0123 0x53	s	115 0163 0x73
dc4	20 0024 0x14	4	52 0064 0x34	T	84 0124 0x54	t	116 0164 0x74
nak	21 0025 0x15	5	53 0065 0x35	U	85 0125 0x55	u	117 0165 0x75
syn	22 0026 0x16	6	54 0066 0x36	V	86 0126 0x56	v	118 0166 0x76
etb	23 0027 0x17	7	55 0067 0x37	W	87 0127 0x57	w	119 0167 0x77
can	24 0030 0x18	8	56 0070 0x38	X	88 0130 0x58	x	120 0170 0x78
em	25 0031 0x19	9	57 0071 0x39	Y	89 0131 0x59	y	121 0171 0x79
sub	26 0032 0x1a	:	58 0072 0x3a	Z	90 0132 0x5a	z	122 0172 0x7a
esc	27 0033 0x1b	;	59 0073 0x3b	[	91 0133 0x5b	{	123 0173 0x7b
fs	28 0034 0x1c	<	60 0074 0x3c	\	92 0134 0x5c			124 0174 0x7c
gs	29 0035 0x1d	=	61 0075 0x3d	]	93 0135 0x5d	}	125 0175 0x7d
rs	30 0036 0x1e	>	62 0076 0x3e	^	94 0136 0x5e	~	126 0176 0x7e
us	31 0037 0x1f	?	63 0077 0x3f	_	95 0137 0x5f	del	127 0177 0x7f

A.11   Idioms of C Programming

Certain constructions of C are familiar patterns to experienced programmers but puzzle the novice. Herewith, a few of the common ones. Each brief discussion references a section number of *Learning to Program in C.*

c   i   j   n   p   s   (*as variable names*)

Conventional variable names: c is a *character*, i and j are *integer indexes*, n is a *number of something*, p is a *pointer*, and s is a *string*. (2.6)

for (n = 10; n >= 0; --n) (*or*) for (c = 0; c <= 127; ++c)

In an ordinary for loop that counts from a high limit to a low limit, or vice versa, the limit values appear in the control line. (3.2, 3.3)

d != 0 && n / d < 10

The "short-circuit" logical operator && prevents the second expression from being evaluated if the first expression tests *false*. (3.3)

for (i = 0; s[i] != '\0'; ++i)

Run the loop until a terminating value is hit. (3.14)

for (i = 0, j = MAX; i < j; ++i, --j)

Two indexes, i and j, are given equal status in the loop. (3.15)

if (c) (*or*) if (iswhite) (*or*) if (p)

The comparison against zero is implied by the "test" of an if, for, while. In programs that will be maintained by C novices, such abbreviations are considered cryptic. In any event, comparisons of *numeric* data against zero should always be written in full. (4.2, 7.5)

while ((c = getchar()) != EOF)

The "initialization" of the loop is the same as the "step" to the next case. (4.6)

for (;;)

A "forever" loop, perhaps terminated by a break in the body. We suggest the definition of FOREVER. (4.7)

for (i = 0; i < NCARDS; ++i)

A loop over the elements of an array, with a "test" that compares the subscript with the number of array elements, using <, not <=. (5.9)

static short ndisks[3] = 0;

The initialization = 0 when applied to an array or structure fills the entire aggregate with zeroes (a special case). (5.11)

for (p = s; *p; ++p)

A loop over the characters in the string s, using a pointer p. (7.5)

APPENDIX B.1: COMPUTERS AND C

1.1 Igor and the Numbers Game

1.2 Basics of a Real Computer

1.3 Basic Architecture

1.4 A Common Environment

[1-1 mach] [1-2 os] [1-3 cc] *Your own environment:* Appendix B gives information on how C is dependent on its environment. We have tried to report every dependency, and any topic *not* marked as environment-dependent should be valid for all environments. Please consult your compiler vendor for the specifics of your environment. Your vendor may be able to give you information sheets keyed to this appendix and punched with three holes so you can insert them in the right place among these pages in a binder.

1.5 A Sample Program

This section of Appendix B will contain more environment-specific information than any other section, because we are giving detailed recipes here for compilation and linking.

All program listings are reproduced in this Appendix B, in the same format that they appeared in the text. If this Appendix B was provided to you by your compiler vendor, the programs may have been changed to reflect environmental details which the vendor has marked with comments.

```
hello.c [1-4]:
    main( )
        {
        write(1, "hello, world\n", 13);
        }
```

[1-5 os] *Source file names:* Some operating systems restrict the names of files to no more than six letters, optionally followed by a period (.) and no more than three more letters. In this book, we will restrict our source file names to this form, even though longer names are allowed in our Common Environment.

Another convention you may have noticed is the pervasive use of lower-case names such as hello.c. If your system speaks to you in upper case, you should probably type all your file names in upper case. The C programs themselves, however, should be faithfully entered with letters exactly in lower or upper case just as they appear in the text.

[1-6 os] [1-7 mach] [1-8 cc] We give here the details for editing and compiling, in our Common Environment.

(1) Editing the source file: The following steps will create a file named hello.c, using the UNIX text editor ed.

1. Invoke the editor by typing the command ed hello.c. (You must type a carriage-return — RETURN, NEWLINE, or whatever your terminal provides — after each command.) The editor replies with a question-mark message, saying that you currently have no such file.

2. Put the editor into "text mode" with the command a (for "append").

3. Type the text of the program. The indentation at the left-hand side of the program is achieved by typing one TAB character for each indent. (If your system has no TAB, use consistent spacing instead; your file will contain a few more characters this way.)

4. Leave text mode by typing a line consisting only of one period.

5. Write the accumulated text into a file by typing the command w (for "write"). At this point, the editor puts all this text into a file named hello.c and replies 46, the number of characters in the file.

6. Type q to quit the editor.

This entire sequence of 6 steps looks like this:

```
ed hello.c
?hello.c
a
main()
   {
   write(1, "hello, world\n", 13);
   }
.
w
46
q
```

(2) Changing the source file: If you made a mistake in typing the text, or want to change the program, you can change it with this sequence of commands:

1. Find the line with the mistake by typing the incorrect word surrounded by slash-marks. Suppose we had misspelled "hello" as "hellp". Then we would type /hellp/.

2. Substitute new text by typing the command **s** followed by two slashes, the new text, another slash, and the letter **p** (for "print"). The computer will print out the resulting line.

This recipe for substitution would look like this:

```
/hellp/
    write(1, "hellp, world\n", 13);
s//hello/p
    write(1, "hello, world\n", 13);
```

After doing any such substitutions, write the file again using the **w** command.

(3) Compiling: Next, compile the program by typing the command

```
cc hello.c
```

The compiler then goes to work. During its work, it produces a file of assembler code, a human-readable version of the machine instructions needed for the program. You could see the assembler code with this line:

```
cc -S hello.c; cat hello.s
```

which would produce this output:

```
hello.s:
        .globl  _main
        .text
    _main:
    ~~main:
        jsr r5,csv
        jbr L1
    L2: mov $15,(sp)
        mov $L4,-(sp)
        mov $1,-(sp)
        jsr pc,*$_write
        cmp (sp)+,(sp)+
    L3: jmp cret
    L1: jbr L2
        .globl
        .data
    L4: .byte 150,145,154,154,157,54,40,167,157,162,154,144,12,0
```

You are not expected to be able to read this assembler code, nor would you need to read it while working in C. It serves merely to illustrate the translation that the compiler makes into machine instructions.

Some C compilers do not go through the step of generating assembler code — they produce object code directly. And depending on your system, the assembler code may look different. (We have manually improved the layout of the assembler sample shown.) If you can read assembler, produce the assembler output from `hello.c` on your system and compare it with the output above.

If you did not specify the -S flag for "assembler only," the compiler goes on to produce an object file — `hello.o`, in the UNIX style. The linker then combines this file with other files in a link library. (The cc command automatically specifies certain standard link libraries for your compilation.) The final result is a file conventionally named `a.out` (on UNIX systems) which contains all the instructions to execute the program: it is the *executable program*. (On non-UNIX systems, there will likely be a different name for the executable program that results from the

```
cc hello.c
```

command.)

(4) Executing the program: Still seated at your terminal, you could then execute `a.out` by simply typing

```
a.out
```

and you would be rewarded by the message

```
hello, world
```

appearing on your screen or printout (with the cursor or carriage properly returned after the last printed character). (On some non-UNIX systems you may have to say **run** `a.out` or **exec** `a.out` to run the program.)

APPENDIX B.2: DATA

2.1 Bits and Numbers

Question [2-1] What is the decimal value of the following binary numbers?

00001111	01010101	10000001
15	*85*	*129*

[2-2 mach] *Twos complement signed numbers:* At the time of printing, the machines known to use twos complement signed numbers include all processors made by DEC, IBM, Intel, Motorola, Intel, BBN, Zilog, National Semiconductor, and Interdata. If your machine is not on this list, inquire of your vendor whether it uses ones or twos complement.

Question [2-3] What is the 8-bit sum? What does each number equal in decimal? Do each problem both in unsigned and twos complement signed interpretation.

```
   binary        unsigned      signed
                 decimal       decimal (twos complement)

   00101011 =       43            43
 + 10000011 =      131          -125
 -----------
   10101110         174          -82

   11110000 =      240           -16
 + 00001111 =       15            15
 -----------
   11111111         255           -1

   10000000 =      128          -128
 + 00001010 =       10            10
 -----------
   10001010         138          -118
```

Now compute these 8-bit sums, using ones complement interpretation:

```
   binary         signed
                  decimal (ones complement)

   00101011 =        43
 + 10000011 =      -124
 -----------
   10101110          -81

   11110000 =       -15
 + 00001111 =        15
 -----------
   11111111           0

   11111101 =        -2
 + 11111110 =        -1
 -----------
   11111100          -3
```

2.2   Integer Variables

[2-4 mach] *Byte sizes of* char, short, *and* long: On some C machines (the *word-oriented* machines like Honeywell 6000), short variables have 4 bytes just as long variables do. Even if you use such a machine, you should henceforth program as if the short variables might contain no more than 2 bytes, so that your code could be run on other computers. After this cautionary note, we will henceforth assume that char is one byte, short is two bytes (or more), and long is four bytes.

[2-5 mach] [2-6 cc] *Range of* char *variables:* On some combinations of machine and compiler, char variables are never negative; they behave just like the unsigned char variables. We show signed variables here for simple consistency; the details will not matter until Chapter 3.

8-bit char *variables:* Some word-oriented machines (Honeywell 6000, Univac 1100) have 9-bit char variables, and the *byte* is 9 bits. One C machine (BBN C/70 machine) has a 10-bit byte. Again, if you use such machines, your code will be portable to other machines only if you assume that bytes might be no larger than 8 bits.

[2-7 mach] *The size of an* int *in bytes:*

int size	machines
2	PDP-11, 8080, Z80, 8086, etc.
4	VAX, 370, 68000, etc.

[2-8 cc] *Unsigned types:* The types unsigned char, unsigned short, and unsigned long are not available from some compilers. All standard compilers do have unsigned int, and we will steer clear of the others in this volume.

2.3   Floating-point Variables

2.4   Constants

Question [2-9] What is the type of each constant:

123	*int*	1.2	*double*
'x'	*char*	1.5E4	*double*
5L	*long*	'2'	*char*

What does this string constant look like in memory:

"000"

```
| 48 | 48 | 48 |  0 |
| '0'| '0'| '0'|'\0'|
```

2.5   Octal and Hexadecimal Numbers

Question [2-10] Write down the octal equivalent for each binary number:

     10110010   11111111

      0262   *0377*

     1101100100110110   1111111111111111

      0154466   *0177777*

Question [2-11] Write down the binary equivalent (8 or 16 bits) for each octal number:

     014   0177

   00001100   *01111111*

     0200   014662   052525

   10000000   *0001100110110010*   *0101010101010101*

Question [2-12] Write down the hexadecimal equivalent for each binary number:

     10110010   11111111

      0xB2   *0xFF*

     1101100100110110   1111111111111111

      0xD936   *0xFFFF*

Question [2-13] Convert from the hexadecimal to the corresponding binary?

     0xFE   0x40

   11111110   *01000000*

     0x7FFF   0x9A6E

   0111111111111111   *1001101001101110*

2.6   Atoms of a C Program

[2-14 cc] *Keywords of C:* The keyword entry has never actually been used, and may be discontinued. Some compilers reserve the additional keywords enum, fortran, and asm, none of which will be mentioned in this book.

```
hello2.c [2-15]:
    /* hello2 - print greeting
     */
    main()
        {
        write(1, "hello, world\n", 13);
        }
```

```
hello3.c [2-16]:
    /* hello3 - print greeting */
    main
    (
    )
    {
    write
    (
    1
    ,
    "hello, world\n"
    ,
    13
    )
    ;
    }
```

Question [2-17] Write the category of atom next to each line of hello3.c.

```
comment   /* hello3 - print greeting */
name      main
separator (
separator )
separator {
name      write
separator (
constant  1
separator ,
string    "hello, world\n"
separator ,
constant  13
separator )
separator ;
separator }
```

2.7   Flow of Control

```
asst.c:
    1   /* asst - examples of assignment
    2    * (No output is produced)
    3    */
    4   main()
    5      {
    6      char c;
    7      short i;
    8
    9      c = 'A';
   10      i = 65;
   11      c = 'X';
   12      i = -4;
   13      }
```

2.8   Output and Printf

```
asst2.c [2-18]:
    /* asst2 - print assigned values
     */
    main()
        {
        char c;
        short i;

        c = 'A';
        i = 65;
        printf("c: dec=%d oct=%o hex=%x ASCII=%c\n",
            c, c, c, c);
        printf("i: dec=%d oct=%o hex=%x unsigned=%u\n",
            i, i, i, i);
        c = 'X';
        i = -4;
        printf("c: dec=%d oct=%o hex=%x ASCII=%c\n",
            c, c, c, c);
        printf("i: dec=%d oct=%o hex=%x unsigned=%u\n",
            i, i, i, i);
        }
```

[2-19 cc] *The default executable file name* a.out: With compilers other than the UNIX cc, this name may be different.

[2-20 cc] *Compilation into a named executable file:* Non-UNIX compilers may need a different command.

Executable file names: The UNIX convention for executable files is simply to drop the .c suffix from the program name. Thus the executable form of asst2.c is simply named asst, with no suffix. On other operating systems, there may be different suffix conventions, such as .EXE. Consult the manual for your system to determine the appropriate name convention, and follow it in your further programming.

Even if you are working on a UNIX system, you may find it useful to adopt a suffix convention for executable files which you will wish to remove from your directory. If, for example, you routinely name the executable file from pgm.c by the name pgm.x, you can readily remove all these files with the command

```
    rm *.x
```

Question [2-21] What does the output of asst2.c look like?

```
c: dec=65 oct=101 hex=41 ASCII=A
i: dec=65 oct=101 hex=41 unsigned=65
c: dec=88 oct=130 hex=58 ASCII=X
i: dec=-4 oct=177774 hex=fffc unsigned=65532
```

Question [2-22] If each format in `asst2.c` is changed to a 6-position width, what does its output look like?

```
c: dec=    65 oct=    101 hex=    41 ASCII=     A
i: dec=    65 oct=    101 hex=    41 unsigned=    65
c: dec=    88 oct=    130 hex=    58 ASCII=     X
i: dec=    -4 oct=177774 hex=  fffc unsigned= 65532
```

2.9   Program Size

[2-23 os] *Finding the size of a program:*   In a non-UNIX environment, you may need a different command.

2.10   Define and Include

```
hello4.c [2-24]:
    /* hello4 - print greeting
     */
    #define STDOUT  1
    #define MESSAGE "hello, world\n"
    #define LENGTH  13
    main()
        {
        write(STDOUT, MESSAGE, LENGTH);
        }
```

local.h:

```
/* local.h - definitions for use with
 *          Learning to Program in C
 */
#ifndef FAIL
#include <stdio.h>
#define FAIL        1
#define FOREVER     for (;;)
#define NO          0
#define STDERR      2
#define STDIN       0
#define STDOUT      1
#define SUCCEED     0
#define YES         1
#define bits        ushort
#define bool        int
#define metachar    short
#define tbool       char
#define ushort      unsigned  /* use unsigned short, if available */
#define void        int
#define getln(s, n) ((fgets(s, n, stdin) == NULL) ? EOF : strlen(s))
#define ABS(x)      (((x) < 0) ? -(x) : (x))
#define MAX(x, y)   (((x) < (y)) ? (y) : (x))
#define MIN(x, y)   (((x) < (y)) ? (x) : (y))
#endif
```

hello5.c **[2-25]**:

```
/* hello5 - print greeting
 */
#include "local.h"
#define MESSAGE "hello, world\n"
#define LENGTH  13
main()
    {
    write(STDOUT, MESSAGE, LENGTH);
    }
```

APPENDIX B.3: OPERATORS

3.1 Arithmetic Operators

Question [3-1] Draw expression trees for the following expressions:

a + b % c   -a / b   a * -b

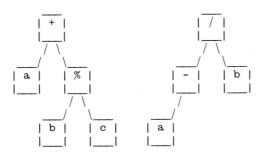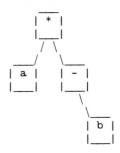

Question [3-2] How many subexpressions are there in this expression? *10* List them.

    (a + b) * (c + d) + e

    1. a
    2. b
    3. c
    4. d
    5. e
    6. a + b
    7. (a + b)
    8. c + d
    9. (c + d)
    10. (a + b) * (c + d)

Question [3-3] What does this program print?

```
arith.c [3-4]:
    /* arith - arithmetic practice
     */
    main()
        {
        printf("%d %d %d %d\n",
            1 + 2, 5 / 2, -2 * 4, 11 % 3);
        printf("%.5f %.5f %.5f\n",
            1. + 2., 5. / 2., -2. * 4.);
        }
```

3 2 -8 2
3.00000 2.50000 -8.00000

Question [3-5] If a equals 8, b equals 2, and c equals 4, what is the resulting value of each expression:

```
        a + b % c              -a / b            a * -b
```

       10   *-4*   *-16*

3.2 Relational Operators

```
blast.c [3-6]:
    /* blast - print countdown
     */
    main()
        {
        short n;

        for (n = 10; n >= 0; n = n - 1)
            printf("%d\n", n);
        printf("Blast off!\n");
        }
```

```
blast2.c [3-7]:
    /* blast2 - print countdown
     */
    main()
        {
        short n;

        for (n = 10; n >= 0; n = n - 1)
            {
            printf("%d\n", n);
            if (n == 3)
                printf("We have ignition!\n");
            }
        printf("Blast off!\n");
        }
```

3.3   Logical Operators

```
codes1.c [3-8]:
    /* codes1 - print ASCII codes
     */
    main()
        {
        short c;

        for (c = 0; c <= 127; c = c + 1)
            {
            printf("%3d 0x%02x 0%03o", c, c, c);
            if (' ' <= c && c <= '~')
                printf(" '%c'", c);
            if ('0' <= c && c <= '9')
                printf(" digit");
            if ('A' <= c && c <= 'Z')
                printf(" uppercase");
            if ('a' <= c && c <= 'z')
                printf(" lowercase");
            printf("\n");
            }
        }
```

Output of codes1.c:

```
 0 0x00 0000                          64 0x40 0100 '@'
 1 0x01 0001                          65 0x41 0101 'A' uppercase
 2 0x02 0002                          66 0x42 0102 'B' uppercase
 3 0x03 0003                          67 0x43 0103 'C' uppercase
 4 0x04 0004                          68 0x44 0104 'D' uppercase
 5 0x05 0005                          69 0x45 0105 'E' uppercase
 6 0x06 0006                          70 0x46 0106 'F' uppercase
 7 0x07 0007                          71 0x47 0107 'G' uppercase
 8 0x08 0010                          72 0x48 0110 'H' uppercase
 9 0x09 0011                          73 0x49 0111 'I' uppercase
10 0x0a 0012                          74 0x4a 0112 'J' uppercase
11 0x0b 0013                          75 0x4b 0113 'K' uppercase
12 0x0c 0014                          76 0x4c 0114 'L' uppercase
13 0x0d 0015                          77 0x4d 0115 'M' uppercase
14 0x0e 0016                          78 0x4e 0116 'N' uppercase
15 0x0f 0017                          79 0x4f 0117 'O' uppercase
16 0x10 0020                          80 0x50 0120 'P' uppercase
17 0x11 0021                          81 0x51 0121 'Q' uppercase
18 0x12 0022                          82 0x52 0122 'R' uppercase
19 0x13 0023                          83 0x53 0123 'S' uppercase
20 0x14 0024                          84 0x54 0124 'T' uppercase
21 0x15 0025                          85 0x55 0125 'U' uppercase
22 0x16 0026                          86 0x56 0126 'V' uppercase
23 0x17 0027                          87 0x57 0127 'W' uppercase
24 0x18 0030                          88 0x58 0130 'X' uppercase
25 0x19 0031                          89 0x59 0131 'Y' uppercase
26 0x1a 0032                          90 0x5a 0132 'Z' uppercase
27 0x1b 0033                          91 0x5b 0133 '['
28 0x1c 0034                          92 0x5c 0134 '\'
29 0x1d 0035                          93 0x5d 0135 ']'
30 0x1e 0036                          94 0x5e 0136 '^'
31 0x1f 0037                          95 0x5f 0137 '_'
32 0x20 0040 ' '                      96 0x60 0140 '`'
33 0x21 0041 '!'                      97 0x61 0141 'a' lowercase
34 0x22 0042 '"'                      98 0x62 0142 'b' lowercase
35 0x23 0043 '#'                      99 0x63 0143 'c' lowercase
36 0x24 0044 '$'                     100 0x64 0144 'd' lowercase
37 0x25 0045 '%'                     101 0x65 0145 'e' lowercase
38 0x26 0046 '&'                     102 0x66 0146 'f' lowercase
39 0x27 0047 '''                     103 0x67 0147 'g' lowercase
40 0x28 0050 '('                     104 0x68 0150 'h' lowercase
41 0x29 0051 ')'                     105 0x69 0151 'i' lowercase
42 0x2a 0052 '*'                     106 0x6a 0152 'j' lowercase
43 0x2b 0053 '+'                     107 0x6b 0153 'k' lowercase
44 0x2c 0054 ','                     108 0x6c 0154 'l' lowercase
45 0x2d 0055 '-'                     109 0x6d 0155 'm' lowercase
46 0x2e 0056 '.'                     110 0x6e 0156 'n' lowercase
47 0x2f 0057 '/'                     111 0x6f 0157 'o' lowercase
48 0x30 0060 '0' digit               112 0x70 0160 'p' lowercase
49 0x31 0061 '1' digit               113 0x71 0161 'q' lowercase
50 0x32 0062 '2' digit               114 0x72 0162 'r' lowercase
51 0x33 0063 '3' digit               115 0x73 0163 's' lowercase
52 0x34 0064 '4' digit               116 0x74 0164 't' lowercase
53 0x35 0065 '5' digit               117 0x75 0165 'u' lowercase
54 0x36 0066 '6' digit               118 0x76 0166 'v' lowercase
55 0x37 0067 '7' digit               119 0x77 0167 'w' lowercase
56 0x38 0070 '8' digit               120 0x78 0170 'x' lowercase
57 0x39 0071 '9' digit               121 0x79 0171 'y' lowercase
58 0x3a 0072 ':'                     122 0x7a 0172 'z' lowercase
59 0x3b 0073 ';'                     123 0x7b 0173 '{'
60 0x3c 0074 '<'                     124 0x7c 0174 '|'
61 0x3d 0075 '='                     125 0x7d 0175 '}'
62 0x3e 0076 '>'                     126 0x7e 0176 '~'
63 0x3f 0077 '?'                     127 0x7f 0177
```

Question [3-9] When the variable c reaches the value 0x20 (ASCII blank, or
' ') how many of the relational expressions in codes1.c evaluate to a *true*
(1) result? *2*

        ' ' <= c

        c <= '~'

     (Remember that if the left-hand operand of && evaluates to *false*, the
right-hand operand is not even evaluated.)

How many evaluate to *true* for the value 126 (tilde, '~')? *5*

        ' ' <= c

        c <= '~'

        '0' <= c

        'A' <= c

        'a' <= c

Write the value of each expression (0 or 1):

       1 < 4 && 4 < 7   *1*

       1 < 4 && 8 < 4   *0*

       !(2 <= 5)   *0*

       !(1 < 3) || (2 < 4) *1*

       !(4 <= 6 && 3 <= 7) *0*

3.4   Character Input/Output

[3-10 os] *The end-of-file character:* If you are not working in a UNIX environment, you will need to consult the user manual for your operating system to find the character which serves as end-of-file from the keyboard.

[3-11 cc] *Including* `stdio.h` *from within* `local.h`: Some compilers will not include one file from within another include-file. If yours is among them, your best approach is probably to have the source program itself include all the files needed. In any event, we will later (in Section 5.18) discuss a technique for being sure that each include-file is included only once per compilation.

`codes2.c` [3-12]:

```
/* codes2 - print ASCII codes
 */
#include "local.h"
main()
    {
    short c;

    while ((c = getchar()) != EOF)
        {
        printf("%3d 0x%02x 0%03o", c, c, c);
        if (' ' <= c && c <= '~')
            printf(" '%c'", c);
        if ('0' <= c && c <= '9')
            printf(" digit");
        if ('A' <= c && c <= 'Z')
            printf(" uppercase");
        if ('a' <= c && c <= 'z')
            printf(" lowercase");
        printf("\n");
        }
    }
```

Question [3-13] If you typed one line of input to this program, consisting of the characters 1aA! followed by a newline, what would its output be?

```
49 0x31 0061 '1' digit
97 0x61 0141 'a' lowercase
65 0x41 0101 'A' uppercase
33 0x21 0041 '!'
10 0x0a 0012
```

The fifth line of output comes from the newline (\n) at the end of your typed input line.

codes3.c **[3-14]**:

```
/* codes3 - print ASCII codes
 */
#include "local.h"
main()
    {
    metachar c; /* return from getchar: char or EOF */

    while ((c = getchar()) != EOF)
        {
        printf("%3d 0x%02x 0%03o", c, c, c);
        if (' ' <= c && c <= '~')
            printf(" '%c'", c);
        if ('0' <= c && c <= '9')
            printf(" digit");
        if ('A' <= c && c <= 'Z')
            printf(" uppercase");
        if ('a' <= c && c <= 'z')
            printf(" lowercase");
        printf("\n");
        }
    }
```

copy.c **[3-15]**:

```
/* copy - copy input to output
 */
#include "local.h"
main()
    {
    metachar c;

    while ((c = getchar()) != EOF)
        putchar(c);
    exit(SUCCEED);
    }
```

3.5   Character-type Tests

```
codes4.c [3-16]:
    /* codes1 - print ASCII codes
     */
    #include "local.h"
    #include <ctype.h>
    main()
        {
        metachar c;

        for (c = 0; c <= 127; c = c + 1)
            {
            printf("%3d 0x%02x 0%03o", c, c, c);
            if (isprint(c))
                printf(" '%c'", c);
            if (isdigit(c))
                printf(" D");
            if (isupper(c))
                printf(" UC");
            if (islower(c))
                printf(" LC");
            if (isalpha(c))
                printf(" L");
            if (isalnum(c))
                printf(" AN");
            if (isspace(c))
                printf(" S");
            if (ispunct(c))
                printf(" P");
            if (iscntrl(c))
                printf(" C");
            printf("\n");
            }
        }
```

Output from `codes4.c`:

```
  0 0x00 0000 C                    64 0x40 0100 '@' P
  1 0x01 0001 C                    65 0x41 0101 'A' UC L AN
  2 0x02 0002 C                    66 0x42 0102 'B' UC L AN
  3 0x03 0003 C                    67 0x43 0103 'C' UC L AN
  4 0x04 0004 C                    68 0x44 0104 'D' UC L AN
  5 0x05 0005 C                    69 0x45 0105 'E' UC L AN
  6 0x06 0006 C                    70 0x46 0106 'F' UC L AN
  7 0x07 0007 C                    71 0x47 0107 'G' UC L AN
  8 0x08 0010 C                    72 0x48 0110 'H' UC L AN
  9 0x09 0011 S C                  73 0x49 0111 'I' UC L AN
 10 0x0a 0012 S C                  74 0x4a 0112 'J' UC L AN
 11 0x0b 0013 S                    75 0x4b 0113 'K' UC L AN
 12 0x0c 0014 S C                  76 0x4c 0114 'L' UC L AN
 13 0x0d 0015 S C                  77 0x4d 0115 'M' UC L AN
 14 0x0e 0016 C                    78 0x4e 0116 'N' UC L AN
 15 0x0f 0017 C                    79 0x4f 0117 'O' UC L AN
 16 0x10 0020 C                    80 0x50 0120 'P' UC L AN
 17 0x11 0021 C                    81 0x51 0121 'Q' UC L AN
 18 0x12 0022 C                    82 0x52 0122 'R' UC L AN
 19 0x13 0023 C                    83 0x53 0123 'S' UC L AN
 20 0x14 0024 C                    84 0x54 0124 'T' UC L AN
 21 0x15 0025 C                    85 0x55 0125 'U' UC L AN
 22 0x16 0026 C                    86 0x56 0126 'V' UC L AN
 23 0x17 0027 C                    87 0x57 0127 'W' UC L AN
 24 0x18 0030 C                    88 0x58 0130 'X' UC L AN
 25 0x19 0031 C                    89 0x59 0131 'Y' UC L AN
 26 0x1a 0032 C                    90 0x5a 0132 'Z' UC L AN
 27 0x1b 0033 C                    91 0x5b 0133 '[' P
 28 0x1c 0034 C                    92 0x5c 0134 '\' P
 29 0x1d 0035 C                    93 0x5d 0135 ']' P
 30 0x1e 0036 C                    94 0x5e 0136 '^' P
 31 0x1f 0037 C                    95 0x5f 0137 '_' P
 32 0x20 0040 ' ' S P              96 0x60 0140 '`' P
 33 0x21 0041 '!' P                97 0x61 0141 'a' LC L AN
 34 0x22 0042 '"' P                98 0x62 0142 'b' LC L AN
 35 0x23 0043 '#' P                99 0x63 0143 'c' LC L AN
 36 0x24 0044 '$' P               100 0x64 0144 'd' LC L AN
 37 0x25 0045 '%' P               101 0x65 0145 'e' LC L AN
 38 0x26 0046 '&' P               102 0x66 0146 'f' LC L AN
 39 0x27 0047 ''' P               103 0x67 0147 'g' LC L AN
 40 0x28 0050 '(' P               104 0x68 0150 'h' LC L AN
 41 0x29 0051 ')' P               105 0x69 0151 'i' LC L AN
 42 0x2a 0052 '*' P               106 0x6a 0152 'j' LC L AN
 43 0x2b 0053 '+' P               107 0x6b 0153 'k' LC L AN
 44 0x2c 0054 ',' P               108 0x6c 0154 'l' LC L AN
 45 0x2d 0055 '-' P               109 0x6d 0155 'm' LC L AN
 46 0x2e 0056 '.' P               110 0x6e 0156 'n' LC L AN
 47 0x2f 0057 '/' P               111 0x6f 0157 'o' LC L AN
 48 0x30 0060 '0' D AN            112 0x70 0160 'p' LC L AN
 49 0x31 0061 '1' D AN            113 0x71 0161 'q' LC L AN
 50 0x32 0062 '2' D AN            114 0x72 0162 'r' LC L AN
 51 0x33 0063 '3' D AN            115 0x73 0163 's' LC L AN
 52 0x34 0064 '4' D AN            116 0x74 0164 't' LC L AN
 53 0x35 0065 '5' D AN            117 0x75 0165 'u' LC L AN
 54 0x36 0066 '6' D AN            118 0x76 0166 'v' LC L AN
 55 0x37 0067 '7' D AN            119 0x77 0167 'w' LC L AN
 56 0x38 0070 '8' D AN            120 0x78 0170 'x' LC L AN
 57 0x39 0071 '9' D AN            121 0x79 0171 'y' LC L AN
 58 0x3a 0072 ':' P               122 0x7a 0172 'z' LC L AN
 59 0x3b 0073 ';' P               123 0x7b 0173 '{' P
 60 0x3c 0074 '<' P               124 0x7c 0174 '|' P
 61 0x3d 0075 '=' P               125 0x7d 0175 '}' P
 62 0x3e 0076 '>' P               126 0x7e 0176 '~' P
 63 0x3f 0077 '?' P               127 0x7f 0177 C
```

3.6   Bitwise Logical Operators

Question [3-17] Convert each number to 16-bit binary, and then negate it:

0x40 = *0000000001000000*   01 = *0000000000000001*

~0x40 = *1111111110111111*   ~01 = *1111111111111110*

Question [3-18] Write the binary result of these operations:

```
   0000000001111111        0000000011000000         1111111111111100
 & 0111010110011010      | 1000000000000100      &  1000000001111111

   0000000000011010        1000000011000100         1000000001111100
```

Question [3-19] Write the ones complement and twos complement of these numbers:

9 = 0000000000001001   0xFF00 = 1111111100000000

1111111111110110   *0000000011111111*
(ones complement)   (ones complement)

1111111111110111   *0000000100000000*
(twos complement)   (twos complement)

[3-20 mach]: *Machines with more than 16 bits per* int: On such machines, the int constants 9 and 0xFF00 would have extra 0 bits on the left, and their complements would have extra 1 bits on the left.

3.7   Shift Operators

[3-21 mach] Machines with more than 16 bits per int: Although the int sized temporary in which shift is performed on these machines is larger and involves more bits, the principles remain the same. For example, if int is 32 bits on your machine, the diagrams would look like this:

```
 _____
|                                           |
| 00000000000000000000000000010000          |
|_____|
```

[3-22 mach]

```
 _____
|                                           |
| 00000000000000000000000010000000          |
|_____|
```

[3-23 mach]

```
 _____
| 00000000000000000000000000010000 |
|_____|

        >> 3

 _____
| 00000000000000000000000000000010 |
|_____|
```

getbn.c **[3-24]**:
```
/* getbn - get a binary number and print it
 */
#include "local.h"
#include <ctype.h>
main()
    {
    metachar c;
    short n;

    n = 0;
    c = getchar();
    while (c != EOF && isspace(c))
        c = getchar();
    while (c == '0' || c == '1')
        {
        n = ((n << 1) | (c - '0'));
        c = getchar();
        }
    printf("%5u 0x%04x 0%06o\n", n, n, n);
    }
```

Question [3-25] What output will the program produce for input 100001?

33 0x0021 0000041

For input 1111111111111111?

65535 0xffff 0177777

3.8   Functions

```
getbn2.c [3-26]:
    /* getbn2 - get and print binary numbers
     */
    #include "local.h"
    #include <ctype.h>
    main()
        {
        short getbin();
        short number;

        while ((number = getbin()) != 0)
            printf("%5u 0x%04x 0%06o\n", number, number, number);
        }
    /* getbin - get binary input number
     */
    short getbin()
        {
        metachar c;
        short n;

        n = 0;
        c = getchar();
        while (c != EOF && isspace(c))
            c = getchar();
        while (c == '0' || c == '1')
            {
            n = ((n << 1) | (c - '0'));
            c = getchar();
            }
        return (n);
        }
```

[3-27 cc] *Returned values in registers:* On all compilers known at the
time of printing, integer return values are returned in a register. On some
machines and some compilers, long and double returned values may be returned in *simulated* registers. The mechanism is important only if C functions
are interfaced with assembler code.

Question [3-28] If the input to getbn2 consists of these three lines

```
101
1111
00000
```

what does the output look like:

```
5 0x0005 0000005
15 0x000f 0000017
```

(Remember that a return of 0 from getbin is taken as end-of-file, so the line 00000 generates no output.)

Question [3-29] (Using the printf manual page) How can the output be printed *left-adjusted* in its field width?

By prefixing a minus-sign to its field width.

```
putbin [3-30]:
    /* putbin - print number in binary format
     */
    void putbin(n)
        short n;
        {
        short i;

        for (i = 15; i >= 0; i = i - 1)
            {
            if ((n & (1 << i)) == 0)
                printf("0");
            else
                printf("1");
            }
        }
```

[3-31 cc] The type name void: This type name was added to the language relatively recently, in the UNIX System III compiler and others based on it, but it is a good idea to use it with all C compilers. It gives you portability to future compilers that you may use, and produces good documentation for the reader. In the header file local.h you will find a definition of void as simply int. If you are using one of the new compilers, you can remove this definition of void.

```
bdrill.c [3-32]:
    /* bdrill - binary arithmetic practice
     */
    #include "local.h"
    #include <ctype.h>
    main()
        {
        short a, b;
        short getbin();
        void putbin();

        while ((a = getbin()) != 0 && (b = getbin()) != 0)
            {
            printf("\n    a = ");
            putbin(a);
            printf("\n    b = ");
            putbin(b);
            printf("\na + b = ");
            putbin(a + b);
            printf("\na & b = ");
            putbin(a & b);
            printf("\na | b = ");
            putbin(a | b);
            printf("\na ^ b = ");
            putbin(a ^ b);
            printf("\n");
            }
        }
    (getbin function goes here)
    (putbin function goes here)
```

Question [3-33] What output will bdrill produce from this input?

```
10101
11001
```

```
    a = 0000000000010101
    b = 0000000000011001
a + b = 0000000000101110
a & b = 0000000000010001
a | b = 0000000000011101
a ^ b = 0000000000001100
```

3.9   Lvalue, Rvalue, Increment, Decrement

3.10   Assignment Operators

[3-34 cc] *Assignment operators and early C compilers:* Some antique compilers, such as that from UNIX Version 6, accept a different form of assignment operators — the equal-sign appears first, followed by the operator. Thus the operator += appears as =+. Some of the more recent compilers accept both forms. Avoid the older ones if you possibly can.

3.11   Nesting of Operators

3.12   Address-of Operator and Scanf

[3-35 cc] short *formats for* scanf: Some versions of scanf may not have the %h formats. In this case, you cannot write portable code which will read values into short variables. If short is the same as int on your machine, you could write

```
#define SHORTFMT "%d"   /* change to "%hd" if available */
```

and code your program using

```
scanf(SHORTFMT, &n);
```

(The format codes for scanf have evolved historically, with less than perfect completeness and consistency. In the Reader Reply Form in the back of the book, we are surveying our readers on possible replacements for the scanf function.)

Question [3-36] Write a program, pr2a.c, to read two hexadecimal numbers into long variables, and print the two variables and their sum.

```
pr2a.c:
    /* pr2a - print the sum of two long inputs
     */
    #include "local.h"
    main()
        {
        long a, b;

        scanf("%lx %lx", &a, &b);
        printf("    a = %8lx\n", a);
        printf("    b = %8lx\n", b);
        printf("a + b = %8lx\n", a + b);
        }
```

Make another such program, pr2b.c, with double variables, using the proper formats.

```
pr2b.c:
    /* pr2b - print the sum of two double inputs
     */
    #include "local.h"
    main()
        {
        double a, b;

        scanf("%lf %lf", &a, &b);
        printf("    a = %12.6e\n", a);
        printf("    b = %12.6e\n", b);
        printf("a + b = %12.6e\n", a + b);
        }
```

3.13   Conditional Operator

Question [3-37] Modify your pr2b.c program to create maxmin.c which prints the max and min of the two input numbers.

```
maxmin.c:
    /* maxmin - print the max and min of two double inputs
     */
    #include "local.h"
    main()
        {
        double a, b;

        if (scanf("%lf %lf", &a, &b) == 2)
            {
            printf("  a = %12.6e\n", a);
            printf("  b = %12.6e\n", b);
            printf("max = %12.6e\n", a < b ? a : b);
            printf("min = %12.6e\n", a < b ? b : a);
            }
        }
```

[3-38 cc] *The functions* toupper *and* tolower: In versions of UNIX more recent than Version 7, these functions are part of the standard library. They behave just as we have shown, but they may require

```
#include <ctype.h>
```

in your program. Unfortunately for portability, in several releases of Version 7 the <ctype.h> file provided toupper and tolower, but the Programmer's Manual makes no mention of them (undocumented "features"). Worse yet, they behave in an unfriendly way, different from what we have shown: they add the offset (such as 'a' - 'A') without doing any checking. If you are programming on such a system, you should ask your system administrator to remove toupper and tolower from <ctype.h> and add the properly protected functions to the standard library. The change cannot impair the functioning of any existing code and will facilitate portability to later versions of the library.

```
toupper [3-39]:
    /* toupper - convert lower-case letter to upper case
     */
    metachar toupper(c)
        metachar c;
        {
        return (islower(c) ? c + 'A' - 'a' : c);
        }
```

```
tolower [3-40]:
    /* tolower - convert upper-case letter to lower case
     */
    metachar tolower(c)
        metachar c;
        {
        return (isupper(c) ? c + 'a' - 'A' : c);
        }
```

3.14   Arrays and Subscripting

```
sizes.c [3-41]:
    /* sizes - report the size of some types and expressions
     */
    #include "local.h"
    main()
        {
        char c;
        char s[512];
        short n;
        short m[40];

        printf("%3d %3d\n", sizeof(c), sizeof(char));
        printf("%3d %3d\n", sizeof(s), sizeof(char[512]));
        printf("%3d %3d\n", sizeof(n), sizeof(short));
        printf("%3d %3d\n", sizeof(m), sizeof(short[40]));
        }
```

[3-42 cc] [3-43 mach] sizeof *examples:* sizeof(char) is 1 byte in all known compilers, and you can take this fact as a de-facto standard. A few word-oriented machines may define short variables to have 4 bytes instead of 2. You may also find a few compilers that refuse to accept sizeof applied to the type of an array, even though they will accept it for the *name* of the array. **[3-44 mach]** *Machines with different "word" and "byte" address schemes:* An important portability observation is that not all machines use "byte" addresses for data. On some machines, each int sized piece of memory has a "word" address, and the subscripting formula is performed using word addresses for such data. Thus, if the word address of the int array m is 3000, then m[40] is located at word address 3040. And to complicate things further, on some machines like the Honeywell 6000, word addresses are stored in the *leftmost* 18 bits of a 36-bit word. (See Chapter 7 for discussion of *pointer* variables which hold machine addresses.) The moral of all these complications is that portable C programs should never depend upon assumptions about the specific integer value of machine addresses.

```
strcpy [3-45]:
    /* strcpy - copy characters from s2 to s1
     */
    void strcpy(s1, s2)
        char s1[], s2[];

        {
        unsigned i;

        i = 0;
        while (s2[i] != '\0')
            {
            s1[i] = s2[i];
            ++i;
            }
        s1[i] = '\0';
        }
```

Question [3-46] What does the following program print? (The defined constant BUFSIZ comes from stdio.h; it is usually 512 or 1024, large enough for the largest line of input.)

```
string.c [3-47]:
    /* string - practice with character arrays
     */
    #include "local.h"
    main()
        {
        char a1[BUFSIZ];
        char a2[BUFSIZ];

        strcpy(a1, "every ");
        strcpy(a2, "good boy ");
        strcat(a2, "does ");
        if (strlen(a1) < strlen(a2))
            strcat(a2, "fine ");
        else
            strcat(a1, "very ");
        if (strcmp(a1, a2) < 0)
            {
            strcat(a1, a2);
            printf("%s\n", a1);
            }
        else
            {
            strcat(a2, a1);
            printf("%s\n", a2);
            }
        }
```

every good boy does fine

copy2.c **[3-48]**:
```
/* copy2 - copy input to output
 */
#include "local.h"
main()
    {
    char s[BUFSIZ];

    while (getln(s, BUFSIZ) != EOF)
        printf("%s", s);
    }
```

3.15   Comma Operator

revers.c **[3-49]**:
```
/* revers - print input lines reversed
 */
#include "local.h"
main()
    {
    char line[BUFSIZ];   /* the line of input text */
    short len;           /* length of line */

    while ((len = getln(line, BUFSIZ)) != EOF)
        {
        if (line[len - 1] == '\n')
            line[--len] = '\0';
        reverse(line);
        printf("%s\n", line);
        }
    }
void reverse(s)
    char s[];
    {
    char t;
    short i, j;

    for (i = 0, j = strlen(s) - 1; i < j; ++i, --j)
        t = s[i], s[i] = s[j], s[j] = t;
    }
```

3.16   Order of Evaluation

Question [3-50] Mark Y or N whether each of these statements is *vulnerable* to the timing of side-effects:

   Y   `n = n++;`

   Y   `printf("%d %d\n", ++n, ++n);`

   N   `n = ++m;`

   N   `n = y *= 2;`

3.17   Floating-point Computation

mortg.c [3-51]:

```
/* mortg - compute table of payments on mortgage
 */
#include "local.h"
#include <math.h>
main()
    {
    double intmo;    /* monthly interest */
    double intyr;    /* annual interest */
    double bal;      /* balance remaining */
    double pmt;      /* monthly payment */
    double prinpmt;  /* payment allocated to principal */
    double intpmt;   /* payment allocated to interest */
    double dnpmts;   /* number of payments, in double */
    short i;         /* loop index */
    short npmts;     /* number of payments */
    short nyears;    /* number of years */

    printf("Enter principal (e.g. 82500.00): ");
    scanf("%lf", &bal);
    printf("Enter annual interest rate (e.g. 16.25): ");
    scanf("%lf", &intyr);
    printf("Enter number of years: ");
    scanf("%hd", &nyears);
    printf("\nprincipal=%.2f  interest=%.4f%%  years=%d\n\n",
        bal, intyr, nyears);
    intyr /= 100.;
    intmo = intyr / 12.;
    npmts = nyears * 12;
    dnpmts = npmts;
    pmt = bal * (intmo / (1. - pow(1. + intmo, -dnpmts)));
    printf("%8s %10s %10s %10s %10s\n",
        "payment", "total", "interest", "principal", "balance");
    printf("%8s %10s %10s %10s\n",
        "number", "payment", "payment", "payment" );
    printf("%8s %10s %10s %10s %10.2f\n",
        "", "", "", "", bal);
    for (i = 1; i <= npmts; ++i)
        {
        intpmt = bal * intmo;
        if (i < npmts)
            prinpmt = pmt - intpmt;
        else
            prinpmt = bal;
        bal -= prinpmt;
        printf("%8d %10.2f %10.2f %10.2f %10.2f\n",
            i, intpmt + prinpmt, intpmt, prinpmt, bal);
        }
    }
```

[3-52 cc] *The math library flag* -lm: On some systems this flag is not needed because the math library is scanned by a normal compilation.

Question [3-53] Revise the mortg.c program to make it correct to the penny. (Hint: forget the decimal points and use long arithmetic.)

```
mortg2.c:
    /* mortg2 - compute table of payments on mortgage
     */
    #include "local.h"
    #include <math.h>
    #define ROUNDING .5 /* on machines that do rounding, make it 0 */
    main()
        {
        double dbal;    /* balance, in double - dollars */
        double dnpmts;  /* number of payments, in double */
        double intmo;   /* monthly interest */
        double intyr;   /* annual interest */
        long bal;       /* balance remaining - pennies */
        long pmt;       /* monthly payment - pennies */
        long prinpmt;   /* payment allocated to principal - pennies */
        long intpmt;    /* payment allocated to interest - pennies */
        short i;        /* loop index */
        short npmts;    /* number of payments */
        short nyears;   /* number of years */

        printf("Enter principal (e.g. 82500.00): ");
        scanf("%lf", &dbal);
        bal = 100. * dbal;
        printf("Enter annual interest rate (e.g. 16.25): ");
        scanf("%lf", &intyr);
        printf("Enter number of years: ");
        scanf("%hd", &nyears);
        printf("\nprincipal=%10.2f", dbal);
        printf("  interest=%.4f%%  years=%d\n\n", intyr, nyears);
        intyr /= 100.;
        intmo = intyr / 12.;
        npmts = nyears * 12;
        dnpmts = npmts;
        pmt = ROUNDING + bal * (intmo / (1. - pow(1. + intmo, -dnpmts)));
        printf("%8s %10s %10s %10s %10s\n",
            "payment", "total", "interest", "principal", "balance");
        printf("%8s %10s %10s %10s\n",
            "number", "payment", "payment", "payment");
        printf("%8s %10s %10s %10s %10ld\n",
            "", "", "", "", bal);
        for (i = 1; i <= npmts; ++i)
            {
            intpmt = ROUNDING + bal * intmo;
            if (i < npmts)
                prinpmt = pmt - intpmt;
            else
                prinpmt = bal;
            bal -= prinpmt;
            printf("%8d %10ld %10ld %10ld %10ld\n",
                i, intpmt + prinpmt, intpmt, prinpmt, bal);
            }
        }
```

Sample execution of `mortg2.c`:

```
Enter principal (e.g. 82500.00): 10000.00
Enter annual interest rate (e.g. 16.25): 18.00
Enter number of years:  1

principal= 10000.00  interest=18.0000%  years=1
```

payment number	total payment	interest payment	principal payment	balance
				1000000
1	91680	15000	76680	923320
2	91680	13850	77830	845490
3	91680	12682	78998	766492
4	91680	11497	80183	686309
5	91680	10295	81385	604924
6	91680	9074	82606	522318
7	91680	7835	83845	438473
8	91680	6577	85103	353370
9	91680	5301	86379	266991
10	91680	4005	87675	179316
11	91680	2690	88990	90326
12	91681	1355	90326	0

3.18   Precedence and Associativity

Question [3-54] Parenthesize to show the binding:

```
(a   ==   b)   &&   (c   !=   d)

y   =   (3.14   *   (-   d))
```

3.19   Conversion

[3-55 cc] *The data types in the conversion table:* Not all compilers support all these types. In particular, `unsigned char`, `unsigned short`, and `unsigned long` are not defined in Kernighan and Ritchie [1978].

[3-56 cc] *The cast operator:* The UNIX Version 6 compiler does not have the cast operator. Some other compilers will not cast into types smaller than the machine's preferred types.

3.20   Overflow

[**3-57 mach**] *Overflow:*   There is unfortunately no universal standard regarding C language's treatment of overflow.

3.21   Defined Types and Defined Constants

```
bits.c [3-58]:
    /* bits - examples of bitwise operations
     */
    #include "local.h"
    main()
        {
        bits b1, b2;

        b1 = 0xF0F0 & 0x1234;
        b2 = b1 | 0x60;
        printf("b1=0x%04x, b2=0x%04x\n", b1, b2);
        b1 = ~1 & 0307;
        b2 = (bits)b1 >> 2;
        printf("b1=0%03o, b2=0%03o\n", b1, b2);
        b1 = 0xF001 | 0x8801;
        b2 = b1 & 0xB800;
        printf("b1=0x%04x, b2=0x%04x\n", b1, b2);
        }
```

Question [3-59] What does bits.c print?

```
b1=0x1030, b2=0x1070
b1=0306, b2=0061
b1=0xf801, b2=0xb800
```

```
local.h:
    /* local.h - definitions for use with
     *         Learning to Program in C
     */
    #ifndef FAIL
    #include <stdio.h>
    #define FAIL        1
    #define FOREVER     for (;;)
    #define NO          0
    #define STDERR      2
    #define STDIN       0
    #define STDOUT      1
    #define SUCCEED     0
    #define YES         1
    #define bits        ushort
    #define bool        int
    #define metachar    short
    #define tbool       char
    #define ushort      unsigned  /* use unsigned short, if you can */
    #define void        int
    #define getln(s, n) ((fgets(s, n, stdin)==NULL) ? EOF : strlen(s))
    #define ABS(x)      (((x) < 0) ? -(x) : (x))
    #define MAX(x, y)   (((x) < (y)) ? (y) : (x))
    #define MIN(x, y)   (((x) < (y)) ? (x) : (y))
    #endif
```

3.22   More about Input/Output

[3-60 os] *Standard files:* The scheme for these standard files originated on UNIX, but it has been transported to many other systems.

[3-61 os] *Redirection symbols:* These are available on most systems that support the standard files, but on some non-UNIX systems there can be no space between the redirection symbol and the file name.

[3-62 os] *Standard file descriptor numbers:* On most systems, these are the same values (0, 1, and 2) as they are on UNIX, but if they are different on your system, change the file local.h to appropriate values.

[3-63 cc] *The function* remark: On some systems this is provided as part of the standard library. If so, use the library version and do not include error in your compilation.

remark **[3-64]**:
```
/* remark - print non-fatal error message
 */
#include "local.h"
void remark(s1, s2)
    char s1[], s2[];
    {
    write(STDERR, s1, strlen(s1));
    write(STDERR, " ", 1);
    write(STDERR, s2, strlen(s2));
    write(STDERR, "\n", 1);
    }
```

[3-65 os] *Status codes returned to the operating system:* Some simple systems such as CP/M do not have any mechanism for receiving status codes from programs. We would still suggest that you include status codes in your programs if you are concerned with portability to other systems.

[3-66 cc] *The function* error: This also may be already available in your library.

error **[3-67]**:
```
/* error - print fatal error message
 */
#include "local.h"
void error(s1, s2)
    char s1[], s2[];
    {
    write(STDERR, s1, strlen(s1));
    write(STDERR, " ", 1);
    write(STDERR, s2, strlen(s2));
    write(STDERR, "\n", 1);
    exit(FAIL);
    }
```

copy3.c **[3-68]**:

```
/* copy3 - most efficient file copy
 */
#include "local.h"
main()
    {
    char s[BUFSIZ]; /* array for characters */
    short i;        /* number of characters read */

    while (0 != (i = read(STDIN, s, BUFSIZ)))
        {
        if (i < 0)
            error("I/O error on read\n", "");
        else if (i != write(STDOUT, s, i))
            error("I/O error on write\n", "");
        }
    exit(SUCCEED);
    }
/* error - print fatal error message
 */
void error(s1, s2)
    char s1[], s2[];
    {
    write(STDERR, s1, strlen(s1));
    write(STDERR, " ", 1);
    write(STDERR, s2, strlen(s2));
    write(STDERR, "\n", 1);
    exit(FAIL);
    }
```

3.23 Timing a Program

[3-69 os] *Timing a program:* If your system has no `time` command, consult your vendor for possible equivalents.

APPENDIX B.4: STATEMENTS AND CONTROL FLOW

4.1   Statements and Blocks

```
hello.c [4-1]:
    main()
        {
        write(1, "hello, world\n", 13);
        }
```

4.2   If

Question [4-2] Which of these are legal `if` statements according to the syntax descriptions? Which are correct according to the readability format?

	LEGAL?	READABLE?
`if (x < 0)` `    y = x;`	Y	Y
`if (n) ;`	Y	N
`if(c == EOF)` `    done = YES;`	Y	N

4.3   If-else

Question [4-3] What does this `if` statement print, for each value of n:

```
if (n < 5)
    {
    if (n % 2 == 1)
        printf("A\n");
    else
        printf("B\n");
    }
else
    {
    if (n % 2 == 1)
        printf("C\n");
    else
        printf("D\n");
    }
```

```
n = 1    A
n = 2    B
n = 3    A
n = 4    B
n = 5    C
n = 6    D
n = 7    C
```

4.4 Else-If

guess.c [4-4]:

```
/* guess - guess a hidden number between 1 and 15, in 3 guesses
 */
#include "local.h"
main()
    {
    char line[BUFSIZ];    /* input line */
    tbool found;          /* have I found it? */
    short n;              /* how many guesses left */
    short range;          /* how much to ajust next guess */
    short try;            /* next number to try */
    metachar reply;       /* the user's reply */

    found = NO;
    n = 3;
    range = 4;
    try = 8;
    printf("Each time I guess, please answer\n");
    printf(" H if I'm high\n L if I'm low\n E if I guessed it\n");
    while (n > 0 && !found)
        {
        printf("I guess %d\n", try);
        if (getln(line, BUFSIZ) == EOF)
            error("Bye!", "");
        reply = line[0];
        if (reply == 'H' || reply == 'h')
            {
            try -= range;
            range /= 2;
            --n;
            }
        else if (reply == 'L' || reply == 'l')
            {
            try += range;
            range /= 2;
            --n;
            }
        else if (reply == 'E' || reply == 'e')
            found = YES;
        else
            printf("Please type H, L, or E\n");
        }
    printf("Your number is %d\nThanks for the game\n", try);
    exit(SUCCEED);
    }
```

Question [4-5] If the guesser had four tries, how big a range could it handle? *31* Five tries? *63*

4.5   Switch

4.6   While

```
copy.c [4-6]:
    /* copy - copy input to output
     */
    #include "local.h"
    main()
        {
        metachar c;

        while ((c = getchar()) != EOF)
            putchar(c);
        exit(SUCCEED);
        }
```


4.7   For

```
strscn [4-7]:
    /* strscn - return the index of c in string s
     */
    unsigned strscn(s, c)
        char s[];    /* string to be scanned */
        char c;      /* char to be matched */
        {
        unsigned i;

        for (i = 0; s[i] != c && s[i] != '\0'; ++i)
            ;
        return (i);
        }
```


4.8   Do While

4.9   Design of Control Structures

4.10   Break and Continue

4.11   Goto

APPENDIX B.5: FUNCTIONS

5.1 Syntax and Readability

pow **[5-1]**:
```
/* pow - return (positive) x to the power y
 */
double pow(x, y)
    double x;    /* base */
    double y;    /* exponent */
    {
    double exp();    /* exponential function */
    double log();    /* natural log function */

    return (exp(log(x) * y));
    }
```

[5-2 cc] *The* void *type:* If your compiler does support this type, you should remove it from your local.h include-file.

[5-3 cc] *Precise declarations of function returned values:* Some compilers will translate the declaration of returned type into one of the preferred sizes of C. This has sometimes been a minor problem for inter-vendor portability.

[5-4 cc] *Promotion of* float *parameter declarations:* The compilers mentioned above also widen the integer-type parameter declarations to int size.

Question [5-5] What is the type of each expression:

The type of log(x)	*is*	double
The type of log	*is*	double ()
The type of exp	*is*	double ()
The type of exp(log(y) * y)	*is*	double

5.2   Argument Passing

```
powdem.c [5-6]:
    /* powdem - demonstrate power function
     */
    #include "local.h"
    #include <math.h>
    main()
        {
        short i;

        for (i = 0; i < 10; ++i)
            printf("2 to the power %d equals %.0f\n",
                i, pow(2., (double)i));
        exit(SUCCEED);
        }
    /* pow - return (positive) x to the power y
     */
    double pow(x, y)
        double x;    /* base */
        double y;    /* exponent */
        {
        return (exp(log(x) * y));
        }
```

[5-7 cc] *The machine's mechanism for "frame" indication:* The details of argument passing are generally of interest only to programmers who interface C programs with assembler code, but the majority of existing compilers use this scheme: The calling function pushes arguments into the machine's stack and executes a "subroutine call" instruction, which pushes a return location into the stack. The called function receives the machine's stack pointer pointing to a fixed offset from the first parameter. This value of the stack pointer is saved in a register dedicated to the "frame pointer," which all the subsequent code uses to get access to variables in the frame. A portion of the frame may be dedicated to saved registers, and another portion may contain automatic variables. On return, the called function undoes the stack manipulations that it did, and the calling function undoes what it did. Again, a cautionary note: details vary across machines and compilers.

[5-8 cc] *The math library:* On some systems, the math library does not need to be specified separately.

5.3   Parameters and Automatic Variables

```
lpow [5-9]:
    /* lpow - power function (for long data)
    */
    long lpow(lnum, n)
        long lnum;          /* base */
        long n;             /* exponent */
        {
        long p;        /* local ("auto") result */

        p = 1;
        for ( ; n > 0; --n)
            p *= lnum;
        return (p);
        }
```

[5-10 cc] [5-11 mach] *The picture of stack frames:*

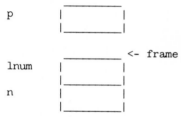

The "empty space" between the local variable and the parameters is meant only to imply that the "frame" may not be contiguous storage. On many machines, the frame is one contiguous region of storage with space in the middle for various bookkeeping details. On other machines, the "frame" may actually be two different regions of memory, one for local variables and one for parameters.

[5-12 cc] *The* lint *command:* You will need to inquire if a lint command is available with your compiler.

badpow.c **[5-13]**:
```
/* badpow - demonstrate power function (argument mismatch error)
 */
#include "local.h"
#include <math.h>
main()
    {
    short i;

    for (i = 0; i < 10; ++i)
        printf("2 to the power %d equals %.0f\n",
            i, pow(2, i));
    exit(SUCCEED);
    }
```

5.4   Array Arguments

strlen **[5-14]**:
```
/* strlen - return length of string s
 */
unsigned strlen(s)
    char s[];
    {
    unsigned i;

    for (i = 0; s[i] != '\0'; ++i)
        ;
    return (i);
    }
```

strncpy **[5-15]**:
```
/* strncpy - copy n bytes from s2 to s1 (using while)
 */
void strncpy(s1, s2, n)
    char s1[], s2[];
    unsigned n;
    {
    unsigned i;

    i = 0;
    while (i < n && s2[i] != '\0')
        {
        s1[i] = s2[i];
        ++i;
        }
    while (i < n)
        {
        s1[i] = '\0';
        ++i;
        }
    }
```

Question [5-16] Assume the following machine state just before calling

```
strncpy(save, line, 4)
```

```
VARIABLE   ADDRESS    STORAGE

line        800       |  97 |  98 |  99 |   0 |
                      |_'a'_|_'b'_|_'c'_|_'\0'_|


save       1800       | 119 | 120 | 121 | 118 |
                      |_'x'_|_'y'_|_'z'_|_'w'_|
```

What does the parameter storage look like when **strncpy** is entered?

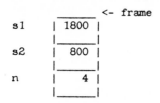

```
         _____  <- frame
 s1    | 1800 |
       |_____|
 s2    |  800 |
       |_____|
  n    |    4 |
       |_____|
```

Question [5-17] At what address is s1[0] located? *1800*

Question [5-18] At what address is s2[3] located? *803*

Question [5-19] What does the storage of **save** look like when **strncpy** returns?

```
save       1800       |  97 |  98 |  99 |   0 |
                      |_'a'_|_'b'_|_'c'_|_'\0'_|
```

[5-20 cc] *The prohibition of address-of on array names:* There has been some controversy in the literature about this point of syntax; see Plauger [1979]. The compilers from Whitesmiths, Ltd., allow the & address-of operator on array names.

dmpdem.c **[5-21]**:

```
/* dump - print memory bytes
 *        (Warning - some usages may be non-portable)
 */
#include "local.h"
#define LINESIZE 16
#define BYTEMASK 0xFF
void dump(s, n)
    char s[];        /* byte address to be dumped */
    unsigned n;      /* number of bytes to dump */
    {
    unsigned i;      /* byte counter */

    for (i = 0; i < n; ++i)
        {
        if (i % LINESIZE == 0)
            printf("\n%08x: ", &s[i]);
        printf(" %02x", s[i] & BYTEMASK);
        }
    printf("\n");
    }
/* dmpdem - demonstrate dump function
 */
main()
    {
    char msg[16];
    double d = 100.;

    strncpy(msg, "testing 1 2 3\n", sizeof(msg));

    /* case 1 - quite proper */
    dump(msg, sizeof(msg));

    /* case 2 - ok, but output will vary with machine */
    dump(&d, sizeof(d));

    /* case 3 - non-portable, may cause hardware error */
    dump(0x40, 4);
    exit(SUCCEED);
    }
```

5.5   Recursive Functions

```
fact.c [5-22]:
    /* factl - return n! (n factorial)
     */
    #include "local.h"
    long factl(n)
        long n;
        {
        if (n <= 1)
            return (1);
        else
            return (n * factl(n - 1));
        }
    /* fact - demonstrate factl function
     */
    main()
        {
        long factl();
        long result;

        result = factl((long)3);
        printf("3! = %ld\n", result);
        exit(SUCCEED);
        }
```

[5-23 mach] *The assumption that* double *can hold all* long *values accurately:* This does not yet seem to be part of any formal standard for C, but you can take it from us as a practical guarantee for two reasons: First, it is true in all compilers known to us. Second, the widening rules of the language would make no sense if it were not true.

5.6   Initializing Automatic Scalars

```
inits.c [5-24]:
    /* inits - initialization examples
     */
    #include "local.h"
    main()
        {
        char c = 'x';
        short i = 1;
        short j = i * 2;

        printf("%d %d %c\n", i, j, c);
        exit(SUCCEED);
        }
```

Question [5-25] What does inits print?

> *1 2 x*

recpt1.c **[5-26]**:

```
/* recpt1 - receipt example #1
 */
#include "local.h"
main()
    {
    short receip();

    printf("First = %d\n", receip());
    printf("Second = %d\n", receip());
    exit(SUCCEED);
    }
short receip()
    {
    short number = 1;

    return (number++);
    }
```

Question [5-27] What does recpt1 print?

> *First = 1*
> *Second = 1*

5.7   Storage Class and Internal Static

[5-28 mach]:   *The picture of program segments:*   In some environments, the relative location of the segments is different.   Also, in UNIX environments, the program storage on the disk (as reported by the `size` command) breaks the *text* segment into two storage areas, one called "text" (for the data with non-zero initializers) and a special one called "bss" (for the data initialized to all zeroes).

stack1.c **[5-29]**:

```
/* stack1 - stack example 1
 */
#include "local.h"
main()
    {
    f1(1);
    }
f1(n)
    short n;
    {
    f2(n + 1);
    }
f2(n)
    short n;
    {
    printf("%d\n", n);
    }
```

recpt2.c **[5-30]**:

```
/* recpt2 - print two receipt numbers
 */
#include "local.h"
main()
    {
    short receip();

    printf("First = %d\n", receip());
    printf("Second = %d\n", receip());
    exit(SUCCEED);
    }
short receip()
    {
    static short number = 1;

    return (number++);
    }
```

Question [5-31] What is the output of recpt2?

  First = 1
  Second = 2

[5-32 mach] *Shorter code on microprocessor from* static: Check with your compiler vendor for details.

5.8   Separate Compilation and Linkage

[5-33 cc] *Assembler code:* Some non-UNIX compilers skip the generation of assembler code and produce object code directly.

[5-34 cc] *The flag* -c *for "compile-only":* On a non-UNIX system, you
may need a different flag for the compiler.

```
recpt3.c [5-35]:
    /* recpt3 - print two receipt numbers
     */
    #include "local.h"
    main()
        {
        short receip();

        printf("First = %d\n", receip());
        printf("Second = %d\n", receip());
        }
```

```
receip [5-36]:
    /* receip - deliver a unique receipt number
     */
    #include "local.h"
    short receip()
        {
        static short number = 1;

        return (number++);
        }
```

[5-37 os] *The suffix* .o *for object files:* In a non-UNIX environment,
you may have a different suffix such as .OBJ or .REL.

[5-38 cc] *The compile command knows what to do from the file suffix:*
On some non-UNIX systems, you may have to tell the compiler more explicitly
whether the files are to be compiled or linked.

5.9   External Static Storage

rand **[5-39]**:
```
/* rand, srand - generate random numbers
 */
#include "local.h"
static long rnum = 0;
void srand(n)
    short n;
    {
    rnum = (long)n;
    }
short rand()
    {
    rnum = rnum * 0x41C64E6D + 0x3039;
    return ((short)(rnum >> 16) & 0x7FFF);
    }
```

nfrom.c **[5-40]**:
```
/* nfrom - return a number between low and high, inclusive
 */
#include "local.h"
short nfrom(low, high)
    register short low, high;
    {
    short rand();
    register short nb = high - low + 1;

    return (rand() % nb + low);
    }
```

Question [5-41] Suppose a program were to call

    nfrom(1, 10)

and rand() were to return 1003. What would nfrom return? *4*

Question [5-42] Suppose a program were to call

    nfrom(1, 6)

and rand() were to return 3605. What would nfrom return? *6*

shuf52.c **[5-43]**:

```
/* shuf52 - shuffle a deck of 52 cards and print result
 */
#include "local.h"
#define NCARDS 52
main()
    {
    short cards[NCARDS];
    short i;

    for (i = 0; i < NCARDS; ++i)
        cards[i] = i;
    shuffl(cards);
    for (i = 0; i < NCARDS; ++i)
        {
        printf("%2d ", cards[i]);
        if (i % 13 == 12)
            putchar('\n');
        }
    putchar('\n');
    }
/* shuffl - permute the cards
 */
void shuffl(deck)
    short deck[];
    {
    short t;          /* temporary for swap */
    short i;          /* index for loop over cards */
    short j;          /* index for swap */
    short nfrom();    /* fn to produce random no. */

    for (i = 0; i < NCARDS - 1; ++i)
        {
        j = nfrom(i, NCARDS - 1);
        t = deck[j], deck[j] = deck[i], deck[i] = t;
        }
    }
```

[5-44 os] *Making a library:* The same capability is available under many different names on systems other than UNIX. Consult your vendor for details.

5.10   Initializing Arrays in Static Storage

Question [5-45] What are the initial values?

```
static char st[5] = "std";
```
```
| 115 | 116 | 100 |  0  |  0  |
| 's' | 't' | 'd' |'\0' |'\0' |
```

```
static char s[2] = "ab";
```
```
|     |     |   (ERROR - WILL NOT COMPILE)
|_____|_____|
```

```
static short a[5] = {1, 2, 3};
```
```
|  1  |  2  |  3  |  0  |  0  |
|_____|_____|_____|_____|_____|
```

```
static short b[] = {1, 3, 5, 7,};
```
```
|  1  |  3  |  5  |  7  |
|_____|_____|_____|_____|
```

5.11   Two-dimensional Arrays

prsam.c **[5-46]**:

```
/* prsam - print sampler
 */
#include "local.h"
#define NROWS 35
#define NCOLUMNS 60
main()
    {
    static char sampler[NROWS][NCOLUMNS + 1] =
        {
        "LOVELOVE ... LOVELOVE",
            /* et cetera, with the rest of the array */
        };
    short i;             /* row index for sampler */
    short j;             /* column index for sampler */
    short len;           /* length of s */
    char s[BUFSIZ];      /* user's message */

    printf("Enter a string:");
    if ((len = getln(s, BUFSIZ)) == EOF)
        error("Bye!", "");
    printf("\n");
    s[--len] = '\0';
    if (NCOLUMNS < len)
        len = NCOLUMNS;
    for (i = 0; i < NROWS; ++i)
        {
        for (j = 0; j < NCOLUMNS; ++j)
            if (sampler[i][j] != ' ')
                sampler[i][j] = s[j % len];
        printf("%s\n", sampler[i]);
        }
    }
```

pegs.c **[5-47]**:

```
/* pegs.c - three functions (push, pop, dumppg) for Towers of Hanoi
 */
#include "local.h"
#include "pegs.h"
static short pegs[3][NDISKS] = 0;
static short ndisks[3] = 0;
/* push - put disk onto peg
 */
void push(peg, disk)
    short peg;    /* which peg: 0, 1, ... */
    short disk;   /* which disk: 1, 2, ... */
    {
    if (peg < 0 || 3 <= peg)
        {
        printf("Cannot push onto peg %d\n", peg);
        exit(FAIL);
        }
    else
        pegs[peg][ndisks[peg]++] = disk;
    }
/* pop - remove disk from peg
 */
short pop(peg)
    short peg;
    {
    if (peg < 0 || 3 <= peg)
        {
        printf("Cannot pop peg %d\n", peg);
        exit(FAIL);
        }
    else if (ndisks[peg] < 1)
        {
        printf("Cannot pop peg %d (it has %d disks)\n",
            peg, ndisks[peg]);
        exit(FAIL);
        }
    else
        return (pegs[peg][--ndisks[peg]]);
    }
/* dumppg - print status of disks and pegs
 */
void dumppg()
    {
    short i; /* index over pegs */
    short j; /* index over disks */

    for (i = 0; i < 3; ++i)
        {
        printf("Peg %d:", i);
        for (j = 0; j < ndisks[i]; ++j)
            printf(" %d", pegs[i][j]);
        printf("\n");
        }
    }
```

```
pegs.h [5-48]:
    /* pegs.h - interface for pegs package
     */
    #define NDISKS 5
    extern void push();
    extern short pop();
    extern void dumppg();
```

5.12   External Variables

5.13   Register Storage Class

[5-49 cc] [5-50 mach] *The number of* register *variables:* Some machines have more than three; some have less; and some compilers allocate the registers as they think best and ignore register declarations.

```
fast.c [5-51]:
    /* fast - count to one million
     */
    #include "local.h"
    main()
        {
        register short units;
        register short thous;

        thous = 0;
        while (++thous <= 1000)
            {
            units = 0;
            while (++units <= 1000)
                ;
            }
        }
```

```
slow.c [5-52]:
    /* slow - count to one million
     */
    #include "local.h"
    main()
        {
        short units;
        short thous;

        thous = 0;
        while (++thous <= 1000)
            {
            units = 0;
            while (++units <= 1000)
                ;
            }
        }
```

[5-53 cc] *The two-for-one improvement with* register *variables:* The improvement factor is remarkably constant over a half-dozen different machine tests that we have made, but obviously each machine and compiler will give a different result.

[5-54 cc] *Handling of* register *variables on microprocessors:* Consult with your compiler supplier if this applies to you.

5.14   Scope Rules

```
x.c:
    #include "local.h"
    short a = 2;
    static short b = 3;
    main()
        {
        short c = a + b;

        xsub(c);
        }
    xsub(d)
        short d;
        {
        short e = 7 * d;

        ysub(e);
        }
```

```
ysub.c:
    #include "local.h"
    ysub(f)
        short f;
        {
        extern short a;

        printf("%d\n", a + f);
        }
```

Question [5-55] What does the program **x** print?

37

5.15   Summary of Initialization

Question [5-56] In this incorrect sample program, which lines have illegal initializers?

```
         /* noinit - some illegal initializers
          */
         #include "local.h"
         short a = 0;
BAD      short b = a + 1;
         short c[5] = {4, 3, 2, 1};
         main()
             {
             short d = a + 2;
BAD          short e[3] = {1, 2, 3};
BAD          static short f = d + 1;
BAD          static short g[2] = {4, 5, 6};

             printf("initializers\n");
             }
```

5.16   Empty Brackets: Three Cases

5.17   Macros with Parameters

5.18   Conditional Compilation

[5-57 cc] *Re-defining a preprocessor symbol:* Some compilers do allow
re-definition of a symbol, but the program thus becomes non-portable to other
compilers. However, the preprocessor can be caused to forget a previous
definition via #undef:

```
#undef FAIL
```

will remove the previous definition of the symbol FAIL.

```
factl.c [5-58]:
    /* factl - return n! (n factorial)
     */
    #include "local.h"
    long factl(n)
        long n;
        {
        if (n <= 1)
            return (1);
        else
            return (n * factl(n - 1));
        }
    #ifdef TRYMAIN
    main()
        {
        long factl();

        if (factl((long)3) != (long)6)
            error("failed 3", "");
        if (factl((long)13) != 1932053504)
            error("failed 13", "");
        exit(SUCCEED);
        }
    #endif
```

[5-59 cc] *Command-line specification of preprocessor definitions:* Some
compilers have other methods for defining these symbols; check with your vendor.

APPENDIX B.6: SOFTWARE DEVELOPMENT

6.1   The Software Development Life Cycle

6.2   Analysis

[6-1 os] *Choices of operating system:* The original popular Blackjack program in our office was /usr/games/bj from the UNIX operating system. The program that we will present here will run on more than a dozen systems, with only one environmental dependency in setting a random seed.

6.3   Design

Question [6-2] Write the program outline of this revised syntax.

> *for each hand*
> > *if (deck is low on cards)*
> > > *shuffle cards*
> >
> > *deal the cards*
> > *if (dealer shows Ace)*
> > > *offer insurance*
> >
> > *while (player can hit and asks for hit)*
> > > *hit player*
> >
> > *while (dealer can hit)*
> > > *hit dealer*
> >
> > *score the outcome*

Question [6-3] Using this syntactic approach, it is fairly easy to modify the design to accommodate multiple players. Do so.

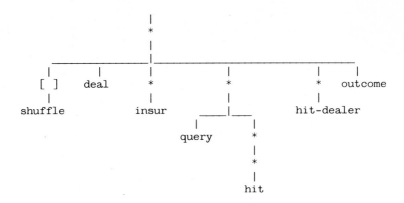

> *for each hand*
>   *if (deck is low on cards)*
>   *shuffle cards*
>   *deal the cards*
>   *if (dealer shows Ace)*
>   *offer insurance*
>   *for each player*
>   *query — split pair, double down?*
>   *for each hand of player*
>   *while (player can hit and asks for hit)*
>   *hit player*
>   *while (dealer can hit)*
>   *hit dealer*
>   *score the outcome*

[6-4 os] *Making a directory:* Some systems have directories, some do not. On some small personal computers, the equivalent concept is a separate diskette devoted to the `bj` project.

Question [6-5] Write a more detailed outline for the main program, `bj.c`. Note any new functions that you discover in the process, and note all data that the top-level program needs to administer. Hand-simulate some simple cases for each function to determine if it has the information it needs. Do not include any miscellaneous `printf` calls that may be needed, but consider whether new functions are needed for printing results.

```
bj/bj.c (partial):
    main()
        {
        CASH action;     /* how much money has crossed the table */
        CASH bet;        /* amount of player's current bet per hand */
        CASH result;     /* net result of this hand, plus or minus */
        CASH standing;   /* how much has player won or lost */
        bool canhit;     /* can player's hand take hit? */
        bool isdbl;      /* did player take DBLDN? */
        bool isinsur;    /* did player take insurance? */
        short hand;      /* current hand number */
        short reply;     /* player's reply to DBLDN, SPLIT */
        short tophand;   /* how many hands is player playing, 1 or 2 */

        Print welcoming messages
        action = standing = 0;
        opndek();
        while ((bet = getbet()) != 0)
            {
            tophand = 1;
            isinsur = isdbl = NO;
            if (deklow())
                shuffl();
            deal();
            if (val(DEALER, 0) == 11)
                isinsur = takes insurance;
            reply = query();
            if (reply == SPLIT)
                tophand = split();
            else if (reply == DBLDN)
                give one hit and double the bet
            for (hand = 1; hand <= tophand; ++hand)
                {
                determine canhit
                while (canhit && takes hit)
                    canhit = hit(hand);
                if (21 < score(hand))
                    printf("Bust\n");
                }
            if (!allbst())
                while (score(DEALER) < 17)
                    hit(DEALER);
            result = outcom(bet, tophand, isinsur, isdbl);
            score and announce standing
            }
        }
```

6.4   Implementation: Writing the Programs

The following pages present the source files of our `bj` program, in the printout format of a UNIX or Idris system. For convenience, line numbers appear at the left of each line.

Fri Jan 14 20:22:12 1983 bj/bj.h Page 1


```
 1   /* bj.h - include-file for blackjack
 2    */
 3
 4   /* defined types
 5    */
 6   #define CASH long    /* dollars */
 7
 8   /* defined constants
 9    */
10   #define DEALER 0        /* which hand is dealer; not modifiable */
11   #define NONE 0          /* no reply */
12   #define DBLDN 1         /* reply: double down */
13   #define SPLIT 2         /* reply: split pair */
14   #define INSUR 3         /* takes: insurance */
15   #define HIT   4         /* takes: hit */
16   #define CASHIN "%ld"    /* input format for CASH data */
17   #define CASHOUT "%ld"   /* output format for CASH data */
```


Fri Jan 14 20:22:14 1983 bj/dekmgr.h Page 1


```
 1   /* dekmgr.h - interface for deck manager
 2    */
 3   bool deklow();
 4   void opndek();
 5   void shuffl();
 6   short tkcard();
```

Fri Jan 14 20:22:20 1983 bj/hndmgr.h   Page 1

```
 1    /* hndmgr.h - interface for hand manager
 2     */
 3    bool allbst();
 4    void deal();
 5    bool hit();
 6    bool isbj();
 7    CASH outcom();
 8    short score();
 9    void show();
10    short split();
11    short val();
```

Sat Jan 15 13:52:33 1983 bj/local.h   Page 1

```
 1    /* local.h - definitions for use with
 2     *        Learning to Program in C
 3     */
 4    #ifndef FAIL
 5    #include <stdio.h>
 6    #define FAIL        1
 7    #define FOREVER     for (;;)
 8    #define NO          0
 9    #define STDERR      2
10    #define STDIN       0
11    #define STDOUT      1
12    #define SUCCEED     0
13    #define YES         1
14    #define bits        ushort
15    #define bool        int
16    #define metachar    short
17    #define tbool       char
18    #define ushort      unsigned  /* use unsigned short, if you can */
19    #define void        int
20    #define getln(s, n) ((fgets(s, n, stdin)==NULL) ? EOF : strlen(s))
21    #define ABS(x)      (((x) < 0) ? -(x) : (x))
22    #define MAX(x, y)   (((x) < (y)) ? (y) : (x))
23    #define MIN(x, y)   (((x) < (y)) ? (x) : (y))
24    #endif
```

Fri Jan 14 20:22:37 1983 bj/ttymgr.h   Page 1

```
 1    /* ttymgr.h - interface for tty manager
 2     */
 3    CASH getbet();
 4    bool takes();
 5    short query();
```

Sat Jan 15 13:40:23 1983 bj/bj.c Page 1

```
 1   /* bj - blackjack
 2    *        Permission is hereby granted to reproduce and use bj
 3    */
 4   #include "local.h"
 5   #include "bj.h"
 6   #include "dekmgr.h"
 7   #include "hndmgr.h"
 8   #include "ttymgr.h"
 9   main()
10       {
11       CASH action;      /* how much money has crossed the table */
12       CASH bet;         /* amount of player's current bet per hand */
13       CASH result;      /* net result of this hand, plus or minus */
14       CASH standing;    /* how much has player won or lost */
15       bool canhit;      /* can player's hand take hit? */
16       bool isdbl;       /* did player take DBLDN? */
17       bool isinsur;     /* did player take insurance? */
18       short hand;       /* current hand number */
19       short reply;      /* player's reply to DBLDN, SPLIT */
20       short tophand;    /* how many hands is player playing, 1 or 2 */
21
22       printf("Copyright (c) Plum Hall Inc, 1983\n");
23       /* permission to copy and modify is granted, provided that
24        * this printout and comment remain intact
25        */
26       printf("\nWelcome to the Blackjack table\n");
27       action = standing = 0;
28       opndek();
29       while ((bet = getbet()) != 0)
30           {
31           tophand = 1;
32           isinsur = isdbl = NO;
33           if (deklow())
34               shuffl();
35           deal();
36           if (val(DEALER, 0) == 11)
37               isinsur = takes("i");
38           reply = query();
39           if (reply == SPLIT)
40               tophand = split();
41           else if (reply == DBLDN)
42               {
43               hit(1);
44               printf("\n");
45               isdbl = YES;
46               bet *= 2;
47               }
48           for (hand = 1; hand <= tophand; ++hand)
49               {
50               if (tophand == 2)
```

Sat Jan 15 13:40:23 1983 bj/bj.c Page 2

```
51                    printf("Hand %d:\n", hand);
52               canhit = !isdbl;
53               canhit &= !isbj(1);
54               canhit &= (reply != SPLIT || val(1, 0) != 11);
55               while (canhit && takes("h"))
56                    {
57                    canhit = hit(hand);
58                    printf("\n");
59                    }
60               if (21 < score(hand))
61                    printf("Bust\n");
62               }
63          printf("Dealer has ");
64          show(DEALER, 0);
65          printf(" + ");
66          show(DEALER, 1);
67          if (!allbst())
68               while (score(DEALER) < 17)
69                    hit(DEALER);
70          printf(" = %d\n", score(DEALER));
71          result = outcom(bet, tophand, isinsur, isdbl);
72          action += ABS(result);
73          standing += result;
74          printf("action = ");
75          printf(CASHOUT, action);
76          printf(" standing = ");
77          printf(CASHOUT, standing);
78          printf("\n");
79          }
80     printf("\nThanks for the game.\n");
81     exit(SUCCEED);
82     }
```

Sat Jan 15 13:32:56 1983   bj/dekmgr.c   Page 1

```
 1   /* dekmgr - deck manager
 2    */
 3   #include "local.h"
 4   #include "bj.h"
 5   #include "dekmgr.h"
 6   #define NCARDS 4 * 52
 7   static short deck[NCARDS] = 0;   /* the deck */
 8   static short nc = 0;            /* subscript of next card */
 9   static short shufpt = 0;        /* subscript of shuffle point */
10   /* deklow - is deck at or past shuffle point?
11    */
12   bool deklow()
13       {
14       return (shufpt <= nc);
15       }
16   /* opndek - initialize the deck
17    */
18   void opndek()
19       {
20       short i;
21       short low;
22       short varnum();
23
24       for (low = 0; low < NCARDS; low += 52)
25           for (i = 0; i < 52; ++i)
26               deck[i + low] = i;
27       srand(varnum());
28       shuffl();
29       }
30   /* shuffl - shuffle the deck
31    */
32   void shuffl()
33       {
34       short t;         /* temporary for swap */
35       short i;         /* index for loop over cards */
36       short j;         /* index for swap */
37       short nfrom();   /* fn to produce random number */
38
39       for (i = 0; i < NCARDS - 1; ++i)
40           {
41           j = nfrom(i, NCARDS - 1);
42           t = deck[j], deck[j] = deck[i], deck[i] = t;
43           }
44       shufpt = nfrom(NCARDS - 52, NCARDS - 36);
45       nc = 0;
46       printf("Shuffle\n");
47       }
48
49
50
```

Sat Jan 15 13:32:56 1983 bj/dekmgr.c Page 2

```
51    /* tkcard - take a card
52     */
53    short tkcard()
54        {
55        if (NCARDS <= nc)
56            shuffl();
57        return (deck[nc++]);
58        }
59    /* varnum - return a varying startoff number
60     */
61    short varnum()
62        {
63        long time();     /* SYSTEM DEPENDENT - NEEDS CLOCK */
64
65        return ((short)time(0));
66        }
```

Fri Jan 14 20:22:16 1983 bj/error.c   Page 1

```
 1   /* error - print fatal error message
 2    */
 3   #include "local.h"
 4   void error(s1, s2)
 5       char s1[], s2[];
 6       {
 7       write(STDERR, s1, strlen(s1));
 8       write(STDERR, " ", 1);
 9       write(STDERR, s2, strlen(s2));
10       write(STDERR, "\n", 1);
11       exit(FAIL);
12       }
```

Fri Jan 14 20:22:16 1983 bj/getbet.c   Page 1

```
 1    /* getbet - get the player's bet
 2     */
 3    #include "local.h"
 4    #include "bj.h"
 5    #define MINBET 2
 6    #define MAXBET 1000
 7    CASH getbet()
 8        {
 9        char line[BUFSIZ];  /* input line */
10        short retn;         /* return from getln and sscanf */
11        CASH bet;           /* player's bet */
12
13        printf("\n\nYour bet (amount): ");
14        FOREVER
15            {
16            retn = getln(line, BUFSIZ);
17            if (retn == EOF)
18                return (0);
19            retn = sscanf(line, CASHIN, &bet);
20            if (retn != 1 || bet < MINBET || MAXBET < bet)
21                printf("Number from %d to %d please: ",
22                    MINBET, MAXBET);
23            else
24                return (bet);
25            }
26        }
```

Sat Jan 15 13:31:43 1983 bj/hndmgr.c   Page 1

```
 1   /* hndmgr - hand manager
 2    */
 3   #include "local.h"
 4   #include "bj.h"
 5   #include "hndmgr.h"
 6   #include "dekmgr.h"
 7   static char spots[13][3] =
 8       {"A", "2", "3", "4", "5", "6", "7", "8", "9",
 9       "10", "J", "Q", "K"};
10   static char suits[4][2] = {"S", "H", "D", "C"};
11   static short hands[3][12] = 0;  /* three hands */
12   static short ncards[3] = 0;      /* how many cards in each hand */
13   static short tophand = 0;        /* how many player hands active */
14   /* allbst - are all player's hands busted?
15    */
16   bool allbst()
17       {
18       if (score(1) <= 21 || (tophand == 2 && score(2) <= 21))
19           return (NO);
20       else
21           return (YES);
22       }
23   /* deal - initialize the hands
24    */
25   void deal()
26       {
27       hands[1][0] = tkcard();
28       hands[DEALER][0] = tkcard();
29       hands[1][1] = tkcard();
30       hands[DEALER][1] =tkcard();
31       ncards[DEALER] = ncards[1] = 2;
32       tophand = 1;
33       printf("The dealer shows ");
34       show(DEALER, 0);
35       printf("\nYou have ");
36       show(1, 0);
37       printf(" + ");
38       show(1, 1);
39       printf("\n");
40       }
41
42
43
44
45
46
47
48
49
50
```

Sat Jan 15 13:31:43 1983 bj/hndmgr.c   Page 2

```
51    /* hit - add a card to a hand
52     */
53    bool hit(h)
54        short h;         /* which hand */
55        {
56        hands[h][ncards[h]] = tkcard();
57        printf(" + ");
58        show(h, ncards[h]);
59        ++ncards[h];
60        if (21 < score(h) || h == DEALER && 17 <= score(h))
61            return (NO);
62        else
63            return (YES);
64        }
65    /* isbj - is hand a "natural" 2-card blackjack?
66     */
67    bool isbj(h)
68        short h;         /* which hand */
69        {
70        if (h == DEALER)
71            return (ncards[DEALER] == 2 && score(DEALER) == 21);
72        else if (h == 1)
73            return (tophand == 1 && ncards[1] == 2 && score(1) == 21)
74        else
75            return (NO);
76        }
77    /* score - tell blackjack value of hand
78     */
79    short score(h)
80        short h;         /* which hand */
81        {
82        short aces = 0; /* number of aces in hand */
83        short i;         /* card counter */
84        short sum = 0;   /* accumulated value of hand */
85
86        for (i = 0; i < ncards[h]; ++i)
87            {
88            sum += val(h, i);
89            if (val(h, i) == 11)
90                ++aces;
91            }
92        for (i = aces; 0 < i; --i)
93            if (21 < sum)
94                sum -= 10;
95        return (sum);
96        }
97
98
99
100
```

Sat Jan 15 13:31:43 1983 bj/hndmgr.c Page 3

```
101   /* show - print a card
102    */
103   void show(h, i)
104        short h;     /* which hand */
105        short i;     /* which card */
106        {
107        printf("%s", spots[hands[h][i] % 13]);
108        printf("%s", suits[hands[h][i] / 13]);
109        }
110   /* split - split the players pair if allowed
111    */
112   short split()
113        {
114        if (val(1, 0) != val(1, 1))
115            return (1);
116        hands[2][0] = hands[1][1];
117        hands[1][1] = tkcard();
118        hands[2][1] = tkcard();
119        ncards[2] = 2;
120        printf("Hand 1: "); show(1, 0); printf(" + "); show(1, 1);
121        printf("\n");
122        printf("Hand 2: "); show(2, 0); printf(" + "); show(2, 1);
123        printf("\n");
124        tophand = 2;
125        return (2);
126        }
127   /* val - tell value of card n of hand h
128    */
129   short val(h, i)
130        short h;     /* which hand */
131        short i;     /* which card */
132        {
133        short n;     /* spots value of card */
134
135        n = (hands[h][i] % 13) + 1;
136        if (n > 9)
137            return (10);
138        else if (n == 1)
139            return (11);
140        else
141            return (n);
142        }
```

Fri Jan 14 20:22:22 1983 bj/nfrom.c Page 1

```
 1    /* nfrom - return a number between low and high, inclusive
 2     */
 3    #include "local.h"
 4    short nfrom(low, high)
 5        register short low, high;
 6        {
 7        short rand();
 8        register short nb = high - low + 1;
 9
10        return (rand() % nb + low);
11        }
```

Sat Jan 15 13:21:32 1983 bj/outcom.c Page 1

```c
 1   /* outcom - print outcome of hand(s)
 2    */
 3   #include "local.h"
 4   #include "bj.h"
 5   #include "hndmgr.h"
 6   static CASH value = 0;
 7   /* outcom - print outcome of hand and compute result
 8    */
 9   CASH outcom(bet, tophand, isinsur, isdbl)
10       CASH bet;        /* amount of player's bet */
11       short tophand;   /* how many player hands */
12       bool isinsur;    /* player took insurance? */
13       bool isdbl;      /* is player DBLDN? */
14       {
15       short h;         /* which hand */
16
17       value = 0;
18       if (isinsur && isbj(DEALER))
19           prmsg(1, 1, "Insurance wins\n", bet / (isdbl ? 4 : 2));
20       else if (isinsur)
21           prmsg(1, 1, "Insurance loses\n", -bet / (isdbl ? 4 : 2));
22       if (isbj(DEALER) && !isbj(1))
23           prmsg(1, 1, "Dealer BJ beats all but BJ",
24               -bet / (isdbl ? 2 : 1));
25       else if (isbj(DEALER) && isbj(1))
26           prmsg(1, 1, "Both BJ: push", (CASH)0);
27       else if (isbj(1))
28           prmsg(1, 1, "Your BJ wins 3 for 2", (3 * bet) / 2);
29       else
30           {
31           for (h = 1; h <= tophand; ++h)
32               {
33               if (21 < score(h))
34                   value -= bet;    /* "Bust" message printed already */
35               else if (score(DEALER) == score(h))
36                   prmsg(h, tophand, "Push", (CASH)0);
37               else if (score(DEALER) < score(h) || 21 < score(DEALER))
38                   prmsg(h, tophand, "Win", bet);
39               else
40                   prmsg(h, tophand, "Lose", -bet);
41               }
42           }
43       return (value);
44       }
45
46
47
48
49
50
```

Sat Jan 15 13:21:32 1983 bj/outcom.c Page 2

```
51    /* prmsg - print appropriate message
52     */
53    static void prmsg(h, tophand, s, delta)
54        short h;          /* which hand */
55        short tophand;    /* how many hands */
56        char s[];         /* message */
57        CASH delta;       /* change of value (+ | -) */
58        {
59        if (tophand == 2)
60            printf("On hand %d, ", h);
61        printf("%s\n", s);
62        value += delta;
63        }
64    #ifdef TRYMAIN
65    static short bj[2] = 0; /* isbj, for each hand */
66    static short sc[3] = 0; /* hand scores, for testing */
67    main()
68        {
69        char line[BUFSIZ];        /* line of test input */
70        short len;                /* returned value from input fn */
71        short ibet;               /* players bet, as short int */
72        short ins;                /* isinsur? */
73        short toph;               /* tophand */
74        short dbl;                /* isdbl? */
75        CASH value;               /* return from outcom */
76
77        FOREVER
78            {
79            printf("%-8s %-8s %-8s %-8s %-8s %-8s %-8s %-8s %-8s\n",
80                "bet", "toph", "ins", "dbl",
81                "bj[0]", "bj[1]", "sc[0]", "sc[1]", "sc[2]");
82            len = echoln(line, BUFSIZ);
83            if (len == EOF)
84                break;
85            if (9 != sscanf(line, "%hd %hd %hd %hd %hd %hd %hd %hd %hd",
86                &ibet, &toph, &ins, &dbl,
87                &bj[0], &bj[1], &sc[0], &sc[1], &sc[2]))
88                error("outcom input error", "");
89            value = outcom((CASH)ibet, toph, ins, dbl);
90            printf("outcom() = ");
91            printf(CASHOUT, value);
92            printf("\n");
93            }
94        }
95
96
97
98
99
100
```

Sat Jan 15 13:21:32 1983 bj/outcom.c Page 3

```
101   /* score - dummy version for testing
102    */
103   short score(h)
104       short h;     /* which hand */
105       {
106       return (sc[h]);
107       }
108   /* isbj - dummy version for testing
109    */
110   bool isbj(h)
111       short h;     /* which hand */
112       {
113       return (bj[h]);
114       }
115   /* echoln - get and echo an input line
116    */
117   short echoln(line, size)
118       char line[];
119       short size;
120       {
121       short len;
122
123       if ((len = getln(line, size)) != EOF)
124           printf("%s", line);
125       return (len);
126       }
127   #endif
```

Sat Jan 15 12:07:07 1983 bj/ttymgr.c   Page 1

```
 1   /* ttymgr - tty (terminal) manager
 2    */
 3   #include "local.h"
 4   #include "bj.h"
 5   #include "hndmgr.h"
 6   #include "ttymgr.h"
 7   #define NMSGS 4
 8   #define LENMSG 15
 9   static bool askedhit = NO;
10   static bool wanthit = NO;
11   static char qchar[NMSGS+1] = "dsih";
12   static char qmsg[NMSGS][LENMSG+1] =
13       {
14       "Double down",
15       "Split pair",
16       "Insurance",
17       "Hit",
18       };
19   static short nmsg[NMSGS] = 0;
20   /* query - get players response for DBLDN, SPLIT, HIT
21    */
22   short query()
23       {
24       short ask();
25       short ret;       /* return from ask() */
26
27       if (val(1, 0) == val(1, 1))
28           ret = ask("dsh");
29       else
30           ret = ask("dh");
31       askedhit = (ret != SPLIT);
32       wanthit = (ret == HIT);
33       if (wanthit)
34           ret = NONE;
35       return (ret);
36       }
37   /* takes - get a YES or NO reply to question
38    */
39   bool takes(s)
40       char s[];
41       {
42       short ask();
43
44       if (askedhit && strcmp(s, "h") == 0)
45           {
46           askedhit = NO;
47           return (wanthit);
48           }
49       return (ask(s) != NONE);
50       }
```

Sat Jan 15 12:07:07 1983 bj/ttymgr.c Page 2

```
51   /* ask - get a choice among alternatives
52    */
53   static short ask(s)
54       char s[];
55       {
56       bool isbrief;                    /* is prompt brief? */
57       char ans[BUFSIZ];                /* player's reply line */
58       char c;                          /* player's one-char answer */
59       short i;                         /* index over chars of s */
60       short j;                         /* index over chars of qchar */
61       short slen;                      /* length of s */
62       static short msglim = 5;         /* verbosity limit */
63       unsigned strscn();               /* gives the index of c in s */
64
65       isbrief = YES;
66       slen = strlen(s);
67       for (i = 0; i < slen; ++i)
68           {
69           j = strscn(qchar, s[i]);
70           if (++nmsg[j] <= msglim)
71               isbrief = NO;
72           }
73       if (isbrief)
74           {
75           for (i = 0; i < slen; ++i)
76               printf("%c?", s[i]);
77           printf("\n");
78           }
79       FOREVER
80           {
81           if (!isbrief)
82               {
83               printf("Type\n");
84               for (i = 0; i < slen; ++i)
85                   printf("%c      For %s\n",
86                       s[i], qmsg[strscn(qchar, s[i])]);
87               printf("RETURN For None\n");
88               }
89           if (getln(ans, BUFSIZ) == EOF)
90               error("Bye!", "");
91           c = tolower(ans[0]);
92           if (c == '\n')
93                   return (NONE);
94           for (i = 0; i < slen; ++i)
95               if (s[i] == c)
96                   return (1 + strscn(qchar, c));
97           isbrief = NO;
98           }
99       }
100
```

Sat Jan 15 12:07:07 1983 bj/ttymgr.c Page 3

```
101    /* strscn - return the index of c in string s
102     */
103    unsigned strscn(s, c)
104        char s[];    /* string to be scanned */
105        char c; /* char to be matched */
106        {
107        register unsigned i;
108
109        for (i = 0; s[i] != c && s[i] != '\0'; ++i)
110            ;
111        return (i);
112        }
```

6.5   Implementation: The Latter Phases

Question [6-6] Apply these three methods to designing test cases for the outcom function in bj/outcom.c.

bet	toph	ins	dbl	bj[0]	bj[1]	sc[0]	sc[1]	sc[2]
2000	1	1	1	1	0	21	20	0
4	1	1	1	0	0	21	21	0
1000	1	1	0	1	0	21	20	0
2	1	1	0	0	0	20	22	0
2	1	0	0	1	1	21	21	0
4	1	0	1	0	1	20	21	0
2	1	0	0	0	0	20	21	0
2	1	0	0	0	0	22	21	0
2	1	0	0	0	0	21	20	0
2	2	0	0	0	0	20	20	21

Question [6-7] Predict what values outcom should give for each of your test cases. Compile outcom.c with the symbol TRYMAIN defined, to obtain the test driver for outcom. Run the driver, using your file of test cases as input. Compare the output with your predictions.

bet	toph	ins	dbl	bj[0]	bj[1]	sc[0]	sc[1]	sc[2]
2000	1	1	1	1	0	21	20	0

Insurance wins

Dealer BJ beats all but BJ
outcom( ) = -500

bet	toph	ins	dbl	bj[0]	bj[1]	sc[0]	sc[1]	sc[2]
4	1	1	1	0	0	21	21	0

Insurance loses

Push
outcom( ) = -1

bet	toph	ins	dbl	bj[0]	bj[1]	sc[0]	sc[1]	sc[2]
1000	1	1	0	1	0	21	20	0

Insurance wins

Dealer BJ beats all but BJ
outcom( ) = -500

bet	toph	ins	dbl	bj[0]	bj[1]	sc[0]	sc[1]	sc[2]
2	1	1	0	0	0	20	22	0

Insurance loses

outcom( ) = -3

bet	toph	ins	dbl	bj[0]	bj[1]	sc[0]	sc[1]	sc[2]
2	1	0	0	1	1	21	21	0

Both BJ: push
outcom( ) = 0

bet	toph	ins	dbl	bj[0]	bj[1]	sc[0]	sc[1]	sc[2]
4	1	0	1	0	1	20	21	0

Your BJ wins 3 for 2
outcom( ) = 6

bet	toph	ins	dbl	bj[0]	bj[1]	sc[0]	sc[1]	sc[2]
2	1	0	0	0	0	20	21	0

Win
outcom( ) = 2

bet	toph	ins	dbl	bj[0]	bj[1]	sc[0]	sc[1]	sc[2]
2	1	0	0	0	0	22	21	0

Win
outcom( ) = 2

bet	toph	ins	dbl	bj[0]	bj[1]	sc[0]	sc[1]	sc[2]
2	1	0	0	0	0	21	20	0

Lose
outcom( ) = -2

bet	toph	ins	dbl	bj[0]	bj[1]	sc[0]	sc[1]	sc[2]
2	2	0	0	0	0	20	20	21

On hand 1, Push
On hand 2, Win
outcom( ) = 2

bet	toph	ins	dbl	bj[0]	bj[1]	sc[0]	sc[1]	sc[2]

[6-8 os] *Packaging the compilation procedures:* On a system without the make command, you can still automate repetitive compilations. Just take the commands that you use to build the program, and put them into a "shell script," "command file," or whatever similar facility your system has.

6.6   Maintenance

APPENDIX B.7: POINTERS

7.1 Basics

[7-1 mach] [7-2 mach] *The pictures of pointers:* On a machine with 4-byte pointers, the pictures would have different addresses, and larger boxes.

Question [7-3] Which of the following are *illegal?*

> *GOOD* p = &i;
>
> *BAD*   p = &(i + 1);
>
> *BAD*   p = &++i;

7.2 Declaring and Using Pointers

Question [7-4] Assuming the following initial configuration of memory, after this series of statements is executed, what is the resulting configuration of memory?

```
1100    |    9  |              |    9  |
        |_____|              |_____|

pi  1300    |  1100 |          |  1350 |
            |_____|          |_____|

t   1350    |  14   |          |   2   |
            |_____|          |_____|
            |  20   |          |  21   |
            |_____|          |_____|

pj  1380    |  1350 |          |  1352 |
            |_____|          |_____|

pl  1400    |  1410 |          |  1410 |
            |_____|          |_____|

1410    |         7  |        |         7  |
        |_____|        |_____|

1430    |           0.0  |    |           9.0  |
        |_____|    |_____|

pd  1440    |  1430 |          |  1430 |
            |_____|          |_____|
```

7.3   Pointers as Function Parameters

```
swap [7-5]:
    /* swap - interchange two short integers
     */
    #include "local.h"
    void swap(pi, pj)
        short *pi, *pj;
        {
        short t;

        t = *pi, *pi = *pj, *pj = t;
        }
```

Question [7-6] At the time that swap is entered, what is the value of *pi? *5*
What is the value of *pj? *10*

Question [7-7] At the time the swap returns, what is the value of *pi? *10*
What is the value of *pj? *5*

7.4   Pointers and Arrays

Question [7-8] If we now write

```
i = *pq;
```

what value will i be given? *5*

7.5   Functions using Pointers

index0 **[7-9]**:
```
/* index0 - return index of first occurrence of char c in string s
 *   subscripted version
 */
#include "local.h"
char *index0(s, c)
    char s[], c;
    {
    unsigned i = 0;

    while (s[i] != '\0' && s[i] != c)
        ++i;
    return (s[i] == c ? &s[i] : NULL);
    }
```

index **[7-10]**:
```
/* index - return index of first occurrence of char c in string s
 *   pointer version
 */
#include "local.h"
char *index(s, c)
    char s[], c;
    {
    while (*s != '\0' && *s != c)
        ++s;
    return (*s == c ? s : NULL);
    }
```

```
strcpy2 [7-11]:
    /* strcpy2 - copy characters from s2 to s1
     */
    #include "local.h"
    char *strcpy2(s1, s2)
        register char s1[], s2[];
        {
        char *s0 = s1;

        while ((*s1++ = *s2++) != '\0')
            ;
        return (s0);
        }
```

7.6   Pointer Arithmetic

7.7   Arrays of Pointers

Question [7-12] Write the *type* and *value* of each expression:

	type	value
cities[1][1]	char	'H'
&cities[1][1]	char *	1104
*cities[1]	char	'P'

7.8   Command Line Arguments

[7-13 mach]: *The picture of* ac *and* av: On machines with 4-byte addresses, the addresses would step upward by 4 bytes:

```
ac     1400      |   3   |
                 |_____|
av     1404      | 1440  |
                 |_____|


av[0]  1440      | 1662  |      1662   | c | m | d | \0 |
                 |_____|             |___|___|___|____|
av[1]  1444      | 1666  |      1666   | a | 1 | \0 |
                 |_____|             |___|___|____|
av[2]  1448      | 1669  |      1669   | a | 2 | \0 |
                 |_____|             |___|___|____|
av[3]  1452      |   0   |
                 |_____|
```

[7-14 cc] *The null-terminated list* av: In UNIX Version 6 systems, the argument list is terminated by -1.

[7-15 os] *Passing command arguments:*   The details of mechanisms for passing command arguments depend upon the environment.   On RSX, for example, programs must be "installed" before they can receive command arguments (although the mechanism can be simulated using a special "prompt").

echo.c **[7-16]**:

```
/* echo - print command-line arguments
 */
#include "local.h"
main(ac, av)
    unsigned ac;
    char *av[];
    {
    unsigned i;

    for (i = 1; i < ac; ++i)
        printf(i < ac-1 ? "%s " : "%s\n", av[i]);
    exit(SUCCEED);
    }
```

Question [7-17] If we execute echo with the command

echo abc xyz 123

how many pointers are passed in the array that av points to? *5 (Including the command name and the null terminator.)* What is the value of ac? *4*

APPENDIX B.8: STRUCTURES

8.1 Basics

Question [8-1] What is the size of `ti` on a machine with 2-byte addresses? With 4-byte addresses?

```
                    2-byte      4-byte
                    machine     machine

     sizeof(ti)      14           16
```

task.h **[8-2]**:
```
    /* task.h - include-file for TASK structure
     */
    #define TIME long
    #define TASK struct task
    TASK
        {
        char *desc;
        TIME plan;
        TIME start;
        TIME finish;
        };
```

8.2 Members

[8-3 cc] *Unique structure member names:* Although Kernighan and Ritchie [1978] do not say so, all UNIX systems starting with Version 7 do treat member names as unique per structure. Earlier compilers, such as UNIX Version 6, lack this treatment, causing programmers to put prefixes on member names to ensure uniqueness.

8.3   Initialization

Question [8-4] Write a short program vacat.c containing this declaration for vacation. In the program, assign the value 1983 to the members start and finish. Print the resulting values of all members, using printf.

```
vacat.c:
    /* vacat - structure practice
     */
    #include "local.h"
    #include "task.h"
    main()
        {
        static TASK vacation =  {"leave for Hawaii", 1984, 0, 0};

        vacation.start = vacation.finish = (long)1983;
        printf("vacation.desc = %s\n", vacation.desc);
        printf("vacation.plan = %ld\n", vacation.plan);
        printf("vacation.start = %ld\n", vacation.start);
        printf("vacation.finish = %ld\n", vacation.finish);
        }
```

Output:

```
    vacation.desc = leave for Hawaii
    vacation.plan = 1984
    vacation.start = 1983
    vacation.finish = 1983
```

8.4   Nested Structures

```
task2.h [8-5]:
    /* task2.h - include-file for TASK structure (using days and mins)
     */
    #define TIME struct time
    TIME
        {
        short days;
        short mins;
        };
    #define TASK struct task
    TASK
        {
        char *desc;
        TIME plan;
        TIME start;
        TIME finish;
        };
```

8.5   Arrays of Structures

loadtt.c **[8-6]**:

```
/* loadtt - read data into the task table
 */
#include "local.h"
#include "task.h"    /* the original include-file: TIME == long */
#define TSIZE 5
main()
    {
    TASK tt[TSIZE];                  /* task table */
    char tstring[TSIZE][21];         /* string storage */
    short i;                         /* index for printing */
    short n;                         /* number of successful reads */
    short ret;                       /* returned value from scanf */

    n = 0;
    FOREVER
        {
        tt[n].desc = tstring[n];
        ret = scanf("%20s%ld%ld%ld",
            tt[n].desc, &tt[n].plan, &tt[n].start, &tt[n].finish);
        if (ret == EOF)
            break;
        else if (ret != 4)
            error("Data error", "");
        else if (++n >= TSIZE)
            break;
        }
    for (i = 0; i < n; ++i)
        printf("%20s %8ld %8ld %8ld\n",
            tt[i].desc, tt[i].plan, tt[i].start, tt[i].finish);
    }
```

task3.h **[8-7]**:

```
/* task3.h - include-file for TASK structure
 */
#define TIME long
#define DSIZE 20
#define TASK struct task
TASK
    {
    char desc[DSIZE+1];
    TIME plan;
    TIME start;
    TIME finish;
    };
```

8.6   Pointers to Structures

```
gettt.c [8-8]:
    /* gettt - read data into the task table (using gettask function)
     */
    #include "local.h"
    #include "task3.h"   /* revised to include storage for desc */
    #define TSIZE 5
    main()
        {
        TASK tt[TSIZE];              /* task table */
        short gettask();             /* function to get one TASK */
        short i;                     /* index for printing */
        short n;                     /* number of successful reads */

        n = 0;
        while (n < TSIZE && gettask(&tt[n]) == 4)
            ++n;
        for (i = 0; i < n; ++i)
            printf("%20s %8ld %8ld %8ld\n",
                tt[i].desc, tt[i].plan, tt[i].start, tt[i].finish);
        }
    /* gettask - get one TASK
     */
    short gettask(ptask)
        TASK *ptask;
        {
        short ret;                   /* returned value from scanf */

        ret = scanf("%20s%ld%ld%ld",
            ptask->desc, &ptask->plan, &ptask->start, &ptask->finish);
        return (ret);
        }
```

[8-9 cc] *Structure assignment, argument, and return:* If one considers
Kernighan and Ritchie [1978] Appendix A to be the best current standard for
C, then these extensions must be considered "non-standard" C. Many existing
commercial compilers do not support them, so they are in that sense non-
portable. If you happen to know what "re-entrant code" is, you should be
warned that some of the current implementations of functions returning structures are not re-entrant and can also produce bugs when a function is called
several times in one expression. However, there *are* adequate schemes for implementing the structure return.

complex.h **[8-10]**:

```
#define COMPLEX struct complex
COMPLEX
    {
    double real;
    double imag;
    };
```

cadd **[8-11]**:

```
/* cadd - add two COMPLEX numbers
 */
#include "complex.h"
COMPLEX cadd(x, y)
    COMPLEX x, y;
    {
    COMPLEX z;

    z.real = x.real + y.real;
    z.imag = x.imag + y.imag;
    return (z);
    }
```

BIBLIOGRAPHY

Ahl, David H [1976].
The Best of Creative Computing, Volume I. Morristown, NJ, Creative Computing Press.

Clavell, James [1975].
Shogun. New York, Dell Publishing Co.

Feldman, S. I. [1979].
"Make — A program for Maintaining Computer Programs," *Software — Practice and Experience,* Vol 9, No. 4, April 1979, Pp. 255-265.

Feuer, Alan R. [1982].
The C Puzzle Book. Englewood Cliffs, NJ, Prentice-Hall.

Gilbreath, Jim, and Gary Gilbreath [1983]
"Eratoshtenes Revisted: Once More through the Sieve." *BYTE,* Vol. 8, No. 1, January 1983.

Hamming, R. W. [1973].
Numerical Methods for Scientists and Engineers. New York, McGraw-Hill.

Kernighan, Brian W., and Dennis M. Ritchie [1978].
The C Programming Language. New Jersey, Prentice-Hall.

Kernighan, Brian W., and P. J. Plauger [1978].
The Elements of Programming Style (Second Edition). New York, McGraw-Hill.

Kernighan, Brian W., and P. J. Plauger [1981].
Software Tools in Pascal. Reading, MA, Addison-Wesley.

Myers, Glenford [1979].
  The Art of Software Testing, New York, John Wiley & Sons.

Parnas, David L [1972].
  "On the Criteria to be used in decomposing systems into modules." *Communications of the ACM,* December, 1972.

Plauger, P. J. [1979].
  Review of Kernighan and Ritchie [1978], in *Computing Reviews,* January 1979.

Plum, Thomas [1981].
  C Programming Standards and Guidelines: Version U (UNIX and offspring). Cardiff, NJ, Plum Hall.

Plum, Thomas [1981].
  C Programming Standards and Guidelines: Version W (Whitesmiths). Cardiff, NJ, Plum Hall.

Ritchie, D. M., S. C. Johnson, M. E. Lesk, and B. W. Kernighan [1978].
  "The C Programming Language." In *The Bell System Technical Journal,* Vol. 57, No. 6, July-August 1978.

Walston, C. E., and C. P. Felix [1977].
  "A Method of Programming Measurement and Estimation." In *IBM Systems Journal,* Vol. 16, No. 1, Pp. 54-73, IBM G321-5045.

Yourdon, Edward, and Larry Constantine [1978].
  Structured Design. Englewood Cliffs, NJ, Prentice-Hall.

Zahn, Carrol [1978].
  C Notes. New York, NY, Yourdon Press.

INDEX

In this index, the symbols that appeared in "program" font, such as the names `read` and `strlen`, appear first. All the keywords of C, for example, are found in this part of the index. After them come the symbols in more-or-less ordinary English, such as "portability" and "expression."